Multi Asset Class
Investment Strategy

For other titles in the Wiley Finance Series
please see www.wiley.com/finance

Multi Asset Class
Investment Strategy

Guy Fraser-Sampson

John Wiley & Sons, Ltd

Other Wiley Editorial Offices

Wiley have other editorial offices in the USA, Germany, Australia, Singapore and Canada.

Wiley also publishes its books in a variety of electronic formats. Some content that appears in
print may not be available in electronic books.

Library of Congress Cataloging-in-Publication Data
Fraser-Sampson, Guy.
    Multi asset class investment strategy / Guy Fraser-Sampson.
      p.   cm.
    Includes bibliographical references and index.
    ISBN-13: 978-0-470-02799-8 (cloth : alk. paper)
    ISBN-10: 0-470-02799-1 (cloth : alk. paper)
  1. Portfolio management.   2. Investment analysis.   3. Institutional investments.
  4. Risk.   5. Investments.   I. Title.
    HG4529.5.F746   2006
    332.6 – dc22

                                                                          2006011293

British Library Cataloguing in Publication Data

A catalogue record for this book is available from the British Library

ISBN 978-0-470-02799-8 (HB)

Typeset in 11/13pt Times by SNP Best-set Typesetter Ltd., Hong Kong
Printed and bound in Great Britain by TJ International Ltd, Padstow, Cornwall, UK
This book is printed on acid-free paper responsibly manufactured from sustainable forestry in
which at least two trees are planted for each one used for paper production.

Contents

Introduction

The field of investment strategy is huge, and when one adds into the mix the question of the measurement and adequacy of pension funding then it rapidly becomes unmanageable within the confines of a single book. It may therefore be useful if we are clear from the outset what this book does and does not cover.

WHAT THIS BOOK IS ABOUT

It is first and foremost a book about investment strategy, and in particular about asset allocation based on a Multi Asset Class model. The most famous of such models is undoubtedly that used by the Yale Endowment and described by its creator, David Swensen, in his book *Pioneering Portfolio Management*. In this book, I will be describing my own model, which I have dubbed 'MAC investing'. Thus, while I will be describing and commenting on, where necessary, the Yale Model, the main purpose of this book is not simply to spread Swensen's message to a wider audience, but rather to offer my own arguments for and observations upon Multi Asset Class investing. I have a huge respect both for Swensen and for the model that he created, but anyone who wishes to study it in detail can do so from the horse's mouth by reading his book, and there seems little point in my merely recycling what he has to say.

I will attempt to explain the various aspects of financial theory that underpin MAC investing, some of which may be obvious, but others less so. Among the former are such things as correlation and benchmarking of returns. Among the latter might be numbered liquidity and risk. Some of these may seem such settled and established concepts that there can be little new to say about them. In fact, I will endeavour to show that this is not the case and that a radically new and different approach is required to how we look at investment theory in order to accommodate Multi Asset Class models.

Having examined the conceptual framework that encloses MAC investing I then move to discussing the different asset classes that should be considered. Again, within the confines of a few chapters of a single book the list is not exhaustive, nor is it meant to be. There is, for example, no room to consider some of the interesting new currency and commodity-based products that are being launched, nor to do more than mention things such as the Private Finance Initiative and Public Private Partnerships in which some UK pension funds are becoming involved. Given the limitations of space I have deliberately limited myself to what I consider to be the mainstream areas of quoted equities (both domestic and foreign), hedge funds, private equity and property. Again in the interests of balance, I have limited my consideration of property to the UK. Had I not done so then this chapter would have become unmanageably large and complex; indeed, any one of these asset class chapters could easily have become a book in its own right. In mitigation, I would plead that while the property figures I use are UK specific, the principles are not, and are indeed capable of universal application. It will be an easy matter for a US investor to have access to US property data.

There are various matters that are sometimes put forward as possible alternatives to a Multi Asset Class approach, most notably Liability Driven Investment and Portable Alpha, and I deal with each of these specifically.

Finally, I will attempt to pull everything together and show how different portfolios might have performed over time. I concede that this is a speculative 'what if' exercise, but it is based on real historic performance figures and on asset mixes that could actually have been adopted at the time. Again, given the figures I have used for property investment performance, it seemed only logical to perform this exercise on the basis of a UK (or, at least, sterling-based) portfolio such as would be appropriate for, say, a UK pension fund, but it can very easily be duplicated using, for example, US dollar-based numbers.

WHAT THIS BOOK IS NOT ABOUT

I had not originally meant to deal with the question of pension funding at all. Indeed, this was at one time intended to form the subject of a separate book based on my Total Funding Model for pension funds. Within such a book, it would have been possible to look in detail at such things as the relative maturity of different pension funds, differing situations in various countries, and the difference between Defined Benefit (DB) and Defined Contribution (DC) schemes. This book is about investment strategy, not pension funding.

However, it rapidly became apparent that this was a pious intention to which it would not be possible to adhere to religiously. In considering investment strategy one must discuss the setting of strategic objectives, and the only possible strategic objective of a pension fund can be to place itself in a position from where it will be able to discharge its funding obligations.

I therefore had to stray into this territory in Chapter 1, in which I give a condensed explanation of Total Funding and consider how a pension fund should go about assessing its funding requirement and fixing its target rate of investment return. This can be thought of as 'the demand side' of investment strategy, while the remainder of the book is concerned with 'the supply side'. Thereafter, I largely ignore the question of, for example, the specific maturity of a pension fund although I do make various references to differing liability profiles, by which I mean the same thing as maturity where the investor concerned is a pension fund.

Early reviewers of the manuscript however, while acknowledging that the subject of the book was investment strategy rather than pension funding, felt that this left two unanswered questions hanging over the rest of the text. How should a MAC investment approach differ for (1) a DC as opposed to a DB scheme, and (2) a mature, possibly very mature scheme?

The problem is that to discuss this topic in the length that any proper consideration would demand would require at least an extra chapter and possibly two (for example, different situations apply in different countries – in the USA, for example, many employers have always run a DC scheme alongside a DB one, and many employees run their own hybrid personal pension scheme), and would definitely unbalance the book.

It is yet possible that the original book idea may see the light of day, but in the meantime I am very concerned at the widespread conception that I encountered during my research, namely that a DC scheme and/or a mature scheme had no place in their investment strategy for alternative assets, and so I have very briefly set out my views on DC schemes and on the question of mature pension funds in a separate note which appears as Appendix 2, immediately after the tables of performance figures. For those who have a specific interest in the subject, I would recommend reading it immediately after Chapter 1. Those whose interest lies primarily in portfolio theory may happily disregard it entirely.

Briefly, my view is that there is little difference in funding (as opposed to legal) terms between a DB and a DC scheme save in the way in which the retirement benefit is actually delivered, and that the pension scheme's investment strategy should be much the same in each case. As for mature pension funds, for all except the extreme case of a scheme that is confidently expecting to pay out all its assets within the next decade and is fully funded on the basis of that assumption, then assets such as private equity still have a role to play. You will see, however, that the MAC investing model automatically compensates in any event for a shortening timescale by increasing the amount of the portfolio held in such things as bonds.

It lies beyond the scope of this book to comment on the current switch from DB to DC schemes but let me say that in purely financial terms, and specifically ignoring the various ethical and legal considerations that are involved, this seems to me to make little sense and, indeed, is likely to make it harder rather than easier to fulfil the scheme's funding obligations (which in my view remain the same regardless of the legal form employed).

WHY DO WE NEED MAC INVESTING?

It may seem strange, given the consistent success in recent years of the Yale Model, as described in David Swensen's best-selling book,[1] that a Multi Asset Class approach to investment strategy for institutions such as pension funds should still be a controversial subject, and require justification. Certainly many in the investment management industry have been arguing the case for Multi Asset Class investing for many years (in my own case for more than the last decade). However, institutions and their advisers have been slow to respond – tragically slow in some cases.

As I mention above, I will be demonstrating that the deficits now afflicting UK pension funds could have been almost entirely avoided had they been practising MAC investing (my own Multi Asset Class model, which I offer as an example of what might have been

---

[1] *Pioneering Portfolio Management* (2001).

achieved) during the relevant period, since such a strategy would have protected them from their massive overexposure to public equity markets and to bond yields during a period when both have fallen dramatically.

Perhaps this has something to do with the fact that at first glance the Yale Model appears to turn established thinking and investment practice on its head. Swensen's concept, at its simplest, is to divide a portfolio into about five roughly equal parts and invest each part in a separate asset class, with each class being as little correlated to the others as possible. Thus, so-called 'alternative' assets such as private equity and hedge funds, which do not feature in some portfolios at all, take pride of place on equal footing with more traditional investments such as quoted equities. We will be looking at MAC investing in general, and the Yale Model in particular, in much more depth later in the book, and you will see that I will be putting forward an individual model of my own, but I think it will be useful to have the basic idea in mind from the outset.

While it is dangerous to generalise, the situation varies with geography. I have referred in various articles and conference speeches to the equivalent of an international postcode lottery which affects members of pension schemes. The USA leads the pack, as so often with investment. In countries such as the Netherlands, Sweden and Australia progress may be discerned in moving away from the old 'what should our bond/equity mix be?' nursery talk towards something more intellectual. However, ignoring countries that do not have what might be termed the Anglo-Saxon pension model (the most obvious examples being France and Germany), UK pensioners find themselves at the very bottom of the heap in terms of investment thinking.

I use the word 'thinking' in the last paragraph deliberately, for the adoption of MAC investing does not only represent a progression from the 'old' to the 'new', but from the 'unthinking' to the 'thinking'. The old approach assumes that one's asset mix (and thus also the investment return which it produces) is essentially a given that cannot be changed, whereas the new approach calculates the investment return required and then sets out to adopt an asset mix appropriate to that target return (a process to which I have given the term Total Funding).

It also represents a change from a 'relative' or 'benchmarked' approach to returns, where one is striving to match the performance of one's peer group, to an 'absolute return' outlook, where one is striving to outperform by selecting those asset classes which, viewed entirely rationally and dispassionately, seem likely to produce the best returns.

Finally, it marks a change from a short-term viewpoint obsessed with annual returns to a recognition that institutions such as pension funds are driven by the nature of their liabilities to take a long-term view, and to set targets not in terms of individual periodic returns but as a compound return to be earned over many years, within which annual fluctuations are largely irrelevant.

I will be developing all these points in more detail, but it is my firm contention that even if the precise Yale Model itself may not be ideal for all investors whatever and wherever they may be (because of different liability profiles, local differences in returns in some asset classes, exchange rate risk, etc.), nonetheless the basic approach of which it is a product (which I have chosen to call MAC investing) most certainly *is* of universal application. In this book I will be demonstrating how the returns of different asset classes may be analysed and compared meaningfully against each other, how a MAC investment strategy may be implemented, and why this can be shown to be infinitely superior to any existing approach.

Finally, I have mentioned briefly already the funding deficit currently afflicting the UK pension industry (and, to a lesser extent, those of other countries) but it would be wrong not to refer to it specifically at least this once, since this overshadows all investment discussion today. Pension funds, who are after all the overwhelming majority of institutional investment by size, simply no longer have the option of continuing with bond-type returns. They have no choice but to seek out asset classes that offer higher rates of return (sometimes much higher) but feel the lack of the expertise required meaningfully to consider them. It is precisely this area that this book is designed to address.

Unfortunately there are many who have a vested interest in traditional views not being disturbed, and they can and will attempt to denigrate and ridicule this book. In a sense I have made this easy for them since you will see that I reject, for example, accepted notions of risk as being simply immaterial to modern investment needs, and this is the financial equivalent of claiming that God does not exist. However, if any readers can suspend their scepticism long enough to follow my arguments with an open mind, then I am confident that they will become further converts to the cause of MAC investing.

ADDENDUM

Very shortly before this book was due to be published one of the major
pension consultancy firms (Watson Wyatt) announced that henceforth
they would be advising all their DC pension scheme clients to adopt
Multi Asset Class investment strategies. Shortly afterwards another
(Mercer) indicated that, while not prepared to go this far, they were
now advocating this strategy. As the book was already at final proof
stage it has not been possible to record this change of attitude in the
body of the main text. However, I trust the reader will agree that any
step in the right direction is to be welcomed.

Given that these very recent developments render the subject of
Multi Asset Class investing more topical than ever, it is entirely likely
that events may now move more quickly than originally anticipated. In
these newly changed circumstances, could I beg the reader to bear in
mind that the task of writing this book was completed in December
2005.

Acknowledgements

In the course of preparing this book (over about a two-year period) I spoke with many people who gladly gave me their time and the benefit of their experience and advice. These included pension trustees, pension professionals, pension consultants, academics and investment managers. It is a sad sign of the rather Orwellian times in which we live that the vast majority did so only on condition of strict anonymity, but they know who they are, and I thank them. Happily, I am at liberty to single out some specific contributions.

I would like gratefully to acknowledge the assistance in the writing of this book of my friend and colleague Joe Schorge, who has been my constant sounding board and sanity check, as well as preparing a number of the graphics.

Philip Jones of the London Pension Fund Authority kindly reviewed the entire publishers' draft text within a very tight timescale and made a number of helpful suggestions. Other individuals made time in their busy schedules to review particular chapters.

Alice Kaye, engineer, mathematician and bridge player of Lady Margaret Hall, Oxford, generously helped me with the phi calculations that form the basis of my risk measurements.

This book could not have been written unless various data providers had been prepared to release the copyright in their benchmark performance figures for the purposes of this publication. I would like to acknowledge the unselfish behaviour of Thomson Financial (particularly Nisha Patel and Bob Keiser) in making available the Venture Xpert system for my private equity returns, CSFB/Tremont for providing my hedge fund returns and IPD (particularly Rob Carpenter, who uncomplainingly accommodated what became a very cramped timetable) for making available the UK property figures.

A big 'thank you' to Rachael Wilkie of John Wiley & Sons Ltd for suggesting the book in the first place, and to her and her colleagues Chris Swain, Jenny McCall, Julia Bezzant and Rowan Stanfield for all their hard work subsequently.

Last, but by no means least, I would like to pay tribute to my wife, who has lived with 'Multi Asset Class Investing' and the MAC investing model as well as with me for the last couple of years, and who has been her usual perfect mix of solace and support.

1
Investment Strategy

WHAT IS STRATEGY?

It will come as no surprise, having read the title of this book, that it is going to deal with investment strategy, and a particular approach to investment strategy at that. Before we dive into our deliberations, however, it might be a good idea to consider briefly what strategy is, or should be, since I have been continually surprised over the years to find the basic concept so widely misunderstood.

In his classic work *On War*,[1] Von Clausewitz points out that strategy must have a tactical result in mind, which in turn is a means to achieving its ultimate objective. In military terms – the field in which strategy was most often applied until recently – this means that, to use his words, strategy has victory as its desired tactical outcome, which is the means to achieving the strategic objective, which is peace. My own definition of strategy would be: 'an action plan designed to achieve specific objectives', which I think is consistent with Von Clausewitz's view.

Considerable confusion arises as to the difference between strategy and tactics, particularly in the world of investment, and this is such an important distinction that it is worth taking a little time to consider it, since it is in the failure to distinguish between tactics and strategy that most corporate 'strategic plans' fall down.

Tactics are the steps laid out in the action plan which, if properly carried out in the proper sequence, are designed to lead to the objective being achieved. Strategy is the totality of the whole process, which needs to take a broad view of the whole environment within which the plan has to operate, rather than the individual circumstances within which a particular action takes place. All too often one sees a particular approach being cited as a 'strategy' when it is not; it is an individual course of action that should be performed within the framework of an overall long-term plan, not seized upon as the totality of what is

---

[1] Penguin Books, London, 1982.

required. To go overweight in Japanese equities, for example, is not a strategy, though it may frequently be represented as one. It is a tactic. Whether or not it is successful must be judged by how well it helps to achieve the overall objective, whatever that may be.

I do not have the original German text available, but I suspect that what is translated in the English version as 'a tactical result' may well be one of those compound German words that could be equally well interpreted as 'the result of tactics'. It is these individual tactical results that form the stepping stones by which we cross the river and achieve our objective of reaching the other side.

I introduced the phrase 'long term' deliberately since I think this is another valid distinction between tactics and strategy. Tactics often take the form of fairly instant action (the shifting of troops from one part of a battlefield to another) whereas strategy implies something that will take place over time (the winning of a war by the successive outcomes of a whole series of battles). In investment terms this is often a stumbling block, with most investors being obsessed with the cult of annual returns and short-term results, rather than recognising that investment objectives are essentially long term, and that individual annual returns within any given period are at best a distraction, and at worst immaterial, and we will be returning to this point in much more detail at various times.

So, if we can adopt as a working assumption the concept of strategy as an action plan designed to achieve specific objectives over time, then we can turn our attention to what investment strategy is, or should be. There are two parts to the exercise. We need to analyse our environment and identify our objective, and we will be covering this first part of the exercise in this chapter. In the following chapters we will be looking at what steps we might take to achieve our objective.

WHAT IS INVESTMENT STRATEGY?

As we have already seen, strategy does not operate in a vacuum. It can only be formulated with regard to the specific objectives to be achieved, and to the environment in which we find ourselves. The objectives must be precisely laid down so that there can be no possible misunderstanding about what they are, or what has to happen for them to be judged to have been achieved. They must be realistic, having regard to the environment, since there is no point in setting a strategic plan that cannot succeed, having regard to all the surrounding circumstances. Most of all, they must be *vital*.

It is possible for an investor to think of many things he or she would like to achieve. To plan successfully, however, we need to clear away the mental clutter and identify those things that absolutely *have* to be achieved, things which, if not achieved, would perhaps threaten the very *raison d'être* and survival of the organisation. It is these things (and preferably just one thing, so as to allow total focus upon it) that will drive the investment strategy. This will form the end to which whatever tactics we lay out in our action plan will be the means.

Let us think in terms of an institutional investor. The institution may take many forms, but we will usually be adopting an occupational pension plan as our model for illustrative purposes. What does a pension fund absolutely *have* to achieve? I think the answer is obvious: a pension fund must be able to meet its liabilities to pensioners as they fall due. This is the only thing that matters, and everything else must be subordinated to it. This is the strategic end to which we need to find the means.

The objective has been identified. However, as yet it is stated in very general terms. We need to analyse further exactly what it is that needs to be achieved in order for our strategy to be judged to have succeeded. We need to think about the length of period over which our strategy needs to operate. We should try to understand how the objective fits into its surrounding environment. All of this will, of course, be done where possible by reference to the circumstances of the individual investor.

One final point before we move on. Strategic planning is a rational process. It requires the rigorous application of logic, and the ruthless suppression of emotional responses. Logic can be cruel and can produce unpleasant conclusions, but the fact that they may be unpleasant is not a reason for ignoring them. Throughout this book we will be attempting to find a simple starting point grounded in the real life circumstances of real world investors, and then to use logic to arrive at the correct outcome. There is no room in this process for blind prejudice. In particular, there is no room for unthinking support for, or dislike of, a particular asset class. We must be prepared where necessary to think the unthinkable, and not shirk from questioning accepted notions as illogical, even where these may have assumed the form of religious dogma. I ask you to bear this point in mind particularly when we consider the concept of risk in later chapters.

PLANNING TO ACHIEVE THE OBJECTIVE

1. Real and Artificial Liabilities

A pension fund has a stream of liabilities stretching out before it into time. It seems logical, therefore, to suggest that when a pension fund begins to plan its investment strategy it needs to think in these terms: cashflows over a long period. Unfortunately we immediately encounter an apparent problem here as pension funds do not exist in isolation. They are attached to a sponsoring employer (sometimes several sponsoring employers) and these have issues of their own which require them to take a very different view. It is most important that we should understand why this is, and why we need to keep the two totally separate.

Briefly, sponsors tend to deal in artificial liabilities whereas pension funds, which have the obligation of actually paying liabilities as they fall due, cannot afford to do this. Their planning process must be based on real liabilities. Unfortunately in practice the difference – and, in many cases, the conflict of interest between the sponsor and the pension plan – is often fudged, and the pension plan finds itself looking at discounted figures that are convenient for the sponsor's accounting purposes, but inappropriate for the pension fund's planning purposes.

This is not intended in any way as a criticism of those corporations and public bodies who sponsor pension plans. It is simply that their needs and requirements are separate and different. This ranges from the obvious to the relatively subtle. It is obvious that a company cannot make additional contributions to its pension fund without depriving either commercial projects of working capital or shareholders of dividend income. Similarly a Local Authority, say, cannot increase its pension fund contributions without either diverting money from public spending programmes (health, education, policing, etc.) or raising additional taxes. Thus in both cases the sponsoring organisation faces a conflict between the interests of different groups, to all of whom it owes a separate duty. That is not their fault. It is rather their misfortune that they are required to play God and attempt to resolve these conflicts of interest in the least objectionable way.

It is not so obvious that sponsor and pension plan should view the stream of future liabilities in different ways, because each is subject to different imperatives. For the sponsor, any deficit in the pension plan is both technically and legally a debt owed by the company to the pension fund. Their need is to find a figure to place in their accounts, in respect of this liability, that is both as low as possible and acceptable to their auditors. This need has been met by the introduction of 'new world' accounting standards (FRS 17 in the UK, but similar schemes have been introduced both in the USA and in some European countries, the latter under the aegis of a European Union standard) which bring consistency and uniformity.

Both of these are admirable qualities in their own way and in the right context – and the world of financial accounting is undoubtedly such a context. Nobody can disagree that it is surely a good thing if all pension fund sponsors are required to account for their pension liabilities in the same way. Unfortunately, however, there is always a trade-off inherent in such situations, and here consistency and uniformity have been achieved at a price. That price is real world accuracy, and it is this lack of real world accuracy that makes them unsuitable for use by the sponsored pension plan.

All these accounting standards work in the same way. They look at the liabilities of the pension fund (and, arguably, not all the liabilities but only those that have already vested) and then discount them, usually by the relevant Government bond (Gilt) rate. Now, that is all very well for accounting purposes. Indeed, it is difficult to think of any way of treating them for accounting purposes that does *not* involve discounting. I have no problem, therefore, with FRS 17 and similar schemes as accounting standards.

Therein lies the crux of the problem, though. I take no issue with them *as accounting standards*, but the problem is that pension funds forget that this is what they are. Worse, it never seems to occur to them that not only are they accounting standards, but accounting standards of third parties. They do not apply to pension funds, but only to organisations that sponsor pension plans. Pension funds should simply ignore them as irrelevant when embarking upon their own planning process.

The conflicts of interest inherent in the system to which I refer above show graphically the importance of sponsor and pension plan being viewed totally separately[2] and this is a wonderful illustration of one

---

[2] Sadly, the UK Government does not agree and has recently passed a new Pensions Act which, rather than sweeping the conflicts away by requiring the appointment of independent trustees and in-house investment professionals, as recommended by the Myners Report, decided instead to perpetuate the existing conflicts by requiring that potentially all the trustees of a scheme should be either employees or directors of the sponsoring company.

specific example of this. A pension fund needs to know exactly what its future liabilities are likely to be. It needs to know, so far as is possible, the actual amounts and dates of future cashflows. It needs to consider future liabilities that have not yet accrued, not just the net present value of present liabilities projected into the future. I hope it will be clear from all this that FRS 17 and the like may do a great job as accounting standards, but as investment planning tools they are useless – worse, misleading.

All of which is rather a shame, because in the talks I have had with pension trustees and managers in the preparation of this book, they all seemed simply to be adopting the sponsor's accounting position and assuming it as their own. It did not seem to occur to them that their responsibility was to their members and to their liabilities, and not to the sponsoring employer. It is not their job to cause the sponsor as little trouble as possible. It is their job to safeguard the pension funds' abilities to pay all future liabilities as they fall due.

In all of these discussions, they were all able to tell me more or less instantly what 'their' obligations were under FRS 17 (these discussions all took place in the UK). Yet none of them was able to say what the real liabilities were, or what shortfall this implied in the overall funding of the scheme. Of course FRS 17 does not state 'their' liabilities at all, but the accounting treatment of the liabilities of the sponsor. My recognition that they seemed incapable of distinguishing between the position of the sponsor (a third party for their purposes as trustees) and the fund, and between an accounting position based on discounting and a real life situation based on actual liabilities, was one of many moments during the preparation of this book when I felt the mental equivalent of a bucket of cold water being poured over my head. (Another was when the NAPF released figures showing that the average UK pension trustee spent just four hours a year discussing investment matters. One pension professional told me: 'I'd be happy to get their attention for half of that'!)

So what we need are the real figures, the actual liabilities, not just a single figure that has been artificially arrived at – 'artificially' in the sense that it has been discounted on some arbitrary basis. I do not mean to imply that all systems that discount pension liabilities are simplistic; far from it. Some consultants have extremely complex models and, indeed, it was these very models that first drew attention to the staggering scale of the deficits to which many pension schemes are currently subject. Yet they all operate by discounting, and as part of this discounting process they take account of notional investment performance during the period under review. This is the essential and fundamental problem with the system, and the one factor above all that condemns the strategic planning of pension funds as artificial.

We need to plan to achieve our objective. Our objective is to meet our liabilities as they fall due. We also need to calculate what target rate of investment return is required during the period under review to enable us to do that. We then need to plan our asset allocation in such a way that the target rate of return can be achieved. This is the crux of the matter, and where I part company intellectually from all that seems to be happening in practice.

In practice, it seems that the fund's rate of return is assumed to be a 'given', fixed and immutable. Either it is plucked out of the air as an arbitrary figure (for example, the Gilt rate used by FRS 17, or perhaps as some margin over the Gilt rate, or over inflation) or, at best, assessed on the basis of the fund's existing asset mix. This is nonsense. The target rate of return determines the asset mix, not vice versa. The target rate of return is not fixed and immutable; the asset mix operates as a dial on the dashboard which can be turned one way or another to alter the rate of return. It is not an arbitrary number; it can only have any meaning if it is calculated as the rate that will allow the fund to meet its liabilities. The present system is a perfect example of the tail wagging the dog.

Nor is it strategy. We need to be proactive, not reactive. Strategy is about planning how to shape the future as we would wish it to be. The present system consists of little more than being swept along passively by events.

2. Mapping the Liability Cashflows

Let us assume that we have finally got our hands on the real figures. We can now simply map these out into the future. What I have in mind here are the net outflows of the fund.

It may be convenient to think about this as a projection into the future of the fund's financial statements. These will show (1) the level of contributions (and value of transfers in), (2) the cost of administering the scheme and (3) the level of benefits payable (and the cost of any withdrawals). For example, the publicly available accounts of the London Pension Fund Authority for 2003/4 show:

	£000
Contributions and transfers in	141066
Costs of administration	4040
Benefits payable and withdrawals	198780
Net liabilities before investment return	(61754)

There are two things to note here. Firstly, we have stated the liability position before considering the effect of investment performance. Note please that this is not a term that appears in the accounts, and the omission shows that this is not the way in which pension funds have been encouraged to think about their financial position. This is highly significant because only by viewing accounts in such a way can they be used as a platform for investment strategy, rather than as a matter of financial record.

Secondly, the LPFA is already in a negative cashflow position before the impact of investment performance. In other words, the cost of benefits payable exceeds the value of the contributions which it is receiving. This is in fact typical of the current position of occupational pension funds in the UK, as may be seen from their membership profile. Scheme members may be thought of as 'active' if they are still in employment and having contributions made for them. The others are either 'pensioners', in which case they are retired and are receiving benefits payable by the fund, or 'inactive' (sometimes called 'deferred'), in which case they have left the employment of the sponsor but have accrued rights that will kick in at some date in the future when they retire. The LPFA's 2003/4 membership breakdown was broadly typical of UK pension funds:

Members	% of total
Current	29
Inactive	27
Pensioners	44

Thus it is hardly surprising that the cashflow situation is negative. Positive cashflow is attributable to just 29% of the membership, while negative cashflow is attributable to 44%. Given anticipated demographic changes and the fact that there will be a steady movement of 'inactive' members to 'pensioner' status, then this situation can only get worse.

Now imagine that we can give these figures not just for the current year but for future years as well. Why should this be so difficult? Companies which come to a public stock market by way of a flotation (IPO) are required to make such projections, usually for at least three years, and all companies routinely make such projections both for the purposes of their own internal strategic planning and for use by financial analysts. In fact, I would argue that it should be easier to do in the case of a pension plan than in the case of a company. The level of uncertainty surrounding any business must be greater than that experienced by an organisation where the future is broadly predictable by means of arithmetic and statistical analysis. After all, if one can predict the likely changes in the relative percentages of the three member types, assisted by data on the average age of the members of each group and current longevity assumptions, then the figures should more or less fall into place.

Naturally there will still be some level of uncertainty inherent in the situation. Suppose, for example, that the sponsor decides for its own business reasons to launch an early retirement programme, or to close a particular plant or subsidiary. However, we can handle uncertainty, at least to some extent, by introducing an 'uncertainty factor', notionally increasing the likely impact of liabilities (or the range of such possible impact) as they stretch further into the future.

The important thing, however, is that at the end of this process we will have a table of actual liabilities that we can use, stretching out as far as we want to be able to predict. For ease of calculation we will restate these simply as a percentage of the present value of the pension fund. To continue our actual example, the value of the LPFA fund at the end of the 2003/4 period was £2.7 billion, and so the net liabilities (£61.754 million) represented about 2.3% of this figure. From now on, we will generally be talking about liabilities in this way, as a percentage of present fund value.

The main difference, then, between Total Funding and actual practice is that we are using real liabilities instead of artificial, discounted liabilities. I hope that the argument for this is obvious. If you are sitting down to initiate a strategic planning process then it helps if the data on which you are basing your analysis is accurate.

3.   Total Funding

Because it plans to meet all of a pension plan's liabilities, I call my planning concept Total Funding, and the very simple arithmetic behind it the Total Funding Model (TFM). Total Funding assumes that any pension fund will plan to meet all its future liabilities as they fall due, while preserving the relative purchasing power of the fund to safeguard the interests of future pensioners.

While I refer specifically to pension funds, this process could equally well be adopted by any institution with specific future funding needs. Endowments and Foundations would be obvious examples.

Having worked out our basic inputs we are now in a position to put the first element of the TFM in place.

We know our predicted future outflows. Where they are due to occur a long time in the future we will increase them slightly to allow for uncertainty. This is a purely subjective matter and you can take any figures that seem sensible to you. Personally, my preference would be to increase them by about 10% if they are more than 10 years in the future, and then with one extra percent for every extra year, up to a maximum of about 25%.

What else do we know? Clearly we know the present value of our pension fund. So remembering that we are stating the outflows as percentages of our present value, we can carry out a simple compounding exercise to find out what the future value of the fund would have to be at the end of the period:

$$FV = PV\left(\frac{1+O}{1}\right)^n$$

where O is the annual outflow, adjusted where necessary by the uncertainty factor, and n is the number of years under review.

However, O will be different each year (in the nature of things it will increase if only as a function of the growing maturity of the scheme) and so I think it could more correctly be stated thus:

$$FV = PV\left(\frac{1+O^2}{1} \cdots \frac{1+O^n}{1}\right)$$

Of course, in practice one would simply map the individual cashflows on a spreadsheet, but I think the formula does at least set out the general principle.

One important point that deserves to be made if only in passing is that the model can of course also be used to estimate the effect of different levels of contribution. Since O will be calculated as explained above, then increasing the amount of contribution will have the effect of decreasing the value of O. This would flow through into a decreased future value.

The Target Rate of Return can now be calculated quite simply by finding the IRR which is required to turn PV into FV over the number of years in question. This would of course be the same as the IRR of the intervening cashflows.

4. The Escalator Factor

Institutional investors need to plan their investment strategy to meet the objective of being able to meet their liabilities as they fall due, but without diminishing the relative purchasing power of their fund. We have looked in outline above at how we might consider the first requirement. What do we need to know about in considering the second?

A pension fund's liabilities might be compared to annuities, since they are payable for the life of an individual, or the joint lives of two individuals. It is therefore of great importance for our planning process that we should be able to predict the number of years, on average, for which our liabilities are likely to continue. Sadly, this is not possible because of demographic change. What we are seeing in most Western countries is an ageing population due mainly to three factors:

- A 'baby boom' caused by a bulge in the number of babies being born in the late 1940s as servicemen returned home from the Second World War.
- A falling birth rate ever since.
- Advances in medical science and lifestyle changes resulting in people living longer.

As a result, with every year that passes the average age of the population increases slightly. It has been calculated that by the year 2020 half of the UK's electorate will be over the age of 50, which gives a strong indication that pensions should be an ever more important political issue in the years to come.

At the time of writing (2005) government figures state that men and women aged 65 in the UK can expect to live to 81 and 84 respectively. Each of these figures is expected to increase by three years over the course of the next 16 (having increased by about four years over the last 20). I think it will be obvious from this that there is a clear upward trend in life expectancy generally; a boy born in the UK in 1901 could expect to live to only 45.

Similarly, a debate is currently raging in the USA around the future provision of Social Security benefits. (In the USA, this is much more than just an old age pension; it also embraces disability payments and financial support for the spouses and dependents of deceased and retired workers.) In the year 2000 there were 35 million Americans over the age of 65, but by 50 years later, in 2050, that number will have more than doubled to over 80 million. To put that in context, in 1950 the burden of each retired person's Social Security entitlement was spread across 16 taxpayers. By 2050 it will have to be borne by just 2.

The latest US Social Security Trustees' Report states:

> After 2000, the reductions in death rates . . . are assumed to change rapidly from the average reductions by age, sex and cause of death observed between 1979 and 2000.

Grim though this picture may be for those who have to plan for the provision of retirement benefits world wide, it may tell only part of the story. Recent press articles claim that if stem cell therapy works as some scientists claim it might, then within 30 years we may have the medical technology to allow people to live routinely not just to 100 or 120 but for literally hundreds of years. An article in *The Sunday Times* in March 2005 suggested that the first thousand-year-old human being may already have been born.

However fanciful claims of this nature may seem, there can be little doubt that we are living in a period of rapid technological progress in the Life Science area. Even a few years ago much of the work currently being performed in genetics or nanotechnology would have been regarded as science fiction. Surely this must flow through into increased life expectancy. Indeed, the one thing on which everyone seems able to agree is that life expectancy ('longevity assumptions' in actuarys-peak) will indeed continue to increase. The only area of uncertainty is by how much.

Suppose, for example, that in 30 years' time humans in a developed Western society could expect to live routinely to 100. Given the way things are going this may not be as wildly optimistic as it sounds (indeed, the current debate in the USA hints at exactly such a possibility), and it would render the figures for the UK which I quote above completely obsolete and inadequate. Instead of life expectancy increasing by three years over the course of 16, it would increase by 20 over the life of 30 – nearly four times as quickly as predicted. Against this sort of backdrop, debate about having to work longer before retiring may perhaps seem less controversial.

There are a number of ways in which demographic changes will impact upon pension plans, their funding analysis and their required investment strategy. Some of these are fairly obvious, but others less so. Clearly since a pension fund represents a portion of the overall population then if with every year that passes the average age of the population increases, so with every year that passes, the average age of the pension fund's members will increase slightly (more markedly for those schemes that are closed to new members).

This will, in turn, affect a pension plan in four ways:

- With every year that passes, the ratio of pensioners to contributors will increase slightly.
- With every year that passes, the retirement age of the average member comes slightly closer.
- With every year that passes, the assumed lifespan of each member increases slightly.
- Additionally, for many final salary (DB) schemes, a member's level of entitlement increases with length of service.

Having read this section you will understand that the future liabilities of any pension scheme (except perhaps an extremely mature one, whose members are all at or around the limit of their life expectancy) must be increasing with each year that passes, and thus its overall funding position must be worsening. This is a very important concept to grasp. Left to its own devices, the funding position of any pension plan will not stand still, but decline.

It follows, then, that a certain amount of investment return must be used simply to offset the draining effect of demographic change before any contribution can be made to actually improving the pension plan's overall funding position. Imagine that you are keeping water in a jug which is marked with lines to measure its contents but which also has a hole in the bottom so that water is running out in a thin trickle. In order to keep the water level at the same measuring line, you will have to pour more water into the jug.

Surprisingly, as we will see when we come to consider the question of asset allocation, many pension funds do not seem to understand this point, and effectively ignore it. Having read this far in the chapter, I hope you can appreciate just how disastrous it may be to ignore **the escalator factor**.

For every year that passes, a pension fund needs to grow in value by a certain amount just in order to stand still in relative terms. I call this 'the escalator factor'. Imagine that for reasons best known to yourself, you have decided to walk up the down escalator and are now approximately halfway up. If you walk quickly you will eventually reach the top. If you stop, or walk very slowly you will eventually find yourself back at the bottom.

It is the same with investment returns. If the amount of your liabilities is increasing with each year that passes, then the value of your fund calculated before payment of those liabilities must increase by the same amount in real terms each year. In other words, if you can walk upwards at exactly the same speed at which the escalator is travelling downwards you will in fact stand still in relative terms; you will stay halfway up.

What we need to know is by exactly how much the size of the fund needs to grow each year to stand still. In the practical example I gave, we could simply use trial and error, adjusting our pace and seeing if we ended up closer or further away from the top until we could find exactly the right pace needed to stay in the same place. With pension funding we can obviously not take this approach. We need to find some way of calculating the rate required, or at least making some sensible assumptions that will give us a rough estimate.

I must make clear a number of things here. Firstly, the things which we are attempting to model are to a large extent uncertain and unpredictable. Secondly, no one has previously attempted to model their effect on a pension scheme in precisely this way. Thirdly, even if we are completely right about their nature, extent and effect, then it would probably take about 10 years of actual observation and analysis to see if the hard numbers that we had decided to ascribe to them were likely to prove valid. Finally, it could be argued that there is an element of double counting, in that the actuaries may already have built various demographic assumptions into their liability estimates. Accordingly, we are in the realm of informed guesswork here, not hard scientific theory, and whatever figures we choose will be completely open to attack by anyone who may have an interest in pretending that nothing is wrong with the present system, or who may just have a conceptual problem with the model as a whole. I acknowledge all of this.

However, I strongly believe that it is infinitely preferable to make some attempt (hopefully as intelligent an attempt as possible) to model these factors in terms of hard numbers than simply to ignore them. In particular, as we will see, it is precisely when investment returns are set *outside* a Total Funding Model, i.e. in isolation, as UK pension schemes currently do, that it is absolutely imperative to consider these factors; indeed, without considering them, investment returns must be completely meaningless in Total Funding terms.

Suggested Treatment of the Escalator Factor

We have identified four different elements of demographic change. Let us give them the symbols d_1 to d_4:

- d_1 the increase in the ratio of pensioners to contributors
- d_2 the time to retirement age getting shorter
- d_3 the increase in life expectancy
- d_4 the level of entitlement increasing with length of service.

As we have already noted, d_4 will apply in some cases but not all, and so the first thing we need to do is to check the terms of our own particular pension scheme to see whether this is so or not. In some cases this will be purely a function of length of service, and in some cases it may be a hybrid of service and age. In all cases there is usually a 'plateau' level of benefits which, once reached, cannot be exceeded.

My suggestion is quite simple. We should ascribe to each of these d factors a value by which it will impact on the pension fund or, to put it the other way round, a value by which the pension fund will have to increase each year in real terms in order to absorb their impact and stay in the same place. The end product of the Total Funding Model is a target rate of return. Therefore it seems to make sense to ascribe to each of the d factors a percentage rate of return which the pension fund will be required to earn in order to offset its effect.

I have said it already, but it is worth repeating. What I am proposing is an intuitive process rather than a strictly mathematical one, and I am not suggesting that whatever figures we use are any sort of mathematical measure of their actual effect in any given year (although they are intended to approximate to it or simulate it from year to year over a lengthy period). Indeed, given the complexities and uncertainties inherent in the situation (how longevity assumptions might change, how the ratio of current, deferred and pensioner members might change, etc.) I do not believe that it is necessarily capable of precise calculation. To anyone who is approaching the situation on a purely scientific basis, and in the expectation of a neat mathematical solution, then my approach will doubtless seem simplistic and open to attack. Yet that same person will ultimately be disappointed in the search for the 'right' answer and in the end will be forced into making assumptions, just as we are doing.

For the same reason, it is completely open to you to discuss and insert your own figures, and it may be that you will suggest completely different ones (particularly if you happen to be working in the sphere of stem cell research!). The important thing is that you should at least insert *some* numbers, because only then will you see the heavy drag of the escalator factor on pension returns, and only then will you in consequence recognise just what little effect on Total Funding your present returns may be achieving.

Let us ignore d_4 for the time being and focus on the other three d factors. I think we would all agree that it is d_3 (the increase in longevity assumptions) that has potentially the most explosive effect. The need to pay the average member pension benefits for 20 years longer than anticipated will clearly be a greater burden to a pension fund than to receive contributions from any one member for a slighter shorter time, or to find overall net cashflow worsening slightly from year to year. Therefore it seems logical that whatever value we ascribe to the others, the value of d_3 should be greater.

Instinctively, there should be some sort of proportionality between the escalator factor and investment return. Intuitively, it does not feel right that it should not be able to offset the escalator factor within the parameters of a reasonable rate of investment return. At the same time, it does not feel right that the d factors should be given such low value that they become numerically insignificant. There must be a compromise solution whereby they have a significant impact, but not such a huge impact that they can never be completely compensated for.

Accordingly, I am going to suggest that we use 0.5% as a starting point for each of the d factors, but then increase d_3 to 1% to take account of its greater likely impact. Thus, assuming for the sake of the example that d_4 does not apply to our scheme, this would give us a total for the d factors of 2%. This means that the fund needs to grow at 2% a year just to stand still in Total Funding terms. Is that correct?

No, it is wrong. Remember that we said 'in real terms'. In other words, we also have to factor in inflation. There is no benefit in our fund size growing by 2% if its actual purchasing power (its ability to pay out pension benefits) has been eroded in the meantime. Thus we can arrive at the formula:

$$E = d_1 + d_2 + d_3 + d_4 + i$$

where E is the rate required to remain in the same relative position ('the escalator factor') and i is the expected rate of inflation. Thus the value of the fund one year from now needs to be:

$$FV = PV\left(\frac{100+E}{100}\right)$$

where FV is the fund value in one year's time and PV is the present fund value.

Let us try an example of this, assuming a present fund value of £100M and an expected rate of inflation of 3.5% (and remembering that $E = d_1 + d_2 + d_3 + d_4 + i$, but that we are ignoring d_4 for these purposes):

$$FV = £100M\left(\frac{100+0.5+0.5+1+3.5}{100}\right)$$

$$FFV = £100M\left(\frac{105.5}{100}\right) = £105.5$$

Following the normal principle of compounding we can also perform the same calculation over n years simply by raising the calculation to the power of n. Let us assume that we need to calculate the required future value in 20 years' time:

$$FV_n = PV\left(\frac{100+E}{100}\right)^n$$

$$FV = £100M\left(\frac{105.5}{100}\right)^{20} = £100M \times 2.92 = £292M$$

This example helps to show the magnitude of the impact of the escalator factor. The fund in this example could grow by very nearly three times over a 20-year period and thanks to compounding still not be any better off in terms of its ability to pay its liabilities as they fall due.

In my experience this issue is not at all well understood by many pension plans and throws into a very dubious light the rates of return expected from their current asset allocation mixes. We will be examining this in more detail in a later chapter, but suffice it to say at this point that their expected rates of investment return are frequently barely enough to cover the escalator factor, and therefore can have little or no effect on Total Funding. My case for suggesting that the point is not understood is strengthened by the fact that, to take UK pension funds as an example, they are putting a large portion of their fund (frequently about 30%) into an asset class (bonds) which they must know is most unlikely ever to match the escalator factor (let alone their target rate of return), and therefore can only ever act as a drag on the performance of the rest of the portfolio.

5.   Putting it Together

So now we have all the elements of the TFM that we need. We know what our liabilities are likely to be over a given period, increased where necessary by a prudent uncertainty factor, and we know what additional rate of return is likely to be needed to ensure that the relative purchasing power of our fund at the end of the period is no less than it is now.

All we need to do, then, is to combine the algebra we have been looking at so far:

$$FV = PV\left[\left(\frac{100 + O + E}{100}\right)^2 \cdots \left(\frac{100 + O + E}{100}\right)^n\right]$$

where O is the net outflow of each year, increased where appropriate by the uncertainty factor, and E is the escalator factor. The Target Rate of Return (TRR) will be the IRR that will increase PV to FV over the number of years in question.

Finally we have the output of the first part of our planning process: working out what it is that we need to achieve. The next step is to check that the objective is realistic. This is of course a circular process, and it may be a little unfair to introduce it at this stage since we have not yet started to look at the returns of different asset classes, but clearly if the TFM throws out a TRR of 25% then we need to look very carefully at ways of reducing the objective to more manageable proportions. These issues fall outside the scope of this book, but would obviously include such things as increasing the rate of employer and/or employee contributions and deferring the retirement age. None of these is likely to be an easy discussion to have, but initiating and pursuing all of them as quickly as possible is likely to be a better option than setting off on a quest for an unattainable objective.

CONCLUSIONS

We have covered a lot of ground in this chapter, beginning with the very general and descending fairly quickly to the very specific. It may be considered that I have laboured some of the specific issues unnecessarily, but I felt this to be crucial in the light of the surprising insight that I gained, while preparing for this book, into the way in which investors actually approach this area in practice.

I can think of no logical way in which one can embark upon a strategic planning exercise without knowing exactly what it is one seeks to achieve, and I can think of no logical way of assessing the long-term financial obligations of a pension fund other than by a process such as Total Funding. It is therefore very disturbing to find that in practice exactly the opposite actually occurs.

In reality, investment policy is often set in a vacuum. In the world of institutions there is a supply side and a demand side. The demand side is clearly the need to meet all future liabilities. The supply side is the investment performance of the fund that will hopefully provide the necessary money to satisfy the demand side. Why, then, should one's thinking keep these issues separate rather than connecting them? How can one embark on any sort of planning exercise if one regards the supply side as something over which one has no control, and has no idea of the true size of the demand side?

Total Funding offers a simple and logical way of at least attempting to put some sort of number on the demand side. For the remainder of the book we will be focusing on the supply side, but at the risk of boring my readers to death I must emphasise again and again that there is no point at all in embarking on an asset allocation exercise (the supply side) unless one knows the size of the demand that must be met. The calculation of a Target Rate of Return (the size of the demand) is an essential pre-requisite and it is staggering to me that most investors are not going through this process, but simply plucking a figure out of the air in some arbitrary way. We will be looking at the Yale Endowment in the next chapter as a model of best practice on the supply side, and I would also commend their approach on the demand side. They undertake regular and continuing assessment of their future funding needs, including modelling all sorts of 'what if' scenarios. How many investors can say the same?

I hope you will have noticed one other important point. In looking at how we should plan investment strategy we have been concerned with long periods and with compound returns over long periods. To me this seems an obvious approach since it gels perfectly with the real life situation in which investors such as pension funds find themselves; they have future liabilities for which they need to plan over long periods. I will be developing this thinking in more detail in later chapters, but for the moment suffice it to say that what actually happens in the real world is usually exactly the opposite, with most investors and analysts being obsessed with the short term and, in particular, with annual returns. I trust that, from our brief look at Total Funding, it will already be obvious that annual returns as such are irrelevant for any institution that plans its investment strategy over a long period. Why should I be concerned with how much any particular investment returns in any given year? All I am concerned with is that my portfolio as a whole should achieve the TRR over the whole period in question. This has profound implications not only for asset allocation but also for traditional concepts of financial risk, and later I will be devoting two chapters to this latter issue.

One final point on Total Funding: I am not suggesting that this is an exercise under which one models, say, the next 20 years or so and then sits back and concentrates on investment management. On the contrary, it should be an ongoing process, undertaken at least once a year and preferably quarterly. Assumptions will change, as will the present value of the fund. Each year another group of projected cashflows will be added onto the model. Our thinking should never stand still, and nor should our analysis.

Thus we embark upon what many will probably, and quite properly, regard as the 'real' subject of this book: a Multi Asset Class approach to investment strategy. Please remember, however, that no investment strategy exists in isolation, but only in regard to the environment in which one operates and the objective which one seeks to achieve. Unless both of these are known and understood, then any attempt at investment strategy is meaningless.

I will be summarising the key points at the end of each chapter, as I have personally found this to be a helpful practice when reading other books.

SUMMARY

- Strategy should be thought of as a plan of action designed to achieve a specific objective.
- The steps set out in the action plan are tactics, not strategy. Strategy is essentially long term in nature, and refers to the totality of the process. Tactics are typically short term and deal with specific parts of the whole.
- The first essential of any strategic planning exercise is to identify and specify exactly the objective that is to be achieved.
- The only logical objective of any investor should be to meet whatever the funding requirements may be. In the case of a pension fund this may be expressed as meeting all its future pension liabilities.
- There is great danger in pension funds adopting the discounted, artificial liabilities of the sponsor, expressed for accounting purposes. What is needed for planning purposes are the real, undiscounted liabilities of the pension fund itself, increased by an uncertainty factor if desired.
- Planning cannot ignore the effects of inflation or demographic change. Assumptions in respect of these are incorporated into an escalator factor.
- The liabilities and the escalator factor together form the Total Funding Model. The Total Funding concept states the obligation of any pension fund to be to put itself in a position to be able to discharge all its future liabilities as they fall due, while at the same time preserving the relative purchasing power of the fund.
- The Total Funding Model produces a Target Rate of Return which, once subjected to a reality check, becomes the strategic objective to be achieved. Investment strategy can now be planned in a logical and meaningful way with reference to this specific objective.
- It is essential that the TRR is calculated in this, or some similar, manner. If it is not, then no attempt at investment strategy can be meaningful.

2

Multi Asset Class Investing

THE ASSET ALLOCATION BACKGROUND

As promised at the end of the last chapter, we will from now on be addressing the supply side of investment strategy – how to produce the money that we need to satisfy the demand side. This could equally well be called asset allocation, since that is effectively what investment strategy involves.

Before we delve into the detail of this, however, it may be useful to set out three trends that have combined to bring asset allocation, and particularly Multi Asset Class Investing ('MAC Investing') well and truly into the spotlight over the last few years, a hot topic that seems to feature increasingly at conferences and in pensions and investment journals.

Firstly, there is a growing recognition that investors need to think in terms of absolute returns rather than relative returns. Having read the first chapter you will understand that it is most unlikely that any two investors will ever have exactly the same demand side characteristics, and it is thus most unlikely that they will have exactly the same Target Rate of Return. Why then should it be logical for them to benchmark their investment performance against each other's? If both perform equally, then both could be doing equally badly, or equally well, or one could be achieving its TRR while the other is not. Clearly, this must be a totally meaningless exercise. Yet it may surprise some to know that this is exactly what many UK pension funds do, even to the extent that, for example, Local Authority pension funds in London will benchmark their performance against other London Local Authority pension funds. We will discuss this in more detail shortly.

Secondly, we now live in a new world of widespread pension fund deficits rather than surpluses. This has many implications, not least in a socio-economic context of what quality of retirement employees may expect in years to come. However, the main implication for our purposes is that the old cosy world in which it was assumed that one probably needed to do little more than marginally outperform inflation, has been swept away for ever. In the old world, for example, bonds were often seen as an ideal investment since they did exactly that. In the new world, where the imperative is to claw back the deficit, much higher rates of return are obviously required and bonds have moved from the sublime to the ridiculous; from being an ideal investment to being an ineligible one. 'Ineligible' since they cannot possibly match the TRR of any investor, and thus can only ever act as a drag on performance, meaning that the remaining assets in the portfolio have to work even harder (effectively outperform to make up for the underperformance of bonds). On the other side of the coin, the so-called 'alternative' asset classes are now seen as offering the potential to deliver the higher level of returns that will be required by investors in the future. We will be discussing this too in more detail later.

Thirdly, the collapse of the world's equity markets during the three years from 2000 to 2002 has shaken the cosy old complacency about equities being a safe haven, and a reliable source of outperformance. This makes a move towards MAC investing an inevitable consequence for two reasons. (1) If one cannot invest in bonds, and equities are no longer seen as totally safe and reliable, where can one go other than in the direction of so-called 'alternative' asset classes? (2) If equity markets are not safe then investors need to be offered protection by way of diversification, in which case a MAC investment model is a logical development, with capital being spread across a number of different asset classes with low correlation to each other.

All this has caused a particular culture shock to those investors and consultants who have been clinging grimly to their traditional views on asset allocation despite overwhelming practical experience and real world evidence to the contrary. Until very recently, for example, pension consultants in the UK were actively encouraging their clients not to diversify into alternative assets. In fact, they would often suggest the worst of both worlds, namely purely nominal allocations that could not possibly make any difference to overall portfolio returns but, equally, could not justify the devotion of the necessary time and resources to be run efficiently as investment programmes. As you may tire of hearing as we go through the book, hedge fund and private equity investments, even when lumped together, currently total less than 1% of UK pension plan assets.

From my conversations with them over the last year or so, the message is gradually beginning to percolate, but they find themselves in an embarrassing situation, since to begin preaching the gospel now involves finding some plausible reason for having been so wrong in the very recent past. Some evidence of a slow *volte face* is, however, beginning to emerge. While they cannot bring themselves to accept the need for diversification, they are now at least speaking of 'diversity' of asset allocation!

POTENTIAL PROBLEMS IN MOVING TO A MULTI ASSET CLASS APPROACH

Other than the purely cultural (and these should not be underestimated – in the world of investment strategy, reason often takes a back seat to intellectual cowardice and blind prejudice), there are three practical issues that may at first seem to present stumbling blocks along the road to MAC investing; they have certainly and frequently been presented as such by consultants.

Firstly, it may seem to the uninitiated that there is a lack of proper return information about alternative asset classes such as hedge funds, private equity and property. It is this supposed lack of reliable benchmarks that I have frequently heard presented as a reason for ignoring outperforming asset classes in favour of a 'safer' approach. Well, in the course of my research for this book I had no difficulty at all in finding the performance figures I needed for any particular asset class. Some I knew about already, and others I was able to unearth quite easily by talking to practitioners in the asset class; but, whatever the case, adequate, professionally maintained databases of benchmark figures do indeed exist. Thus, if it ever was the case that performance figures were not available, I can personally vouch for the fact that it is no longer the case, as you will see from the figures presented in later chapters.

Secondly, no one has yet suggested a way of validly comparing the returns of all asset classes directly against each other. As we will be looking at this in more detail later, let me say here that there are particular problems with regard, for example, to private equity, where annual returns are simply not a valid measure of performance, except in very limited circumstances. This is true, and yet it is surprising that it has been seen as a major stumbling block since there is an easy and fairly obvious way of doing so, which will be outlined in this book for the first time.

Thirdly, the idea of Multi Asset Class Investing (or MAC investing) will be alien to many pension funds and other institutional investors around the world who are still labouring with a traditional so-called 'risk-adjusted' investment model. As we will see in coming chapters, the traditional view of risk is simply not equal to the task of dealing with modern asset allocation issues, and in fact was probably always deeply flawed conceptually.

As the notion of 'risk' plays such a key role in portfolio theory I will be devoting three entire chapters to exploring what may properly be meant by the term, and proposing new measures of risk which are relevant to the actual concerns of real world investors. I will therefore leave all that for later, and begin by explaining exactly what is meant by MAC investing and the thinking that lies behind it.

THE YALE MODEL

The Yale Model will be well known to many US investors, but I make no excuse for covering it in some detail, first because I take it as the basis (one might almost say the inspiration) for all MAC investment theory and, secondly, there are a surprising number of investors outside the USA who have never heard of it, despite David Swensen's best selling book on the subject.[1]

At its simplest, Swensen's idea was to split a portfolio into a number of broadly equal tranches and invest each tranche into a different asset class, with as little correlation as possible between the various classes.

There are three main strands of theory that underlie the Yale Model, plus a fourth which, while not explicitly stated in these terms, is I believe implicit in how Swensen describes his investment approach. Let me deal with each of these in turn before circling back to discuss the Yale Model within the wider context of MAC investing as a whole.

Higher Returns as a Goal, not Peer Group Benchmarking

Swensen began implementing the Yale Model in the 1980s, so it would be wrong to credit him with any clairvoyance in predicting the pensions funding crisis that is currently gripping so many countries around the world and has meant that pension funds have no alternative but to consider a higher return investment strategy in order to clawback their deficits and be able to meet their liabilities as they fall due. He seems to have been driven by intellectual curiosity, and a welcome eagerness

---

[1] David Swensen (2000) *Pioneering Portfolio Management*. New York: The Free Press (Simon & Schuster).

not to subscribe to accepted ideas just because they had become common practice.

He recognised that many investors were going about the asset selection process driven not by a desire to obtain the highest return, but by two main desires. The first was to stay in step with their peer group by broadly replicating their portfolios. The second was a desire for liquidity. In his book, he questions both of these and finds them to be illogical.

The desire to benchmark oneself against a peer group is sadly almost universal in the investment world and is often carried to ridiculous lengths. As we have already noted, for example, in the UK, Local Authority (i.e. Public) occupational schemes benchmark themselves against other Local Authority schemes, and there is even a system under which those in the London area benchmark themselves against others in the London area. This occurs both at the general level (virtually identical asset mixes) and at the particular (managers are rarely considered unless they already manage other Local Authority money). As Swensen puts it:

> Many investors simply allocate among the asset classes popular at the time in proportions similar to those of other investors, creating uncontroversial portfolios that may or may not address institutional needs. By relying on the decisions of others to drive portfolio choices, investors fail to consider the function of particular asset classes in a portfolio designed to meet specific goals.

As he points out, the objections to such a system are obvious. First, investment performance should be benchmarked against a target rate of return. Such a return must be scientifically calculated for each individual pension scheme (using Total Funding or some similar system) and will almost certainly not be exactly the same in any two cases, let alone across a large number of cases. Therefore to benchmark yourself against your peers rather than against what you actually need to achieve is clearly meaningless. Secondly, asset classes and individual managers within asset classes should be selected both on the basis of their intrinsic attractiveness, and of their likelihood of helping to meet your target rate of return. The decisions made by others within your peer group are irrelevant on both bases. The selection process of others is likely to be driven at least in part by their own circumstances which will include both individual prejudice and different views of risk, not least because, as we will see, risk is not absolute but varies according to one's target rate of return and, as we have already noted, this is most unlikely to be exactly the same in any two cases.

Sadly this fallacious approach is driven not just by a profoundly mistaken approach to investment strategy but also by rigid internal processes that create inertia and choke any originality of thought. In some parts of the world, such as the UK, a lack of investment knowledge within pension plans, a gross failure to devote enough trustee time to investment matters, and the unnatural grip that pension consultants are able to exert over all stages of the investment process in consequence also play an important part. Thus, while in theory the new world of MAC investing should be available to all, in practice its benefits will continue to be denied to those who lack the intellectual courage and originality of thought to kick over the traces of old world practices and dogma.

LIQUIDITY

The question of liquidity highlights once again the intellectual limitations under which many institutional investors and their advisers labour. What J.M. Keynes called 'the fetish of liquidity' is still alive and well around the world. I will be dealing specifically with the issue of liquidity within a MAC portfolio (real liquidity as opposed to imagined liquidity) in a later chapter but let me here simply set out Swensen's view of impact of liquidity on investment returns – a view with which I would humbly but heartily concur.

Swensen recognises that there is a price, often a very heavy price, to be paid for liquidity in the shape of lower returns. The return expectations of most investors reflect this, varying usually from government bonds at the bottom end to something that is perceived[2] as highly illiquid, such as private equity at the top end. Swensen takes the point that there is no sense in paying a price for something unless you have to, and that accordingly in theory one should keep the amount of liquid assets within the portfolio to a minimum.

> Managers willing to accept illiquidity achieve a significant edge in seeking high risk-adjusted returns. Because market players routinely overpay for liquidity, serious investors benefit by avoiding overpriced liquid securities and locating bargains in less widely followed, less liquid market segments.

---

[2] Wrongly, as we will see in a later chapter.

The content of the Yale portfolio reflects this, having at many times been more than 60% 'illiquid' (although I will be showing later that conventional views of liquidity are outdated and mistaken, and that in any event institutions do not need nearly the level of liquidity which they think they do) but the proof of the pudding is in the eating and the portfolio, once mature, has ranked consistently in the top percentile of US endowment investment performance, with an average return of 17.4% over the last decade. Last year the endowment returned over 22%; the S&P 500 index rose just over 4% during the same period.[3]

Swensen's views on liquidity have been widely accepted and adopted in the USA, where, for example, many pension funds have allocations to private equity of over 20%. (I know of one public pension plan in the USA which has just reduced its private equity allocation from 25% to 15%, not because of disillusionment with the asset class but because so many US pension funds are now running similar allocation levels that accessing quality private equity funds in the USA has become a real problem.)

John Griswold, himself a Yale graduate and now executive director of the Commonfund Institute, is typical of many US investors when he says:

> Something David Swensen has said over and over again is that the yields in the private markets are higher than those in the public markets. Public markets are relatively inefficient, and the efficient market is what the smart investor works for.[4]

Compare and contrast this with the situation in the UK, for example, where private equity and hedge funds, even when lumped together, total less than 1% of UK pension plan assets, and do not even rate a mention in an annual review of Local Authority pension funds, being described simply as 'other investments'.[5]

DIVERSIFICATION

I will be dealing with the idea of diversification of risk in a later chapter. I trust, however, that anyone would accept the notion that, just as the

---

[3] All figures from the Yale Endowment annual report, reported in the *Yale Daily News*, 20 September 2005.

[4] *Yale Daily News* as above.

[5] WM Annual Review 2004.

specific risk of holding any one asset can be diversified away by holding a sufficient number of different assets, the same must hold true for asset classes. If there is a specific risk attached to investing in, say, a US real estate portfolio, then clearly that risk can be diversified away by investing at the same time in a sufficient number of other asset classes. What the risk might be, and what might constitute 'a sufficient number', may be open to debate but the principle surely is not.

The principle has even crept slowly into UK law, being given expression by The Local Government Pension Scheme (Management and Investment of Funds) Regulations 1998:

> 'investment policy must be formulated with a view to the advisability of investing fund money in a wide variety of investments.'

Yet if the principle is so obvious, why is it so widely flouted around the world, not least by the very UK Local Authority pension funds to whom the above legal requirement applies? (Please note the deliberate use of the word 'must' in the above statement – this is a mandatory requirement, not a guideline.) In 2004 they had 69.6% of their assets invested in quoted equities, of which 60% (i.e. about 42% of their total assets) was in the UK public market. (Compare that figure of nearly 70% with Yale's exposure to both domestic and overseas quoted equities together at that time, which was about 28%.)

It does seem incredible that this very basic concept of diversification should be ignored when it requires no real understanding of finance theory at all but only a healthy dose of common sense. Which of us when asked to look after money with the heavy legal responsibility of a trustee would elect to put all our eggs in one basket rather than spread our investment activities over a number of different investment classes?

Yet this is exactly what pension trustees around the world have done, and the damage that their actions have caused is plain to see. The pension funding deficit in the UK, for example, is variously estimated at sums in excess of £700 billion, which I calculate as being roughly equivalent to seven years' total income tax receipts. Yet, as will be demonstrated in the final chapter, a diversification of 20% into only one asset class initially (private equity), with rebalancing into another (absolute return funds) would have effectively prevented this from happening.

LONG-TERM RETURNS

Of all the mistaken mindsets that beset the world of investment, surely the most pernicious must be the obsession with the short term, and with annual returns. Let me use an image of a train journey, to which I will return at various times later in the book. If I am taking a train to travel to a very important meeting that will begin promptly at a stated time and which I cannot possibly miss, then do I really care about how quickly or slowly the train will travel at any time during its journey? No. All I care about is that the train should arrive on time at the end of the journey. I believe that this image encapsulates two totally different attitudes to investment.

The investor who is driven by annual returns (and, to be fair, many compensation schemes are based on such a measure) will be content if a particular asset class delivers a satisfactory return over the course of the current year. The more sophisticated investor will recognise that annual returns as such are irrelevant and will be looking to plan an investment strategy over a long period (20 years? 25 years?) and that all that matters to that investor is that the portfolio as a whole should deliver the target rate of return when measured across the whole of that period. It is rather like thinking about the difference between simple interest and compound interest, and just as fundamental a difference.

Let me now deal with two issues that rear their heads immediately. The first is that there is no available risk model that can handle anything other than periodic (usually annual) returns. However, there are certain asset classes (chiefly private equity), for which annual returns can almost never be a valid performance guide (I will discuss why this is in a later chapter on private equity) which in turn means that it is not possible to arrive at a 'risk-adjusted' return (whatever this might mean) for such an asset class. Even worse, the distinction between annual returns and compound returns is sometimes simply not recognised and people start using things like Monte Carlo analysis (which is dependent on periodic returns as its inputs) and applying them to private equity returns. Thus, if one accepts the need to think in long-term/compound returns rather than short-term/annual returns, one must also accept the need for a totally new approach to 'risk'. I will not develop this point further at this stage since I devote three entire chapters to this issue later.

The second is that there is often a conflict between the short-term/annual returns approach and the long-term/compound returns approach. Beginning a private equity fund investment programme, for example, can actually lead to a dip in annual returns in the short term as a necessary price to be paid for better compound performance measured over the whole term (including the year in question).[6] Unless this point is understood and accepted by all those who are involved in the taking of investment decisions, then it is difficult to see how they can ever embark properly upon a MAC investment strategy.

To sum up, therefore, I think we can identify three main strands in the philosophy of the Yale Model.

- Each investor must set its own investment strategy with regard to its own individual requirements and circumstances, rather than benchmarking itself unthinkingly against its peer group.
- Liquidity is bad not good, in the sense that it comes at a price, often a heavy price, and the sensible investor will avoid it except to the extent that is absolutely necessary.
- An investment institution needs to plan for the long term and thus investment returns should be measured over the long term, not on the basis of individual annual returns, which may fluctuate from year to year.

THE YALE MODEL AND MAC INVESTING

The Yale Model uses six different types of investments: domestic (quoted) equities, foreign (quoted) equities, private equity, real (property-related) assets, absolute return funds (for which hedge funds can be seen as an alternative description), and bonds. However, though Yale refer to six, I believe we can conveniently coalesce these into just four asset classes and I will be devoting a chapter to each of these: quoted equities, private equity, hedge funds, and property. Let me explain my thinking.

Bonds

Such is the requirement for higher investment returns today, particularly with so many pension funds around the world being in deficit, that I simply do not believe that bonds are an appropriate investment. As we will see in the next chapter, a pension fund needs to make a certain

---

[6] Although there are ways of ameliorating this that are not widely used or understood.

return every year just to stand still in real terms (what I have called 'the escalator factor') and a bond portfolio will broadly fall either at or below this rate, according to the assumptions you make about the escalator factor. Whatever the case, they clearly cannot make any impact on the remainder of the required return, that part of it which is necessary to do more than stand still – for example, to pay current liabilities let alone to start making inroads into the deficit. The result of including bonds in your portfolio can only make the job of the remaining assets even more difficult, as they now have to make not only their own target return but also that part of the return that should be being earned by the bonds, but is not. I therefore propose simply to ignore them as an asset class.

Of course, in the unlikely event that a pension scheme was to be in surplus, then a very different state of affairs would prevail and bonds might indeed be an excellent investment for the whole portfolio, since the target investment return would then effectively be the same as the escalator factor. There is a slight problem here in that there are simply not enough government securities and triple A bonds around to fuel such a demand, but we will let that go, particularly as similar issues arise in respect of other asset classes. Sensible though such a scheme might be, it is noteworthy that when some pension schemes *were* running surpluses, their trustees did not in fact match all their liabilities against bonds, leaving whatever surplus there might be to be invested in other classes. Ironically, in many cases the people who refused to use bonds to lock in profits (a legitimate tactic) are now using them to lock in losses (a non-legitimate tactic).

In the circumstances, the best use of bonds should be to provide an emergency liquidity reserve to guard against the possibility of some unexpected short-term adverse event; Swensen describes the Yale bond portfolio as 'a hedge against financial accidents or periods of unanticipated deflation'.[7] I would suggest that a pension fund should look at its predicted net outflows for the next three years and match these against bonds of similar duration; for the typical UK pension fund, for example, this would probably be a figure somewhere between 7% and 10% depending on the maturity and the membership profile of the scheme.

I believe that this provides a prudent measure of short-term liquidity (it would of course be recalculated every year on a three-year rolling

---

[7] Yale Endowment Annual Report 2004.

basis) while holding true to the dictum that one should minimise the amount of the portfolio tied up in liquid (and hence underperforming) assets. This would leave the remainder of the portfolio free to be deployed in a Multi Asset Class portfolio, and I will assume for ease of example throughout the remainder of the book that 8% has in fact been so deployed.

Quoted Equities

From the numbers involved, it would seem as though the Yale Model treats these effectively as two asset classes, since each is usually discussed separately. In the chapter on quoted equities I will explore levels of correlation between US and UK quoted indices, and in particular between the total returns that may be earned on them. We will discuss whether those levels of correlation make it appropriate for them to be treated as two asset classes or one. Also, might the answer vary as between US dollar investors and others?

HOW MUCH SHOULD BE ALLOCATED TO EACH ASSET CLASS?

There are three different considerations here.

First, it must be enough that it can have some meaningful impact on the returns of the portfolio as a whole. Swensen feels that 10% is the minimum but my instinct is that even this figure is on the low side. After all, this means that an asset class would have to double (achieve a 50% rate of return) just to shift the needle by 5%, and it does not seem feasible to think even of private equity turning in a 50% compound return over time. My own preference would be for a minimum of 20% if using four asset classes or as much as possible (presumably at least 15%) if using five.

Secondly, it must be enough that your asset classes can be balanced in such a way as to diversify away their specific asset class risk. This is a somewhat nebulous concept since, as you will see when you read the chapters on risk, it is something of an open question to even ask what constitutes the 'risk' in this situation, let alone how one should measure it. This will also clearly depend on the degree to which the returns of the different asset classes are correlated. My feeling is that, providing the correlation is not too high, then four asset classes will suffice. However, should it be the case that, for example, domestic and quoted equities are in fact highly correlated then you would need to use three other classes rather than two (i.e. five asset classes in total rather than four). To put it another way, if domestic and foreign equities do turn out to be highly correlated then they should be thought of as just one asset class and their combined allocation would have to fall within the maximum weighting for any one class.

Finally, there is the consideration that the allocation to any asset class must be sufficient to justify the expenditure of time and money to do it properly. This is particularly significant in those asset classes in which investment may be seen as particularly complex – hedge funds and private equity being good examples. Outside the USA, this requirement is sadly honoured more in the breach than in the observance, at least in the realm of pension funds. It can be argued that in the USA the large population of trained investment professionals within pension funds makes this easier, but this is really just a manifestation of the problem rather than a reason for it. If one has a proper allocation to an asset class, say 18% to 20%, then one can afford to take on a specialist professional to manage it. If one has a 2% allocation to the class, then one cannot.

HOW IS THE YALE MODEL
CURRENTLY ALLOCATED?

The Yale endowment is no longer allocated as equally as a pure 'equality' model might envisage (Table 2.1). In particular, the allocation to hedge funds rose from 19% in 2000 to 25% five years later, while the allocation to private equity fell over the same period from 25% to less than 15%. With all due respect to Swensen, I find this hard to understand, since the 2004 Annual Report ascribes an expected real return of 11.4% to private equity and just 6% to hedge funds. Perhaps Yale, like other US investors, has been having problems putting such large amounts of money to work in a private equity market where (particularly in US venture) access to quality funds has become a huge issue. As I say above, I know of a large US pension fund that has reduced its exposure to private equity for precisely this reason. This issue has become particularly acute since 2000, with most of the leading US venture firms (an area where Yale is presumably heavily exposed) reducing their fund sizes.

It is also worth noting that Yale do not use the word 'allocation' in its precise sense, at least, not in the way in which it is used by other

Table 2.1 Yale endowment asset allocation as at 30 June

	2004	2003	2002	2001	2000
Domestic Equity	14.8%	14.9%	15.4%	15.5%	14.2%
Absolute Return	26.1%	25.1%	26.5%	22.9%	19.5%
Foreign Equity	14.8%	14.6%	12.8%	10.6%	9.0%
Private Equity	14.5%	14.9%	14.4%	18.2%	25.0%
Real Assets	18.8%	20.9%	20.5%	16.8%	14.9%
Fixed Income	7.4%	7.4%	10.0%	9.8%	9.4%
Cash	3.5%	2.1%	0.3%	6.2%	8.1%

Source: Yale Endowment Annual Report 2004.

investors in different parts of the world, since it also publishes its 'target allocations'. It would surely be more readily comprehensible to talk about 'percent invested' and 'percent allocated'. The 'target allocation' for private equity is 17.5%, which strengthens my suspicion that what we are viewing is partly a difficulty in accessing quality partnerships in the first place, partly the effect of fund size reductions, and partly just the usual pesky unpredictability of the timing of private equity cashflows. In page 5 of the report, Swensen talks of 'shortfalls relative to the target in private equity holdings', and it is probably not a coincidence that the level of cash is roughly equivalent to this amount. (This is actually a good example of the problems surrounding the private equity commitment/investment cycle that we will explore later.)

As we can see from the figures, the allocation to domestic equities has remained fairly constant over the period in question, but the allocations to both foreign equities and hedge funds have increased significantly. Since it is these two asset classes which, as we will see later, have been the two worst performers, this is clear evidence of an investor not believing that past returns are necessarily a good guide to future performance, something that I will be urging you to remember at various points in later chapters. Sadly, Yale do not disclose exactly what it is that leads them to believe this in this particular case, since it would be interesting to learn what lies behind this clearly contrarian approach.

Real assets are what we will be referring to as property, although in fairness Yale's portfolio goes well beyond this in scope and complexity. I have chosen not to include detailed discussion of such things as oil and gas royalties since they lie beyond the scope of a generalist book of this nature and will, in any event, only ever form a very small part of any investor's overall portfolio. Yale's weighting in this class has fluctuated up and down more than any other asset class, but I would guess that this may well have much more to do with changing asset valuations than with changes of investment policy.

WHAT DOES ONE LOOK FOR IN SELECTING AN ASSET CLASS?

There are in the modern world of investment a bewildering range of asset classes available, including, on a global scale, such things as commodities and, increasingly, also local varietals. For example, UK investors may consider PFI transactions or insurance risk-based products or instruments. For ease of reference to the Yale Model, however, I have chosen to focus on quoted equities (both US and other), private equity, hedge funds and property. Selecting these asset classes for investment, however, would probably involve exactly the same criteria.

- Is there a sufficiently robust benchmark available for the asset class?
- Based on the benchmark, does it exhibit an acceptable level of return risk?
- Based on the benchmark, does it exhibit an acceptable level of capital risk?
- Based on the benchmark, does it exhibit an acceptable level of correlation with domestic quoted equities?

Is there a Sufficiently Robust Benchmark Available for the Asset Class?

This requirement poses little problem when viewing public markets since a wide variety of benchmarks is available. Indeed, the only difficulty is likely to be in choosing between them. However, for other asset classes there are views ranging from the understandable to the downright ignorant that, for various reasons, the benchmark returns for different asset classes are not to be relied upon. While I accept that in some limited circumstances there may be some force in these remarks (for example, with regard to hedge funds, where there are numerous different data providers, all using different constituents and time periods), in most cases there is not. For example, I am frequently told by pension funds and their advisers that there is no good benchmark available for private equity returns, a remark which I find completely baffling since there is one universally accepted data provider who has been in the market for many years and whose figures go back about 25 years on a single year basis – longer than the current FTSE 100 index.

I suspect that much of this ill-informed and unhelpful comment springs from the blind prejudice that seems to exist in many quarters against so-called 'alternative' asset classes. If one, for emotional and subjective reasons, has decided not to invest in an asset class then I suppose one may attempt to justify that position by arguing that no rational, objective analysis is possible. I trust that this book will give the lie to this point of view. Not only are the figures for objective analysis available, but I believe it is possible, and indeed simple, validly to compare the returns of any one asset class against another.

Based on the Benchmark, does it Exhibit an Acceptable Level of Return Risk?

I would like to pass quickly on at this point, since to discuss this in any detail would be to pre-empt much of what I am going to say in the risk chapters. Suffice it to say at this stage, that I believe the most material risk to any investor, whatever that person's personal circumstances, will be the risk that a particular asset class will not achieve the target rate of return, and I will be showing how this can be measured.

To do this, we will be using phi calculations based on the normal distribution function and, while Yale do not divulge their own methods for understandable reasons, it is possible that they employ something similar, since they say that their return assessment includes 'mean variance analysis', which is exactly what phi calculations are.

Based on the Benchmark, does it Exhibit an Acceptable Level of Capital Risk?

Again, we will be discussing this in detail in a later chapter, but basically the capital risk is a subset of the return risk. If your target rate of return is, say, 10%, then the return risk will be the probability that the asset class will not return at least 10%, whereas the capital risk will be the probability that it might actually return less than zero, thus leading to some loss of your original capital.

As we will see, these calculations will show that in just about every case, people's instinctive perception of capital risk is in fact dramatically mistaken.

Based on the Benchmark, does it Exhibit an Acceptable Level of Correlation with Domestic Quoted Equities?

I previously mentioned investors' obsession with short-term and annual returns, rather than long-term and compound returns. However, there is one perfectly valid use for annual returns, and that is in the calculation of correlation. In its purest form, the MAC approach would call for asset classes to exhibit, as far as possible, negative correlation with each other. However, this is one area where theory must give way to practical reality (something that does not seem to happen very often in the world of finance).

There is a well-known writer on the game of bridge[8] who talks about 'general truisms', and in researching historic performance figures while preparing this book I was struck by one very obvious general truism, to which I will be referring again in later chapters. Most asset classes increase in value (i.e. exhibit positive returns) most of the time. Yes, we have had some periods of frightening negative returns, particularly in quoted equities in recent years, but the fact remains that over the last 20 years or so (which is the period we will be considering – usually from 1984 onwards where good data is available) the number of years of positive returns have far outweighed the number of years of negative returns, regardless of which of our asset classes you look at. Thus, logically we should actually avoid asset classes that exhibit negative correlation with others rather than be attracted to them, since they are likely to have more periods of negative returns than positive.

If we look at this in practice, it seems to hold good. For example, Dedicated Short Bias hedge funds exhibit consistent negative correlation against all other hedge fund strategies, and have enjoyed (if that is the right word in the circumstances) consistently negative returns. The same is true of the Nikkei index of Japanese public equities. Thus, we will be looking for asset classes that exhibit not negative correlation but low levels of positive correlation. I believe this to be a sensible modification to the strict theory, which may be fine as a matter of pure arithmetic, but does not seem to be practical in the real world. Sadly, as we will discover, those who cling rigidly to the traditional risk model are not prepared to make similar concessions.

I have chosen quoted equities as a convenient yardstick against which to calculate correlation simply because it is likely to form the bedrock of all existing investment portfolios, and is therefore a

---

[8] Mike Lawrence.

convenient starting point. It is worth pointing out, however, that where an investor seeks to have two asset classes comprising quoted equities (e.g. 'domestic' and 'foreign'), then these will actually have to be analysed against each other as well as against other asset classes. We will see that many investors' traditional views in this regard are hard to understand; the FTSE 100 and the S&P100, for example, exhibit very high correlation with each other – much too high to justify consideration as two separate asset classes.

However, at the end of the book we will also be looking at the extent to which all our target asset classes are correlated with each other. This is obviously both important and complex, since each will interact on every one of the others.

CONCLUSIONS

So, MAC investing seems the logical solution to the investment world's needs, and the Yale Model has undoubtedly been outstanding as best of breed, generating returns that place it consistently in the top percentile of US endowments. Since it is natural for the members of any industry to study its leading exponents and attempt to copy (and where possible improve upon) what they are doing, it seems strange indeed that MAC investing is not already widespread around the world.

Ignorance clearly has a major part to play, since outside the USA there are a surprising number of investors who have never even heard of MAC investing or the Yale Model. However, given my comments in the previous paragraph, this does indeed seem difficult to understand. How can one practise in a profession and not keep abreast of the latest developments? And the Yale Model is hardly even a 'latest development', having been around for over 20 years, and Swensen's book having been published in 2000.

Can it be that investors have been deliberately kept in ignorance of the Yale Model by those who advise them, who may have a vested interest in not disturbing their existing analytical methods, or manager relationships? Conspiracy theories are dangerous things, and certainly form no part of the world of investment strategy, but it seems hard to imagine that if consultants had been keeping their clients properly advised of developments in the world of investment (their job, surely?) then those clients would not have been beating a path to the door of MAC investing for the clear advantages which it offers in the shape of higher returns and proper diversification.

There is a saying that a prophet is never properly honoured in his own country, but this is certainly not true in the case of Swensen; just the opposite in fact. In America his views are accepted as mainstream and he is a revered establishment figure and investment guru, yet outside the USA he might as well never have existed as far as many in the investment business are concerned. As we will see when we examine their asset allocation practices, investment institutions can be surprisingly insular, but this is surely carrying things too far. Yet perhaps the 'not invented here' syndrome has also a part to play.

I would venture the suggestion that perhaps the main reason for MAC investing not having found a wider audience lies in its requirement for a totally new way of thinking. To the conservative mind, some of this seems radical. The negative impact of liquidity, the need to think in long-term, compound terms when considering returns, and most of all the inapplicability of accepted notions and measures of risk are all potential show-stoppers. To the enquiring mind this will all offer a fascinating and challenging new exercise in logic, but sadly the conservative mind (which is in many cases the intellectual coward taking refuge in conservatism) predominates.

Today as never before the imperative in the investment world is to think the unthinkable, to explore new frontiers of investment strategy and to rely on logic, common sense, and real world experience to guide us along the path. It is my hope and intention that the remainder of this book will demonstrate to you that there really is a viable alternative view, that any apparent theoretical challenges can be overcome, and that it is in MAC investing that the future of investment will lie.

SUMMARY

- Three things have combined to make MAC investing the logical approach to portfolio construction: (1) the need to move from relative to absolute returns, (2) the need for higher returns in the new world of pension fund deficits, and (3) the need for greater diversity having been underlined by collapses in world equity markets.
- MAC investing consists of splitting the portfolio into a number of equal parts and investing each part in a separate asset class, with the historic returns of the asset classes so chosen having as little correlation with each other as possible.
- Bonds are unlikely to qualify as an asset class given the current need for high returns to claw back pension fund deficits. However

they do have a role to play as a cash substitute, and the MAC model will assume that about 8% of the portfolio will be held in bonds, representing approximately a typical investor's next three years' anticipated outflows, matched to bonds of similar duration.

- The Yale Endowment has been the outstanding example of the genre, with their approach (broadly what is described above) having become known as the Yale Model, and the subject of a best-selling book by its creator, David Swensen.
- Potential obstacles bruited to the implementation of a MAC approach are: (1) the lack of benchmark returns for so-called 'alternative' asset classes; (2) difficulty in comparing the returns of different asset classes directly against each other; and (3) incompatibility of some types of return with traditional risk models. In fact, all of these objections are either false or can be circumvented.
- Asset classes should be selected if they satisfy the following criteria: (1) a reliable professional source of benchmark returns exists; (2) on the basis of that benchmark, the class exhibits acceptable levels of return risk; (3) on the basis of that benchmark, the class exhibits acceptable levels of capital risk; and (4) it exhibits an acceptable level of correlation with other asset classes (initially being measured against quoted equities).
- MAC investing represents the logical future of investment strategy. However, its implementation requires a willingness to think in a new way about asset allocation and to question and abandon where necessary outdated traditional concepts that may no longer be appropriate or material to the investment process.

3
Risk

INTRODUCTION

It is very important to recognise that when investment managers or consultants use the word 'risk' they mean something completely different from what we mean by the word 'risk' in its everyday sense. If we are asked whether a particular investment we are contemplating is 'risky', we would probably understand the question as asking us how likely it is that we might actually lose some or all of our money. In the world of financial theory, however, the concept of 'risk' has a clearly defined but very different meaning, and huge problems arise when people such as pension trustees, who may be highly educated and experienced in their own field but have no financial qualifications and no experience of working within the investment community, are told that a particular investment carries a particular level of 'risk' without any attempt being made to explain exactly what is meant by the term.

Sadly most of us are too timid in such a situation to ask what seems like a very stupid question, and rather than expose our own ignorance we sit quietly and accept whatever the consultant tells us. Yet in this situation, as with so many others in business, what seems like the 'stupid' question to ask is in fact exactly the right one. Ask it, and your colleagues will thank you for it. For you will all be astonished to learn that there has been a very fundamental misunderstanding of what is being discussed. As I am about to demonstrate, what is meant by 'risk' in the rarefied world of portfolio theory bears no connection to any construction that any ordinary person would place upon the word in any everyday context.

If we were left a sum of money to invest as trustee for someone who was entirely dependent on that money for the rest of his or her life (for example, a severely disabled person who was unable to work), then I think we would all adopt the view that whatever we did with that money would have to carry as little risk as possible, since the most unthinkable outcome would be for the capital value of that sum (at least on an inflation-adjusted basis) to decline rather than increase. I would suggest also that it would be common sense if, in pursuance of such a prudent approach, we chose not to put all our eggs in one basket but to spread the money among a number of different and unrelated investments so that the capital sum as a whole would be as little affected as possible by turbulence in the values of any one asset class. Clearly, then, when we see pension funds and other institutions doing precisely the opposite, and effectively putting all their eggs into the one basket of domestic quoted equities – and apparently on the advice of their consultants that this is the correct approach to take on a 'risk-adjusted' basis – something is profoundly wrong. To understand why this should be I am afraid we have to take a short but scenic diversion, in which I trust you will indulge me.

THE ATHEIST CATHEDRAL

It has been said that humankind is distinguished from all other members of the animal kingdom by three things: the female orgasm, the fully opposable thumb and the power of conceptual thought. I do not propose to comment further on the first two, except perhaps to speculate whether there may not be some connection between the female orgasm and manual dexterity. However, in the last of these three qualities lie the seeds of our present problem.

The power of conceptual thought is the ability to process abstract ideas divorced from experience derived from observation. For example, a dog may burn his nose on a steaming kettle and learn thereafter to avoid kettles when steam is coming out of them because they are likely to be hot. A man might observe the steam lifting the lid of the kettle and hypothesise that this must be due to the steam exerting pressure on the lid, and that this same pressure might be used to push a piston, and thus drive an engine. Some writers have referred to this as 'imagination', a usage with which I would quibble as I think that imagination has other shades of meaning that do not happily fit the sense of abstract conceptualising, but let that be. Neanderthal man, for example, did not bury his dead. Since he had no 'imagination' he could not invent the concept of an afterlife, and so did not develop the religious belief required for ritual burial. *Homo sapiens*, on the other hand, seems to have left evidence of religious practices such as ritual burial from the very earliest times of his existence. In order to develop concepts which, by definition, are not experienced empirically (such as spirits and gods), the power of conceptual thought or 'imagination' is required.

However, the power of abstract thought is a curse as well as a blessing, filling us as it does with the obsession to explain conceptually all that we find in our world. The early Greek philosophers, for example, sought the answers to all existence through the use of logic. This could arrive at some surprising conclusions in the wrong hands; Thales, the first recorded member of the Milesian school, came to the view that everything was made out of water (in fairness he did also accurately predict a lunar eclipse in 585 BC – although Babylonian astronomers had already discovered by observation that lunar eclipses happen once every 19 years). However, in due course logic produced Plato's theory of ideas and became the foundation of early science and mathematics. Gradually man discovered that rules could be laid down that would hold true universally wherever that same situation was encountered. An object floating in water will displace its own weight of water; the square of the hypotenuse of a right-angled triangle is equal to the sum of the square of the other two sides; and so on.

All this is well and good. However, the desire to create rules that will provide a universal explanation of why something happens in a particular way, and (even more impressively!) to predict how they may happen in the future, can become a siren call which lures us onto the rocks of dogma, and actually inhibits rather than facilitates progress. The theory that the sun revolved around the earth seemed to explain much that could be discerned by empirical observation, and this became literally an article of religious faith, with those who suggested otherwise being accused of heresy. Elaborate 'rules' were invented to try to provide for what could *not* be explained fully by the theory. Incredibly complex astrolabes were produced, early mechanical computers that sought to calculate and simulate the movement of the sun and the planets by applying these 'rules'. They were masterpieces of the clockmaker's art which still have the power to awe and amaze us when we see them in museums today. But they were all based on a totally false premise. Today we view them as an atheist would view Europe's great cathedrals. They were beautiful but completely misconceived. They are of no practical use whatsoever, and never have been. Our atheist would be stunned by their wonderful architecture and soaring proportions but bemused that thousands of men should have spent (in many cases) their whole lives constructing them as monuments to glorify something which (in his view) has never existed.

When man the rule-maker turned his attention to the world of finance he had a few basic building blocks to hand. The theories of discounting and compounding were known and understood. Also, there was general recognition that there must be some sort of relationship between risk and reward, with a risk premium in the shape of a higher return being expected for a project that was 'riskier' than another. The original fortune of the Rothschild family, for example, was made by standing in the market in London at certain times every day and assessing the rates of discount at which to accept bills of different maturities drawn on different banks and governments (and doing so very successfully!).

However these general principles only took one so far, and certainly nowhere near as far as man the rule-maker wanted. He needed to be able to evolve rules that would hold true in all situations and could be used to predict how things would happen in future. Unfortunately this simply was not possible, reality turning out to be a much peskier little beast than had been hoped. Between the two world wars, for example, various countries experienced periods of 'stagflation' (Germany being the most extreme example) with negative economic growth, and thus high unemployment, coinciding with high inflation. The problem was that this was supposed to be impossible under the prevailing 'rules' dreamed up by economists, which held that there was a direct inverse relationship between unemployment and inflation, and that either could be reduced but only at the risk of increasing the other.

It took John Maynard Keynes to show how the cycle could be broken, at least in the short term, by Government spending albeit at the expense of budget deficits. In the USA, Roosevelt was a belated and reluctant exponent of Keynes's idea, and even then it took Pearl Harbor and America's entry into the Second World War to prompt him to try it on a scale that was likely to be truly effective in banishing the Great Depression (it was!). In more recent times it has been found that even the Keynesian model does not explain every situation. In the UK, for example, during the seventies Government ran high deficits to such an extent that the country was effectively bankrupted and had to ask the IMF to bail it out, and yet production remained low, unemployment remained high, and so did inflation. It has been replaced partially or totally according to local attitude by any number of ideas, including monetarism and supply side economic theories developed by such people as Milton Friedman and J.K. Galbraith, and some would argue that these ideas have in turn been found wanting (witness Mrs

Thatcher's[1] breathtaking *volte face* in asserting that she had never been unduly influenced by monetarism).

So man the rule-maker was in a bit of a fix when it came to finance. He wanted to evolve rules that would be universally true and universally applicable, but reality kept getting in the way.

For example, even if you could show logically how an investor should act in a given situation, when that situation actually arose the individual investor in question might not see things your way and might act totally differently to your prediction, perhaps impelled by motives or concerns that you would not even recognise as being valid. So what is man the rule-maker to do when confronted with a reality that consistently refuses to behave as he believes it should?

In his 'Hitchhiker's Guide to the Galaxy' series, Douglas Adams tells of the inhabitants of a planet called Kriket, who are convinced, and treat it as a matter of religious belief, that they are totally alone in creation. When they are finally presented with incontrovertible proof of the existence of other worlds they decide to bring reality into line with their belief by setting out to destroy the rest of the universe. This is essentially the line that man the rule-maker took when it came to setting out financial theory. He could not create rules that could be guaranteed to work in the real world, so he set out to destroy the real world and create a little unreal world of his own instead.

What he created is basically an astrolabe. It is a beautiful little box comprising an artificial world within which his rules work perfectly, protected as they are by the box from the contaminating influences of reality. The box is built out of a number of assumptions (such as the assumption that all investors are rational, to get around the problem mentioned above) and financial models (such as the Capital Asset Pricing Model), many of which are interdependent (for example, an investor is deemed to be 'rational' if he accepts the outcome of the Capital Asset Pricing Model and 'irrational' if he rejects it!). Like the astrolabes that have come down to us from the time of the Renaissance, the box is a magnificent structure and one can only marvel at the intellectual endeavour that has gone into creating something so complex. But, like those astrolabes, it is based upon concepts that have no foundation in reality.

---

[1] As she then was.

Our criticism of the accepted classical theory of economics has consisted not so much in finding logical flaws in its analysis as in pointing out that its tacit assumptions are seldom or never satisfied, with the result that it cannot solve the economic problems of the actual world.

John Maynard Keynes[2]

Now in the rarefied world of finance faculties in the world's business schools none of this really matters because everyone understands (or should!) that whatever new work they do based upon these theories is valid only in the artificial world they have created. The problems arise when people who should know better either forget this or only half-understand it in the first place, and start encouraging people to use these rules in the real world, outside the artificial environment of the box. The brilliant academics who invented these rules well understood that they were built upon an artificial base that had been created expressly to support them, even if they did not say so explicitly. To pretend that they can, and should, be treated as being of universal application in the real world, does their inventors' reputations no service, and does huge violence to the intellectual integrity of the rules themselves. Sadly this essential distinction has been almost entirely overlooked and the rules have come to have the force of religious dogma, quoted most by those who understand them the least, and any who seek to query their validity being dismissed as dangerous and deluded heretics.

Such is the hold that these rules now have upon the collective investment mind that even clear examples of their fallibility are simply ignored. For example, classic corporate finance theory, as taught to MBA students for years, holds that it is cheaper for a company to finance itself with debt than with equity. This is because two of the many assumptions that support the artificial world contained in the box are: (1) investors hold shares for dividend flows rather than speculatively for capital gain, and (2) a shareholder will always require a risk premium to compensate for a correspondingly lower place in the pecking order for both distributions and liquidation rights. In practice, of course, this is not necessarily always the case. During the late 1980s and early 1990s, for example, dividend yields in the UK were significantly lower than interest rates, and many public companies issued equity in order to retire debt – exactly the opposite of what finance theory taught!

---

[2] *The General Theory of Employment, Interest and Money*, first published in 1935. Currently published by Prometheus Books, London, 1997.

The poet Christopher Fry had a salutary reminder for man the rule-maker:

There may always be another reality
To make fiction of the truth we think we've arrived at.

RISK AND THE CAPITAL ASSET PRICING MODEL

The Albanian language apparently contains 27 different words for 'moustache', and it is a great shame that the English language contains not 27 words for 'risk' but only one, since then financial theorists would not have seized upon a perfectly good word and used it in a very specialised and artificial sense. As we will see, that sense is not the 'risk' that would be understood by any person in the real world, but in the sense of an arithmetical device which is required in the artificial world of the box to enable the Capital Asset Pricing Model (CAPM) to work.

The Capital Asset Pricing Model, which was developed in the early 1960s, forms the basis for the whole of modern investment theory. Though it was first published in 1964 by William Sharpe, similar work was also being done at the same time by others such as Treynor and Lintner, and it built upon the pioneering thinking on portfolio theory already performed by Harry Markowitz in the 1950s (for their work on portfolio theory Sharpe and Markowitz were awarded the Nobel Prize in 1990 jointly with Merton Miller). The measurement and use of 'risk' in its artificial and specialised sense is a key feature of the CAPM.

The CAPM offers a way of theoretically splitting the risk inherent in holding a portfolio of investments into two different sorts of risk: systematic and specific. That is to say, the risk of holding the 'market portfolio' (the 'systemic' risk) contrasted with the risk of holding any one individual investment within it (the 'specific' risk).[3] The 'market portfolio' is really just a notional portfolio representing the market as a whole. For example, a FTSE 100 market portfolio would comprise all the individual shares that make up the FTSE 100, weighted by market capitalisation. However, in order to understand properly how

---

[3] Confusingly, some writers talk about the 'systematic' risk of any individual asset or group of assets as opposed to 'market' risk. They may even say that the systematic risk is the market risk of the individual asset or groups of assets. While there is nothing wrong with these terms, I believe it is less confusing to talk about 'specific' and 'systemic' as representing the asset (or group of assets) and the market portfolio respectively, and will do so throughout.

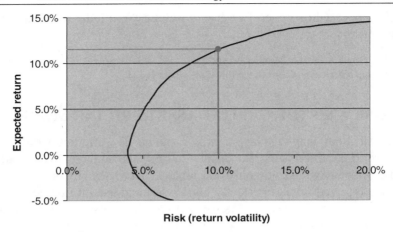

Figure 3.1   The efficient frontier

risk fits into portfolio theory we also need to be aware of the concept of 'the super-efficient portfolio', the brainchild of another writer, James Tobin, in the late 1950s.

Markowitz had already come up with the idea of the 'efficient frontier' in the early 1950s; essentially this is the point at which individual portfolios exhibit a maximum return for a certain level of risk, or, conversely, the minimum level of risk for a certain return.

In Figure 3.1, at least one portfolio can be constructed and mapped at each specific risk/return ratio within the shaded area. The efficient frontier is the curve at the top of the shaded area which shows the logical (because optimal) choice of portfolio for any given level of risk or expected return. Clearly for any given rate of return one would logically choose the portfolio with the lowest risk, and for any given level of risk one would logically choose the portfolio that offered the highest return.

Tobin added into the mix an asset that paid the risk-free rate of return. By drawing a tangent (the 'Capital Market Line'), as shown in Figure 3.2, from the risk-free rate to the efficient frontier, the super-efficient portfolio can be determined as the point at which the two touch. Further, by assuming that investors could either leverage or deleverage their position, it is possible to construct portfolios that are on the Capital Market Line and are superior to the efficient frontier because they offer a higher return for the same level of risk, or a lower level of risk for the same rate of return.

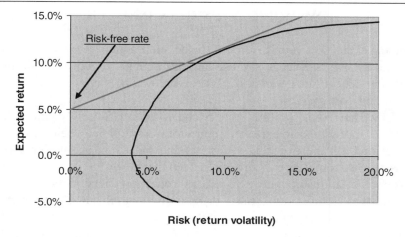

Figure 3.2   The super-efficient portfolio

By making a number of assumptions, Sharpe in his turn was able to show that if all investors have perfect market information, if all agree with the model's view of risk and return, and if all are logical in the sense of being able to arrive at the optimal level of leverage for any desired risk/return ratio, then the super-efficient portfolio and the market portfolio are one and the same. In other words, all investors would hold the market portfolio and simply leverage or deleverage it to arrive at their own desired risk/return profile. This in turn, however, assumes that there is such a thing as one single and identifiable market portfolio, which is of course false, at least unless one can identify a universe that the market portfolio is designed to represent, and this in turn could only be done by arbitrary selection, which could be different for every individual investor. This is yet another example of the sort of desperate mental gymnastics into which financial theorists are forced when reality threatens to intrude. There is a well-known journalistic aphorism: 'never let the facts get in the way of a good story'. In the case of those who cling blindly to the world of the CAPM perhaps it should be: 'never let reality get in the way of a good theory'.[4]

---

[4] I remember reading a press interview with Madeleine Albright in which she recalled her first experience of dealing with French officials. Having outlined what she thought was a very clever solution to a particular problem they shook their heads sadly and said 'Ah yes, it may work in practice but does it work in theory?'

HOW 'RISK' IS USED IN PRACTICE

Having sketched a brief history of the development of portfolio theory, we now have the necessary background against which to show the development of the concept of risk, and how this is commonly calculated and portrayed.

As we have seen, portfolio theory coalesced into Sharpe's idea of the CAPM. Using this, an expected return for a portfolio can be calculated by estimating the expected returns of the individual assets, or asset classes, that comprise the portfolio. Given that portfolio theory assumes a direct relationship between returns (or, more accurately, relative volatility of returns) and 'risk', these individual expected returns can be calculated if one knows exactly the degree of risk to ascribe in each individual case (and vice versa). The expression of this individual risk (the 'specific' risk of holding a particular asset or asset class) has commonly come to be known as 'beta', and so let us use this term (although Sharpe did not).

If one accepts the theory that underpins the CAPM, then it also of course follows that one can change the expected return of a portfolio by substituting assets that have higher or lower betas. We will see later that accepted measures of risk such as beta have no valid application in the real world to a MAC allocation model. However, there is a very important point to note here with regard to asset allocation. Even if those who argue for the universal application of their so-called 'risk-adjusted' model were to be right rather than wrong, then 'in the alternative' (as lawyers say) even they accept as a basic principle of their own belief system that the expected rate of investment return of a portfolio is not a 'given'. It is not a fixed and immutable function of whatever initial asset mix is chosen; rather, by turning a knob on the control panel which changes the overall asset mix (or, as they would see it, the level of 'risk' within the portfolio), it is possible to move the needle on the dial which shows the expected rate of overall return.

I want to be quite clear about what beta is, and there is really no substitute for understanding exactly how it is calculated, as there are some important arithmetical points that have implications that are seldom properly appreciated. Beta is simply the covariance of the individual asset against the market as a whole divided by the variance of the market return (variance being the square of the standard deviation). Thus:

$$\beta = \frac{\text{covar}(r_\text{a}, r_\text{m})}{\sigma^2 r_\text{m}}$$

where r_a is the rate of return of the individual asset, r_m is the rate of return of the market, and σr_m is the standard deviation of the market return.

Remember how the CAPM distinguishes between systemic risk and specific risk? Well, the model assumes that if one has an expected rate of return for the market portfolio (which effectively represents the market as a whole), then having calculated beta for an individual asset[5] we can use it to estimate the expected return of that asset. Let me first describe how this is done before setting it out in a formula. Put simply, beta operates as a function by which the difference between the expected market return and the assumed risk-free return is multiplied; this is then added to the risk-free return to give the expected return of the asset, and is expressed algebraically as follows:

$$\text{Expected } r_\text{a} = r_\text{f} + \beta(\text{Expected } r_\text{m} - r_\text{f})$$

where r_f is the risk-free rate.

It may be helpful to illustrate this with a hypothetical example. Suppose we hold some shares in BP and we want to arrive at an indication of the return we are likely to earn on them relative to simply buying the FTSE index. Let us assume that we expect FTSE to rise 10% over the next year, that the Gilt rate (which we will adopt as the risk-free rate) is 5%, and that we have calculated the beta for BP shares as being 1.5:

$$
\begin{aligned}
\text{Expected } r_\text{BP} &= 5\% + 1.5(10\% - 5\%) \\
&= 5\% + 1.5(5\%) \\
&= 5\% + 7.5\% \\
&= 12.5\%
\end{aligned}
$$

In other words, assuming that FTSE rises 10% during the coming period, we can assume that BP will rise by 12.5%. Now that we can calculate the expected return of each asset (or rather, the volatility of the expected return of each asset relative to the market) we can in turn calculate the overall return, or likely volatility of return, for the portfolio as a whole simply by summing the individual returns pro rata to the size of each holding. This is really all that is meant by 'risk

---

[5] Using historic returns for both the asset and the market portfolio.

adjusted'. If one believes in the basic theoretical framework (a big 'if'!) then it can be used in this way to construct an appropriate portfolio for any desired level of risk or return.

We can see that an asset with a beta of 1 will track the index exactly. An asset with a beta of greater than 1 will tend to rise more than the index ('market') when it rises and fall more than the index when it falls. In other words, it only shows that it will be more volatile than the market, exhibiting bigger movements in each direction.

Thus 'risk' in this sense (beta), though calculated from actual real world data, is itself essentially an artificial construction; an algebraic artifice introduced to permit arithmetical calculation within the assumed world of the CAPM. (Among other artificial assumptions underlying CAPM are (1) a perfect market, (2) all investors sharing the same information and (3) all investors sharing the same investment horizon.)

I hope that, by now, the nature of what is being represented by financial theory as the accepted measure of 'risk' is becoming clear. It is not, for example, the risk of losing some or all of the money we put into an investment. It is rather the probability of being able to predict how any individual investment will perform in any single particular period relative to the market portfolio or market universe of which it forms part, and against which it is being measured. We will see shortly that such 'risk' is quite simply irrelevant for the purposes of long-term asset allocation and can quite safely and properly be ignored.

ARITHMETICAL PROBLEMS WITH BETA

Given the intellectual white heat that went into creating the CAPM and the concept of beta, you would at least expect it to do what it says on the box, i.e. estimate the risk of any individual investment. However, it is my contention that the very arithmetic on which it is based works against it being able to do this. Later, I will have more to say on the conceptual difficulties surrounding beta, but consider this: if, as the CAPM maintains, the 'risk' level of an investment is something that is capable of precise measurement, then would you expect that risk level to be something that would remain the same (barring some significant change in the qualities of the investment) or vary, apparently illogically? The former, naturally. If we calculate something as possessing a precise numeric quantity or size then that number does not change if we look at it differently. The number 2 is still 2, regardless of whether we are looking at it as the square root of 4 or one-third of 6.

Yet this does not happen with beta. Furthermore, not only does the calculation of beta produce different results if applied in different ways, but it can produce results that are actually the opposite of what one would expect. Consider the following situation, which is set out in Table 3.1. Imagine a market portfolio that contains one particular share (XYZ) which is 5% of the portfolio (this is hardly fanciful: I believe that BP has at various times represented much more than 5% of the FTSE 100). Let us call this Portfolio 1. The individual share has a beta to the market portfolio of just over 1.7. In other words, this is what anybody who believes in the CAPM would describe as quite a 'high-risk' (because high beta) investment. The returns of both the XYZ share and Portfolio 1 are as set out in the table over a 10-year period.

Now imagine a market portfolio in which that one share has been boosted dramatically. Just for fun, let us assume that instead of being 5% of the market portfolio it has risen to 50% (maybe XYZ Corporation has just announced a cure for the common cold, or a visible lie detector for politicians). Again, the returns are as set out. All that has changed is the proportion of the market portfolio that the individual share represents. You have probably cheated by looking at Table 3.1 already, but would you expect the risk of the same share now to be represented by a beta of just 1.2? In other words, if the beta represents the specific risk of the investment, then the CAPM is saying that within Portfolio 2 the riskiness of the share is less than 30% of the riskiness of the same investment within Portfolio 1. How do you feel about that?

There are two obvious issues here. Firstly, if the riskiness of an investment is capable of precise calculation then how can it change in such an arbitrary manner? Nothing has changed in the nature of the investment, or of its environment. All that has changed is the number of the shares that are held, and for the purposes of the company and its shares, the number of shares that are held is irrelevant. Yet the CAPM calculates that exactly the same share has a beta of about 1.7 in Portfolio 1 and only 1.2 in Portfolio 2.

Secondly, how would you actually *perceive* the riskiness of the share in the second example compared to the first? If you were prepared to put only 5% of your portfolio into one share, but were happy to commit 50% of your portfolio to another share, would you be looking for them to have the same risk rating? Wouldn't you rather be looking for the second share to carry a much lower risk than the first, because you would be exposed to so much more specific risk in respect of that one

Table 3.1 Worked beta example

	Year 1	Year 2	Year 3	Year 4	Year 5	Year 6	Year 7	Year 8	Year 9	Year 10
Risk-free rate	5.00%	5.00%	5.00%	5.00%	5.00%	5.00%	5.00%	5.00%	5.00%	5.00%
XYZ	15.00%	19.00%	−21.00%	13.00%	25.00%	−17.00%	1.00%	17.00%	15.00%	7.00%
Portfolio 1	10.25%	12.35%	−8.65%	9.20%	15.50%	−6.55%	2.90%	11.30%	10.25%	6.05%
Portfolio 2	12.50%	15.50%	−14.50%	11.00%	20.00%	−11.50%	2.00%	14.00%	12.50%	6.50%
Covariance 1	0.011164									
Covariance 2	0.015948									
Variance 1	0.006512									
Variance 2	0.013290									
Beta 1	1.71									
Beta 2	1.20									

share than in Portfolio 1? In other words, if in fact they are not different shares but the same share, would you not perceive its riskiness in Portfolio 2 to be much higher than in the context of Portfolio 1? Just the opposite, in fact, of what the CAPM actually suggests!

So, in a nutshell, how can a figure that has been arithmetically calculated change in an arbitrary fashion and, furthermore, how can it change in a manner that runs contrary to all our commonsense instincts?

The answer of course lies with the arithmetic that the CAPM uses. Remember the formula we looked at before?

$$\beta = \frac{\text{covar}(r_a, r_m)}{\sigma^2 r_m}$$

Beta is calculated by taking the covariance of the individual asset against the market portfolio *of which it forms part*, and dividing that by the variance of the market portfolio. Herein lies the nub of the issue. You cannot calculate the beta of any asset (or, more precisely, the historic returns of any asset) in isolation but only by reference to (the historic returns of) the market portfolio of which it forms part. As a matter both of simple arithmetic and common sense, the larger a part of the market portfolio that the asset forms, the less will its returns vary from the returns of that market portfolio, and accordingly the beta calculation will show a share as having lower risk if it forms a larger part of the portfolio.

This affects not just an individual share but the overall context too. Suppose that the FTSE 100 decided to create a new subindex comprising only the biggest 50 companies, and you decided that in future you were going to base your portfolio strategy around this new index. Overnight, all your companies would be magically transformed to lower risk ratings as they would now each form a larger part of the overall whole than hitherto. Again we come back to the same two questions: (1) If the CAPM is capable of calculating a precise value in a scientific manner, how can it be valid in these circumstances? (2) How can it be suggesting a lower risk rating for each share when our commonsense instincts cry out for a higher one because of our increased exposure to each?

Think again about what beta represents. It is essentially the degree to which the historic returns of any one asset have varied relative to the way in which the historic returns of its market have varied. It measures not 'risk' in any real sense of the word, but uncertainty, or at least one possible manifestation of uncertainty. Extrapolating from the past into the future (and assuming that it is valid to do so), it measures the degree to which the annual return of any one asset may vary in any one year from the annual return of the market portfolio. This is open to infinite manipulation depending on what 'market portfolio' you represent. If you select the FTSE 100 as your market portfolio, then a fund comprising entirely the FTSE 100 constituent companies in the same weighting as they enjoy within the index will have a beta of precisely 1 and will therefore, in the eyes of CAPM, be entirely free of systemic risk. Yet compare that same fund against a market portfolio comprising the FTSE 100 merely as its pro rata share of all global quoted markets, and you will get a very different result.

If you choose a market portfolio consisting entirely of a particular hedge fund index, then a portfolio exactly matching that index will have a beta of 1 and be free of systemic risk. Fanciful? Perhaps, but then choosing any particular index is self-serving, and is the notion of having all your eggs in one hedge fund basket any less sensible than having all your eggs in one quoted equities basket? If you decide in advance what you want the weighting of your portfolio to be, then choosing the index that represents the largest part of your portfolio will make it look very attractive on a 'risk-adjusted' basis. If you choose the S&P 100, then anything other than a portfolio that comprises a large portion of US blue chip quoted equities will appear high risk.

This is clearly an absurd situation. Let us take a ridiculous example. Suppose you were contemplating putting 75% of your portfolio into Ukrainian property funds. If you were to measure the beta of such an investment programme against a market portfolio comprising 75% Ukrainian property funds then it would seem to have relatively low risk. Yet if it would be wrong to take this as the market portfolio, what would you suggest instead? It would hardly be fair to compare it to US Treasury Bills, and if you do, how valid is the measure of risk at which you arrive? Sadly, pension consultants get away with this foolishness because pension trustees never ask them 'in what sense are you using the word "risk", and on what market portfolio are you basing your calculations, and why?' The choice of the 'market portfolio' for comparative purposes is self-serving, and they know it.

There is a further arithmetical aspect of the beta calculation which presents us with a problem if we try to use it in the real world. You may have spotted it already. Because it uses covariance and variance calculations, it is concerned with volatility of returns – that is, the pattern of fluctuation in two different series of values. It assumes that an investor is uncaring whether the annual return of any individual investment comes in above or below the market return. It is concerned solely with the degree of such fluctuation, which may be seen as a proxy for the level of uncertainty should one attempt to predict such return. Yet in practice an investor would surely have a very different view of the riskiness of any investment if he or she knew that, for example, it tended to fluctuate to relatively higher levels when positive than lower when negative, or vice versa.

None of this bodes well for the notion of a risk-adjusted model offering a scientific approach to asset allocation. The truth is that the so-called 'risk-adjusted' approach is dead; it simply does not work when it comes to Multi Asset Class investing (if indeed it has, or ever had, any validity in any circumstances whatever), and rather than changing their rules to fit reality consultants prefer to reject out of hand those (very large) parts of reality that do not fit their rules. It is like a farmer saying 'I have no use for a tractor because it won't eat hay'.

CONCEPTUAL PROBLEMS WITH BETA

As we have seen, beta is the device that drives the CAPM and is basically an arithmetic expression of the way in which the returns of a particular asset have 'trended' on a historic basis compared with those of the market portfolio of which it forms part. It attempts to express uncertainty or, the other side of the coin, probability. It sets out what seems arithmetically the most probable outcome relative to the market portfolio.

Unfortunately, as we have seen above, there are a number of problems with this approach. Leaving aside the purely mathematical, which I trust I have adequately explained above, there are also two major conceptual problems. The second of these (whether uncertainty is actually a valid thing to express as financial 'risk' at all) I will leave to the next chapter. However, the first of these we must confront now as it leads on from something we encountered at the end of the last section: the question of subjectivity.

Of course the CAPM attempts to get around this by assuming that all investors are 'rational' and share exactly the same knowledge, circumstances and outlook, but once its exponents take it out of the box and claim that it will function perfectly well in the real world, they are saying that it still works when the comforting framework of all these assumptions (and more) is removed, and so it is perfectly valid for us to expose it, and the concept of 'risk' which it promulgates, to real world analysis.

In practice the risk of an investment will be perceived in different ways by different individuals. An experienced specialist hedge fund manager who has worked in the industry for 20 years or so will almost certainly see the 'risk' of investing in any one hedge fund, or of putting a significant part of one's overall portfolio into the hedge fund sector, as less than someone with no experience of the sector, and possibly with no investment knowledge whatever. Levels of knowledge, experience and expertise are therefore clearly relevant in considering how 'risk' will be perceived. Yet the CAPM would say this is not so, and that the 'risk' of the hedge fund or hedge fund portfolio in question would be the same for each investor, provided that it was assessed against the same market portfolio.

In 1905 Albert Einstein[6] argued that

- If two observers are moving relative to each other, their experiences of time will differ.
- All motion is relative, so
- All time is relative, so
- There is no true time.

Why should the same not be true for risk? If two investors do not have the same viewpoint then what they are looking at will not appear the same, just as Einstein demonstrated the theory of time actually slowing down as one approaches the speed of light. If, as Einstein postulates, there is no such thing as true time, then why should there be any such thing as 'true risk'? And if there is no such thing as 'true risk' then how can it be scientifically calculated? And if it cannot be scientifically calculated, then why use a model that pretends that it can?

At a single stroke, Einstein's theory of relativity destroyed the concept of 'absolute time' which had been created by Newton in the seventeenth century[7] (although, to be fair, Newton had considered the existence of both absolute time, which he called 'duration', and relative time). Alas, the same has not occurred in the case of risk (at least, not yet) since those who flourish their risk-adjusted models on a daily

---

[6] In a long article in German with an unpronounceable name, fortunately reprinted in English as *The Principle of Relativity* (1952), New York, Dover.
[7] *Principia Mathematica* (1686) translated as *Newton's Principia* (1848), New York, D. Adee.

basis have a firm grip on the dogma of the industry. Yet discussion of the problems that subjectivity poses for any assessment of risk dates from the early 1920s and actually pre-dates the creation of the CAPM! Perhaps this is why its aseptic world is hedged around with quite so many artificial assumptions, as if its creators were only too well aware of what might happen if reality were allowed to intrude.

There are some obvious examples of situations in which any concept of absolute risk simply does not work. Consider the case of an investor who has never previously invested in anything but government securities, and decides to take a first cautious step into equities by investing in, say, Coca-Cola shares. To her, Coca-Cola shares are likely to seem a high-risk investment since they offer the possibility of significant fluctuation in capital value – not something to which she is accustomed in the world of government bonds. To another investor, who has a portfolio largely based on the S&P or the Dow, Coca-Cola shares will probably be as close to a 'risk-free' investment as she can imagine.

The historian Barbara Tuchman has spotted exactly the same concept in operation in the realm of military strategy; no two staff officers will necessarily view a piece of intelligence in the same way, although the intelligence itself remains exactly the same in each case.

> What a staff makes out of the available evidence depends upon the degree of optimism or pessimism prevailing among them, on what they want to believe or fear to believe, and sometimes upon the sensitivity or intuition of an individual.[8]

Of course, man the rule-maker might well argue that in fact the Coca-Cola shares do have an absolute risk rating which remains the same in each case but either (1) it is differently perceived by each investor because each is looking at it from a different viewpoint or (2) each investor has a different tolerance to risk and will therefore place a different weighting on that absolute value. We have of course already seen that, arithmetically, the argument that there is in fact an absolute value all the time, is almost certainly insupportable, but just for the sake of argument let us consider each of these propositions.

I think the first proposition runs straight into the arms of Einstein. If two investors are at different places on the bond/equity continuum, that is surely analogous to being in different places on the space/time continuum and proves rather than disproves the existence of relative or

---

[8] Barbara W. Tuchman, *The Guns of August*, 1962, London, Constable & Constable.

subjective risk. One person may see a car as coming towards him while another may see it as moving away from him, depending on where they are standing, and one may see it as moving quickly while the other sees it as moving slowly.

As for the second proposition, surely 'risk' is supposed to be (at least largely) a measure of how attractive a particular investment should be to any investor, and if that is not in fact the case (i.e. that one investor may see it as attractive and another as unattractive despite it having the same beta score in each case) then surely it has no absolute application? Would one not need to have a model that could calculate different levels of attractiveness based on the varying circumstances of different investors? But since their circumstances would include such things as risk tolerance, preferences among asset classes, time horizons and target rates of investment return, then surely by definition no numbers arrived at by such a process could be regarded as absolute.

There is a further problem with beta in that it operates by studying historic returns and assuming that the statistical trend they exhibit will persist into the future. Yet, as many of us know from personal experience, this is frequently not the case. For example, if one takes the year end NASDAQ index values for the 10-year period 1990 to 1999 (surely a statistically significant period?) and calculates an exponential growth curve, then the forecast index figure for the end of 2000 is 3584, whereas in fact the NASDAQ index stood at 2470 at the end of 2000; a little matter of a 31% margin of error over one year.

I do not wish to labour this point, because at the end of the day historic data is largely all we have to work with in the world of financial theory and I am sure we all recognise the inherent risks. Yet I have seen any number of papers and articles which confidently assert that analysis based on this historic data 'shows' (or even occasionally 'proves') that some investment is riskier or less attractive than another, whereas in fact it does no such thing. It simply shows that there is a statistical relationship between the various sets of historic data, which, *if repeated in the future*, would tend to lead to a particular outcome. Too often this point is overlooked by those who seize upon risk-adjusted models as a scientific panacea to all the investment world's problems.

I will be developing the conceptual aspects of risk further in the next chapter and we will also be looking elsewhere at the related concept of alpha, but let us leave this area for the time being and turn to the practical considerations that make beta and the CAPM irrelevant and inappropriate for use in the real world.

WHY BETA AND THE CAPM ARE IRRELEVANT

The single most important point to grasp here is that 'risk' within portfolio theory, and beta as an expression of it, relies entirely upon returns for individual periods (be they a day, a month or a year), and from this all else flows.

Let us assume for the sake of argument that these are annual periods, and refer to them as annual returns. There is all the difference in the world between an annual return (*for* a particular year) and a return compounded over a number of years (which we are calling a 'vintage year' return since it is calculated *from* a particular year, i.e. the vintage year). It is as fundamental as the difference between simple interest and compound interest. An annual return looks at the change in value over a single year expressed as a simple percentage of the starting value. A vintage year return looks at the starting value (present value) and the value at the end of the period (the final value) and calculates the IRR, that is the compound return, over the whole period.

We have already seen that when setting a Target Rate of Return (TRR) for a pension plan we are concerned with a target IRR – a compound return over a long period. What happens to any individual asset over the course of any individual year is simply of no relevance or interest to us, since it is impossible to predict in advance and so forms no part of our analysis process. When we set an expected long-term return for each asset class we are taking into account the possibility (indeed, probability when dealing with a long period) of that asset class having good years and bad years. Our expected rate of return is our best guess of how the class will perform over the whole period once these various blips are incorporated into the big picture.

Still less are we interested in how any individual asset might perform in any individual year relative to any other asset or asset class within our portfolio. All we are interested in is the actual IRR to be produced by the portfolio as a whole over a lengthy period. Indeed, we accept when investing in certain asset classes that their initial impact upon the portfolio as a whole may actually be negative in the early years; we accept it because our expectations of much higher returns in later years will more than offset this.

In addition there are some asset classes – private equity funds being a good example – where annual returns are simply meaningless. As we will see when we consider them in detail later, private equity funds suffer from something called the J-curve (Figure 3.3), which simply

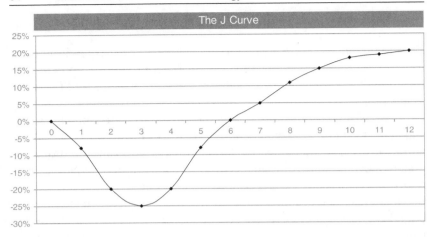

Figure 3.3   The J-curve

means that returns in the early years must necessarily be strongly negative as money is being paid out but no money is yet coming in as the result of investee companies being exited.

Thus, even the best private equity fund the world has ever seen could appear to be a disastrous investment if only the return of, say, Year 2 of its life was measured, while even a weak one would be entirely capable of generating quite a high annual return in, say, Year 8. We will examine this in much more detail in a later chapter.

Since accepted measurements of 'risk' can only operate on annual returns, it follows that they are inappropriate for asset classes such as this. Yet I hear of exactly this approach being attempted, with some assumed beta for private equity being presumably plugged into a pension fund's CAPM. I also hear frequently of Monte Carlo analysis being performed across a pension fund's whole portfolio, or even prospective investment universe. The problem with this, without going into excessive detail, is that Monte Carlo analysis (a wonderful statistical tool developed by Stanislaw Ulam, who worked on the Manhattan Project during the Second World War), like CAPM and beta, operates only on annual or other fixed periodic returns, not compound returns.

All this being so, then it must be obvious on any level that the traditional 'risk-adjusted' model is simply and hopelessly misconceived and that no attempt should ever have been made to apply it to real world situations. Clearly we need to adopt a new mindset based upon what actually happens in reality rather than what should happen in theory in the artificial world of the theorist's box. Similarly, we need to view risk from the standpoint of the issues that would actually worry us were they to occur, rather than those that are conceptually required to make the CAPM work.

For all these reasons, the time has come to give the traditional risk model a decent burial. In fact, this should have been obvious for many years. It has certainly been obvious to those of us who have been urging pension funds from the early 1990s onwards to adopt a much more balanced approach by a sensible exposure to so-called 'alternative' asset classes. However, the risk model has, like the theory that the sun goes around the earth, come to assume the status of religious dogma and has proved illogically resilient. The blame must, I fear, be laid at the door of the consultants, none of whom have the courage to be the first to break ranks and risk being burned at the stake for heresy.

Thus instead of introducing a model that actually works in the real world, consultants continue to fiddle with their astrolabe and simply reject all those aspects of the real world (MAC investing, 'alternative' assets, etc.) that will not fit into its cosy, yet artificial assumptions. As I said earlier, this is analogous to saying 'I have no use for a tractor because it won't eat hay'. Our message to the farmer should surely be: 'get rid of the horse, buy a tractor and find someone to show you how to drive it'.

We will see in the next chapter, that if one starts to think, first, about the portfolio as a whole, and not just individual assets and asset classes within it, and, second, as operating on a long-term, compound return basis, rather than a short-term, annual return basis, then it becomes even more obvious that traditional views of 'risk' are simply inappropriate. We will look at the conceptual nature of risk in more detail, and suggest how we should go about actually assessing risk in real world situations.

SUMMARY

- The way in which the word 'risk' is used by investment theorists and consultants is very different from its everyday meaning. This is highly damaging and dangerous since the difference is usually not understood, or even recognised.

- The everyday meaning of the word 'risk' when applied to an investment would most likely be the risk of losing some or all of our capital.
- The sense in which it is used by traditional financial theory is as a measure of the likely volatility of the annual returns of the investment in any one year relative to those of the market portfolio of which it forms part. Within the context of the Capital Asset Pricing Model (CAPM) this is commonly referred to as beta.
- Beta seeks to calculate the specific risk of a particular asset, i.e. the risk additional to the market portfolio risk (the 'systemic risk') that is incurred by investing in the individual asset.
- The CAPM is an impressive arithmetical construction but can operate only when hedged about with all sorts of artificial assumptions and thus has no place in the real world. Neither does the sort of 'risk' that it purports to demonstrate. Sadly, this point is not usually recognised and many real world investment decisions are made on a 'risk-adjusted' basis which belongs only in the lecture room.
- There are serious theoretical problems with beta – both arithmetical and conceptual.
- Since the arithmetic of the CAPM relies partly upon covariance with the market portfolio, then the choice of what is the market portfolio for any particular purposes will greatly influence the outcome, since what is being measured is not 'risk' in any real sense but rather the difference between the selected asset and the selected market portfolio. This leads to the anomaly that different 'risk' values can be calculated for the same investment depending on its relationship to the market portfolio.
- Conceptually, it cannot be right that the CAPM captures all the risk inherent in any investment. There is in any event no such thing as absolute risk since two investors with different circumstances are likely to view the same investment in different ways. Therefore any attempt to define and analyse 'risk' must take into account this relativity.
- One stumbling block is that all traditional measures of risk use as their input periodic (usually annual) returns, and all they can measure is something that is irrelevant to the needs of real world investors. Therefore any attempt to define risk must use some measure of returns that **IS** relevant to the needs of real world investors.

4
How to Define Risk

At the end of the last chapter I said that the risk model, or risk-adjusted model, was dead. That may seem a controversial statement, and is certainly a very sweeping one, so let us be quite clear about what we are saying.

As I explained, one of the building blocks that man the rule-maker found when he turned his attentions to the world of finance was the concept of the risk premium. This states simply that if there is a notional risk-free rate (which could be assumed for practical purposes to be an appropriate government bond rate)[1] then a rational investor will expect a higher rate of return in respect of a rival investment that carries greater risk than the risk-free investment (e.g. a company share compared to a government bond). I have no trouble at all with this principle. It must logically be the case that a 'risky' investment will have to provide a higher return than a 'non-risky' one, and the difference between that return and the risk-free return will be the risk premium. Thus:

$$\text{Expected } r_a = r_f + r_p$$

where r_a is the return expected to be produced by a particular asset, r_f is the risk-free rate, and r_p is the risk premium.

You may remember something like this formula from Chapter 3. Let me remind you:

$$\text{Expected } r_a = r_f + \beta(\text{Expected } r_m - r_f)$$

where r_f is the risk-free rate.

The market portfolio itself carries a higher degree of risk than the risk-free investment, and so already carries a risk premium over the risk-free rate ($r_m - r_f$). This is what we called systemic risk, or market

---

[1] Of course this is not strictly speaking a risk-free rate since there is the notional risk that the government in question may default on the bond, such as happened historically with Tsarist Russia and the American Confederate States, and more recently with Argentina. This is usually called 'sovereign debt risk'. However for practical purposes the sovereign debt risk of, say, the USA or the UK is assumed to be minimal.

risk in the previous chapter. The risk premium of an individual asset contained within the market portfolio represents the specific risk of investing in that individual asset. Effectively, the CAPM beta expression has simply been substituted for the risk premium.

In other words, the CAPM is saying that the risk premium of an individual asset will (always) be the same as the beta of the particular asset multiplied by the difference between the market return and the risk-free return. Further, since the CAPM claims that the risk premium and its own expression are essentially the same, it must follow that the CAPM expression calculates *all* the risk that the risk premium represents. I will have more to say about this a little later, but for the time being let us take a step back and consider what financial theorists are measuring as 'risk' compared to what one would consider to be the 'risk' of an investment in the real world.

RISK AND UNCERTAINTY

It has long been assumed that there is at the very least a strong relationship between risk and uncertainty, with many writers seeming to assume that they can and should be treated as being the same. At least, they assume that (1) risk and (2) uncertainty of return are the same.

Let me give a couple of concrete examples. Assume that you are evaluating an investment that has only two possible outcomes: it may double in value or it may increase in value a hundred-fold. We in the real world would regard this as a low-risk investment, while financial theory would regard it as a very high-risk investment, since it carries tremendous uncertainty in the form of possible variation in return.

My second example comes from an article on the meaning of risk[2] by Glyn Holton. How would you rate the idea of jumping out of an aircraft without a parachute? We in the real world would regard this as a pretty high-risk occupation. In the artificial world of financial theory, it carries zero risk since there is no uncertainty as to the outcome.

I think it will be self-evident from these two examples that we in the real world and those who live in man the rule-maker's artificial world are using the concept of 'risk' in very different ways. The position of the financial theorist may be summarised as:

---

[2] 'Defining Risk', *Financial Analysts' Journal*, Volume 60, Number 6 (2004), CFA Institute.

the total risk of an investment is expressed by the extent to which its return is likely to vary from the return of the market portfolio of which it forms part . . .

Hold on a minute, though. We know that the CAPM operates on series of periodic (usually annual) returns and it is from these that the relevant variance and covariance calculations are made. So the position properly expressed should be:

the total risk of an investment is expressed by the degree to which its annual return in any one year may vary from the annual return in the same year of the market portfolio of which it forms part . . .

Is that how we in the real world would regard the 'risk' of an investment? Clearly not. Yet I wonder how many pension trustees would expect to receive the reply set out above if they asked a pension consultant the question: What exactly do you mean by 'risk'?

Holton points out, importantly in my view, that even Harry Markowitz never said that risk and volatility of returns were one and the same. In his landmark 1952 article[3] Markowitz says:

the investor does (or should) consider return a desirable thing and variance of return an undesirable thing. (p. 77)

Surely this does no more than state a fact? Faced with a choice between a certain outcome and an uncertain outcome any investor will prefer the former.

Elsewhere Markowitz says:

The concepts 'yield' and 'risk' appear frequently in financial writings. Usually if the term 'yield' were replaced by 'expected yield' or 'expected return', and the term 'risk' by 'variance of return' little change of apparent meaning would result. (p. 89)

Holton interprets this as meaning that other writers have made this assumption but that the great man does not necessarily agree with it. I take the same view, and indeed derive great comfort from the fact that the father of modern portfolio theory should actually have written the whole of his original article on the subject without actually proffering any definition of 'risk' at all! This may have something to do with the fact that he was probably a believer, at least in part, in subjective or relative risk.[4]

---

[3] 'Portfolio Selection', *Journal of Finance*, Volume 7, Number 1 (1952).
[4] See p. 60.

RISK AND DIVERSIFICATION IN
THE ARTIFICIAL WORLD

It may be interesting to follow the path of the CAPM just a little further since, interestingly, even if you accept all its artificial assumptions and constructions, even those who mistakenly propound its use in the real world must accept that in most cases their sort of 'risk' can simply be disregarded.

I am sure we would all agree that risk is capable of being 'diversified away'. The principle is simple. You have a choice between buying one $10 lottery ticket and ten $1 lottery tickets. All individual tickets have an equal chance of winning, but if the $10 ticket wins it pays out 10 times as much as the others. If you wish to diversify away some of the risk of holding just the $10 ticket you would instead buy the 10 individual tickets. (This is exactly the same principle under which a bookmaker will 'lay off' bets.) To carry the idea to its logical yet ridiculous conclusion, if you could theoretically buy all the tickets you could arrive at a situation where you had no risk at all since you would be guaranteed to win the lottery.[5]

The official explanation is, alas, somewhat more complicated, and has to do with something called 'relative non-market risk', which is defined as the ratio of the non-market risk of an actual individual asset to the non-market risk of the typical such asset. This is, of course, a somewhat nebulous concept and, unlike beta, cannot be readily calculated or looked up. Having read this far, however, I am sure you can guess how the theorists get around this. Why yes, they make an assumption! They assume that the relative non-market risk of any asset is equal to its beta.

Actually, this assumption is not quite as unrealistic as it sounds (provided that you buy into the concepts of relative non-market risk and beta in the first place) since according to the law of large numbers it is perfectly possible for a large number of relatively small, inaccurate estimates to combine to produce one large, accurate estimate. Certainly it must be the case that as the number of assets in our portfolio increases, then the more accurate must our estimate of diversification become.

---

[5] Logical because it is true. Ridiculous because you would lose money; any lottery pays out less than it takes in.

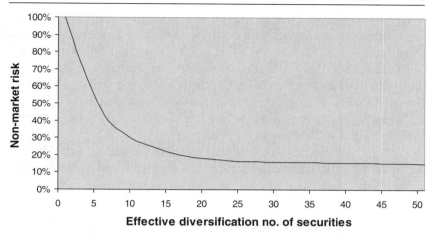

Figure 4.1   Effective diversification versus non-market risk

Sharpe suggested finding non-market risk by:

$$NMR = \frac{1}{\sqrt{D}}$$

where D represents the effective diversification of the portfolio and

$$D = \frac{1}{\sum (V \times R)^2}$$

where V is the relative value of each individual asset in the portfolio and R is the relative non-market risk of that asset.

The non-market risk equation can be graphed as shown in Figure 4.1, where it will be seen that effective diversification can be achieved with a surprisingly small number of individual assets – probably no more than about 25. Remember that Sharpe is talking about his type of risk, not any real world perception of risk, but it is heartening to know that even on the basis of his own theory this should not apply to anyone whose portfolio is adequately diversified. Equally, logically, if any asset class within our portfolio contains a sufficient number of individual investments, then we may disregard the specific risk of any such individual investment and consider simply the systemic risk of the asset class as a whole, however that might be calculated.

If we continue this line of logic it would suggest that, provided one has a sufficient percentage of a portfolio in each of a sufficient number of different asset classes, then this risk too (the risk inherent in any individual asset class), whatever that might be, can also be diversified away. Remember that we are still in the box – in the artificial world of financial theory. I have simply been demonstrating that even using the rules and logic that prevail in the box, their sort of 'risk' is largely irrelevant within a sufficiently diversified portfolio.

It's time to leave the box now, and return to the real world. What do we mean by 'risk' when considering an investment, and how might we measure this, and use it in deciding our investment strategy?

RISK IN THE REAL WORLD: UNCERTAINTY AND MATERIALITY

I will be setting out below two types of risk which I think are relevant to the investment process, and showing how the impact of these might vary from one investor to another. First, let us look again at the general conceptual background of 'risk'. What is it, and how can we assess it? What questions should we be asking to help us to arrive at an assessment?

Well, there seems general agreement that risk has a close relationship with uncertainty, and that any measurement of risk should attempt some calculation of the probability of uncertain outcomes. In an early setback for man the rule-maker, however, Frank Knight, one of the first writers on the nature of risk,[6] drew a distinction between the uncertainty that can be measured, which he defined as 'risk', and the one that cannot be measured, which he referred to simply as 'uncertainty'. This may be nothing more than semantics, but I don't think so. Even if risk is capable of precise measurement (which it isn't in the real world) and even if, as the CAPM suggests, the beta($r_m - r_f$) expression defines it (which it doesn't in the real world), is it really credible that this represents *all* the uncertainty of outcome that we in the real world would perceive as being attached to that individual investment?

Isn't it more likely that, no matter how sophisticated and flexible a risk model we may evolve, we will never be able to measure all the uncertainty that attaches to an investment in the real world? Remember that many of the assumptions that underpin the CAPM, and the

---

[6] *Risk, Uncertainty and Profit* (1921), New York: Hart, Schaffner & Marx.

artificial world in which it operates, themselves cover situations of uncertainty, resolving them conveniently in a way in which the CAPM can cope – that is, by not having to concern itself with them (e.g. the assumption that all markets are perfect, or that all investors are 'rational'). If so, then whatever definitions of 'risk' we may adopt we have to accept that they are at best guidelines or trend indicators and can never provide us with a definitive answer as to whether a particular investment decision makes sense or not. There will always be room for informed instinct born of experience and expertise.

Also, as we have seen in the previous chapter, there is the question of subjectivity, or relativity as I have sometimes referred to it. Markowitz, as we have seen, despite widespread assumptions to the contrary, did not actually provide us with a definition of risk. Interestingly, however, his 1959 book which followed his original article[7] contains an entire chapter on the subject of subjective probability. Is it not likely that in the real world an individual investor's perception of risk generally, and even his or her perception of the degree of probability of various uncertain outcomes in particular, will be conditioned by that person's particular circumstances, such as degree of knowledge, investment time horizon, asset class bias and target investment return? And how can even a small part of this subjective diversity be captured by a neat piece of algebra which looks solely at the relationship between two series of historical data, particularly where the arbitrary selection of one of those series will have a profound effect on the outcome?

I do not want us to become bogged down in a rarefied philosophical debate, but I hope I will by now have shown you enough to enable you to accept that, on a commonsense basis, risk has a close relationship with uncertainty, some of which can in appropriate circumstances be measured or estimated, as long as we accept the limitations of such techniques. Any such measurement or assessment will in turn have a close relationship with probability. However, probability when used in this context will be relative according to the viewpoint adopted, just as perceptions of risk will be subjective according to the particular circumstances of the individual investor. Indeed, it may be the case that the last sentence is actually expressing the same thing in two different ways. Thus we are concerned with five different but interrelated concepts: risk, uncertainty, probability, relativity and subjectivity.

---

[7] *Portfolio Selection: Efficient Diversity of Investments* (1959), New York: John Wiley & Sons.

I suggest that they can be encapsulated in the sort of questions we should be asking ourselves when looking at any situation in which risk may be involved:

- Is the outcome of this investment uncertain?
- Would my decision whether to make the investment be different if I knew in advance which of the uncertain outcomes was most likely to occur?
- Do I care?
- If I care, why do I care?

Other writers have presented slightly more simplistic versions of the above. Holton, for example, suggests that risk consists of what he calls 'uncertainty' and 'exposure'. I prefer to think of the latter as either 'relevance' or 'materiality'. For example, if the terms of my investment mandate specifically prohibit me from investing in hedge funds, then do I care whether it is difficult to predict in advance the likely returns of a particular hedge fund portfolio? Clearly, no. It is irrelevant to me.

In fact, on reflection, the main reason why I draw away from Holton's word 'exposure' is that I have become increasingly convinced that the 'Do I care?' question is actually a symptom not of exposure but of subjectivity and relativity. Hence the supplemental question which, in my view, is the most important of all: 'If I care, *why* do I care?' If one accepts that perceptions of risk will differ according to the individual investor's circumstances, then why not look at those circumstances in attempting to arrive at what the relative risk of his or her investments will be? It is rather like a golfer walking round behind the hole to look at his putt in reverse.

Thus, the correct response to the question 'How risky is this investment?' is itself a question: 'It all depends – what are you looking to achieve?' Or, as Holton says:

> It is meaningless to ask if a risk metric captures risk. Instead, ask if it is useful.

TOWARDS A NEW DEFINITION OF RISK

Nietzsche famously said: 'God is dead' (but then I suppose God would say: 'Nietzsche is dead'). Of course, like most things that are taken for granted in this sound-bite driven world, that isn't really what he meant. Those who have actually read Nietzsche, or even *about* Nietzsche, rather than just their dictionary of quotations, will know that what he meant was that the 'God-hypothesis' was no longer sustainable as a philosophical concept (if indeed it ever had been), and that something that could not be established by logical means (the 'God-hypothesis') could not be used as the ultimate fall-back position in philosophical argument, which was itself supposed to be a purely logical process. Unfortunately Nietzsche, who was apparently always a rather volatile character and eventually had to endure 'a decade of empty madness before the final curtain',[8] tended (like Wittgenstein) to express himself in aphorisms, apparently trusting others to interpret them correctly. When he said 'God is dead' what he meant was that all previous philosophy that had fallen back on concepts of God and/or natural law was now discredited and redundant and that all philosophy in future would have to be formulated to survive critical examination without such artificial props. It is in the same spirit (but hopefully with rather more humility) that I suggest that the traditional risk model is dead and that, in future, financial theory should strive to meet the actual concerns of real world investors rather than evolve complicated universal rules that operate only within the artificial confines of a box safely insulated from all the contaminating and inconvenient effects of reality.

How can we identify and express the risk concerns that real world investors actually experience? Here we come back to the last of our questions which, I submit, is the only really important one: 'If I care, why do I care?' We all know that most investments have uncertain outcomes, and I think we would all accept that any investment decision will be swayed by investors' views of that uncertainty relative to their own particular viewpoints. If investors do not care about the outcome then it is not relevant or material to them, and we need not consider it. But if they do care, *why* do they care? What is it about the range of possible outcomes that concerns them, and why? In the answer to this question lies the explanation of the types of risk we need to examine.

Let us leave the world of finance for a moment and look at a more general example. Suppose I need to travel from London to Edinburgh, arriving in time for an important meeting at midday. Arriving at the station in time for my 7 o'clock train, due to arrive in Edinburgh at 11, I hear three announcements:

- The 10 o'clock train to Birmingham may be subject to delay.
- The midday train to Edinburgh will not be subject to delay.
- The 7 o'clock train to Edinburgh may be subject to delay.

---

[8] Richard Schacht, *Making Sense of Nietzsche* (1995), Chicago: University of Illinois Press.

The first announcement is irrelevant to me. I do not want to go to Birmingham and so I ignore it. The second announcement is also irrelevant. While it is going to the right place it cannot possibly get me there in time, and I so I ignore it too. It is the third announcement that grabs my attention. What do they mean 'may' be subject to delay? How likely is it that the train will be delayed? For how long is it likely to be delayed? I need to be in Edinburgh by midday. Perhaps I should be taking a taxi to the airport in the hope of getting a flight to Edinburgh instead.

Why am I so concerned? Because I have an objective that I must achieve; I must be in Edinburgh by midday. I am concerned because some of the range of possible outcomes now being presented may cause me to fail to achieve my objective. I would welcome some attempt to show the probability of these possible outcomes, as it would help me to decide between different options, for example going to the airport, which is itself subject to a whole different range of uncertain outcomes that I also need to assess.

Let us return, with this example, to the world of finance. Is the investor not likely to react in a similar way? They have an objective that they wish to achieve. They are likely to be very concerned with any perceived risk that puts the attainment of their objective in jeopardy. They are likely to have no interest in risks that are irrelevant to achieving their objective, or, put differently, those that relate to a course of action that can itself never achieve their objective even if successfully performed.

However, an investor also has other valid concerns. If I board a train to Edinburgh there is a slight risk (a fatal train crash) that I may never arrive in Edinburgh at all. However, that risk is so minimal that I would disregard it, which means that in real terms the worst possible outcome is that I will arrive in Edinburgh later than anticipated, perhaps even considerably later. But suppose that risk was not so minimal? Imagine a hypothetical world in which the railways have such an appalling safety record that 50% of all railway journeys end in a fatal accident. Would you still disregard the risk of never arriving in Edinburgh at all? Clearly not. You might, for example, take the view that unless your train could be guaranteed to arrive in Edinburgh in time for your meeting with at least a 90% probability then you would rather not take the risk of never arriving at all, and would go home (although presumably not by train) instead of making your journey to Edinburgh.

All this demonstrates vividly how unfortunate it is that investment theorists and consultants have chosen to base their approach on arcane, artificial theories rather than on real life considerations. Viewed from a real world standpoint, traditional concepts of risk are irrelevant to a long-term investment strategy. We do not care if the train speeds up, slows down, or even stops or goes backwards during its journey; nor do we care about when these events may occur. All we care about is that we should not suffer a fatal train crash, and that we should arrive at our destination on time. Yet traditional measures of risk focus largely upon the former and not at all upon the latter. In reality, investors should be concerned only about two things:

1. Whether a particular proportion of a particular investment (or, more realistically, asset class) within a portfolio is likely to help or hinder that portfolio in achieving its target rate of investment return.
2. Whether that particular investment (or, more realistically, asset class) within a portfolio is likely to suffer a partial or total loss of capital.

Let us call these 'Return Risk' and 'Capital Risk' respectively. In fact there is even an argument that one of these (capital risk) may itself be ignored if one's portfolio is properly diversified between different asset classes, but for the moment let us examine each in turn.

Return Risk

I have explained in an earlier chapter how investors (particularly pension funds) should be estimating their future net liabilities over a long period and using these to calculate a target rate of investment return over the same period; a technique that I call Total Funding. Sadly I am aware that many pension funds, particularly in the UK, do not do so and so the concept of return risk may seem somewhat alien to them. However, I hope they would accept on reflection that their view of being able to take a train journey without having to worry about when they may arrive is fundamentally flawed. A pension fund has a scheduled meeting to attend with its creditors and it is a meeting for which it is legally and morally bound not to be late. It has to be in a position to pay specific benefits at specific points in time, and unless the trustees are basing their investment strategy on achieving the objective of being able to do so, then they are not only behaving illogically but they are in breach of their duty to their beneficiaries.

Let us assume that an investor has gone through the Total Funding process and arrived at a target figure of 13% which must be achieved as a compound return over a 25-year period. The return risk of any candidate asset class, then, is the likelihood, the probability, that it will not in fact achieve at least 13% compound over that period: the probability that it will achieve less than that.

Before we look at ways of embarking upon such an investigation, there are two important things to bear in mind, both of which we have stated before but bear repeating since the traditional risk model mindset conveniently ignores them.

Firstly, any risk metric is attempting to predict the future which, as we all know, is impossible and thus the longer the period for which we attempt to make predictions, the more certain we can be that the accuracy of the prediction cannot be guaranteed. We might quite confidently assert that no alien life form will land on earth tomorrow; there is nonetheless a chance, no matter how small, that we might be wrong. If we assert that humanity will never have any contact with any alien life form of any sort, then the chance of being wrong increases dramatically; in fact, the outcome becomes so uncertain that I doubt whether any two random individuals could ever be expected to ascribe to it the same percentage probability.

So yes, by all means let us do everything we can to predict the future returns of an asset class, but let us not lose sight of our own fallibility. If a risk metric gives an unlikely result, let us question it. If it offers a likely one, let us adopt it but with reservations.

Secondly, all we have to work with is historic data. This is itself subject to two important qualifications. In some cases that data is not perhaps as robust as it might be; witness, for example, the variety of investment benchmarks on offer for the hedge fund industry. The answer here is that it is surely better to make some attempt than none at all, particularly if one can do so based upon a measure of knowledge and experience of the asset class concerned. To say, as many consultants do, that a particular asset class that can be seen quite clearly to be consistently outperforming other investment alternatives, cannot be considered until enough time has passed for it to build up a statistically unimpeachable database of benchmark returns over several decades, is intellectual cowardice of the worst kind.

It also ignores the fact that the quoted indices that they treat with such reverence and deference have themselves been subject to change and restatement over the years. For example, no satisfactory total return data series exists for the UK until at least 1954 and, some would argue, perhaps quite a lot later. A study by the London Business School in 2000[9] shows that the Barclays/CSFB index, which has been used almost universally to look at the period before 1954, had produced an annual return of 8.8%, whereas the real figure was probably less than 4%: an error of over 100%! The constituents of quoted indices have also changed dramatically, perhaps even enough to make them inherently unreliable as statistical data. An attempt in the LBS report to recreate the FTSE 100 index through time sees railway shares making up over 49% of the index in 1900, yet less than half of 1% a hundred years later – a change of more than 100 to 1.

The second qualification to working with historic data is the assumption that one can predict the future by looking at the past. We have also mentioned this before, but it is such a crucial point that I would be negligent not to do so again, not least because this assumption is blithely and routinely made by all who work with traditional risk models, and yet never expressly stated. You will remember that I attempted to address this issue to some extent within Total Funding by suggesting the introduction of an uncertainty factor notionally to increase anticipated liabilities the longer they stretch into the future. I am aware of at least one subasset class[10] where historic returns are almost certainly *not* a good guide to possible future returns, but for the most part I think we have to bear the qualification in mind but proceed anyway, since frankly we have little option. I am aware of at least one investment analyst who uses astrological models to predict market movements – which may be judged by some to be as good a way as any – but at the end of the day all we have to work with is historic data, and so be it.

So how should we look at return risk? How can we look at the available historic data and use it to arrive at some approximation of future return expectations? Let us take by way of example the historic annual returns of the S&P 100 index from 1984 to 2004. Note please that these only capture the potential capital gain represented by the index. It is therefore necessary to add to these figures the percentage dividend yield in order to arrive at a total return. For our present purposes a rough and ready approximation will suffice, since I am concerned only to show how the methodology of such a calculation might work in practice. Let

---

[9] *A Century of Investment Returns* (2000), London: London Business School/ABN Amro.
[10] European venture capital.

us therefore simply add a notional 3% to each year's figures to arrive at a rough total return for the year.

Statistical Analysis

Well, an obvious starting point might be the statistical tools we have at our disposal to measure samples of data. We could, for example, look at the total return figure for each of our 21 sample years, calculate the mean and the standard deviation and then work out the probable range of returns for different levels of confidence. A worked example will be found in Table 4.1. The confidence interval is calculated taking into account the size of the sample, using the formula (in the case of the 95% interval):

$$\mu \pm 1.96\left(\frac{\sigma}{\sqrt{n}}\right)$$

where μ is the sample mean, σ is the sample standard deviation and n is the sample size. Obviously, therefore, the confidence interval, and thus the confidence range, will become smaller with larger sample sizes, and vice versa.

This analysis shows us that the mean annual return for the S&P 100 during this period was just under 14%, and thus would appear at first sight to present little return risk when measured against a target return of 13%. However, the pattern of returns has been very volatile, ranging from about +40% to about −21%, and this is reflected in the high standard deviation (over 17%). In fact all this analysis can lead us to expect with anything like certainty (95% probability calculated on the sample size) is a range of possible outcomes between just under 7% and just over 21%. Yet, of our sample of 21 years, only in 4 of them did the annual return actually fall within this range!

There is actually a more sophisticated way of approaching the data set, but I would prefer to delay consideration of this to the following section. For the moment, let us continue to explore the problem we have just encountered.

I think this anomaly suggests two things. Firstly, statistical tools do a great job in the right conditions but should be treated with caution when we are looking at data sets with very large variation. In fact, this is a classic example of why we should not blindly accept the output of any mathematical process when applied to investment returns if the

Table 4.1 Worked example

	1984	1985	1986	1987	1988	1989	1990	1991	1992	1993	1994
Index return	0.00	24.10	11.65	3.48	10.92	25.00	-6.06	24.52	2.59	8.08	0.00
Dividend yield	3.00	3.00	3.00	3.00	3.00	3.00	3.00	3.00	3.00	3.00	3.00
Total return	3.00	27.10	14.65	6.48	13.92	28.00	-3.06	27.52	5.59	11.08	3.00
Mean	13.97										
Standard deviation	17.07										
90% confidence interval	6.13										
90% confidence range	7.85	to	20.10								
95% confidence interval	7.30										
95% confidence range	6.67	to	21.27								

	1995	1996	1997	1998	1999	2000	2001	2002	2003	2004
Index return	36.92	22.87	27.78	31.30	31.29	-13.49	-14.87	-23.80	23.82	4.36
Dividend yield	3.00	3.00	3.00	3.00	3.00	3.00	3.00	3.00	3.00	3.00
Total return	39.92	25.87	30.78	34.30	34.29	-10.49	-11.87	-20.80	26.82	7.36
Mean										
Standard deviation										
90% confidence interval										
90% confidence range										
95% confidence interval										
95% confidence range										

result is at variance with practical experience and informed instinct. If you were a bookmaker, would you really be prepared to offer someone even odds (let alone 100 to 1) that the S&P 100 annual return would not fall outside the range 4.4 to 23.6 within the next 20 years or so? Yet that is what a 99% confidence range would be, based on our available data.

It is clearly nonsense if a statistician can state with a 95% degree of confidence that the returns for a period will fall within a particular range, whereas in reality this happens less than 20% of the time in the actual historical data on which the prediction is based. As with all mathematical measures, we should not attempt to use them without fully appreciating their possible technical shortcomings. I think the problem here is obvious. Any measure based on a mean and standard deviation will be at the mercy of very wide fluctuations in value, such as we have here. The fact that the sample standard deviation is greater than the sample mean should ring some warning bells.

Perhaps the problem is that we need a larger sample size? Yet if we try this, our problems multiply rather than diminish. Yes, we will obviously achieve a smoother result, yet logically the confidence range should narrow rather than widen and so arguably could be even more misleading when applied to actual recent data. Yes, we will have more data available with which to work, but the further back into history we go, the more we are straining our assumption that past performance figures can simply be extrapolated forwards to give a good guide to possible future performance. Yes, we will be able to look at a longer period, but what good does this necessarily do us if returns for other asset classes (hedge funds, for example) are not available for the same period?

Secondly, it should make us wonder if we are not perhaps barking up the wrong tree in terms of the type of data we are using.

As we have seen in an earlier chapter, the use of periodic returns (i.e. those of a single period such as a month, a quarter or a year) in long-term investment strategy actually makes little sense. All that should concern us is whether we are likely to achieve our target rate of return during the number of years in question across our whole portfolio. We do not care if the annual return of any one asset or asset class is disappointing in any particular year. Still less do we care whether it may be possible to predict this in advance. All we care about is whether that asset or asset class is able to contribute meaningfully to achieving the target rate of return over the whole number of years that we are considering. All we care about is our train arriving on time at the end of its journey.

We do care if the asset or asset class is very unlikely to achieve the target rate of return in *any* year under discussion, but only because this is a good indicator that it may be unable *ever* to produce the target return. At one extreme, if an asset class traditionally produces, say, something close to the risk-free rate of return whereas our target rate of return is twice the risk-free rate, then there is little point in even attempting to analyse it. If we know in advance that the top speed of a train is 10 miles an hour then we know that it cannot possibly get us to Edinburgh in time for our meeting, whatever happens. I will return to this point later with reference to bonds.

However, if we think about how we actually plan and implement investment strategy in the real world then an alternative way of measuring return risk becomes fairly obvious. As we saw earlier, it is more meaningful to look at what has become known as the 'vintage year' basis of returns. There are two main reasons for this.

Firstly, it approximates more closely to actual patterns of investment in the real world. We do not make all our investments at the beginning of January and then sell them all at the end of December ready to start again in the New Year. Rather, there will be a pattern of inflows and outflows, some regular and predictable, others less so. In the world of quoted securities we will need to reinvest our dividend income, and can do so very painlessly. In the world of private equity we may receive cashflows more or less at random, and can only reinvest these as our allocation strategy permits.

The vintage year basis calculates returns throughout a period compounded from year to year. It levels the playing field between those asset classes that may from time to time exhibit spectacular returns on an annual basis (returns which, incidentally, in many cases are never actually realised unless an investor is prepared to stake everything on market timing and 'go liquid') and those where the real level of return becomes apparent only over time.

Secondly, it is the only meaningful way of measuring returns across a large number of years. We saw earlier how pension consultants discount the liabilities of a pension fund over a term of years. Yet discounting is simply the mirror image of compounding, so if it makes sense to discount the liabilities of a scheme, why should it not also make sense to think about compounding the investment returns? As has happened at the Yale Endowment and elsewhere, sophisticated investors are happy to accept a drop in annual returns in the short term if this will lead to a higher compound return in the long term.

We will go into this more deeply later, but for the moment let us circle back and consider the principle of capital risk before getting too bogged down in the various calculative options.

Capital Risk

I hope it will be obvious that capital risk is essentially a subset of return risk. The risk that we might actually lose some or all of our capital in a particular asset class is part of the risk that it will not achieve the target return. It is the risk that the return will be so poor as actually to be negative rather than positive. Since we would expect most asset classes at least to keep pace with inflation, and thus show a positive return no matter how small, then for any capital risk to be present, an asset class would have to perform very badly indeed, at least on a cumulative and/or compound basis over a long period.

The reader should also remember the argument advanced earlier in the chapter (which comes not from me but from Sharpe), which seems self-evidently true, namely that if you diversify your portfolio sufficiently among uncorrelated assets then there comes some logical point where capital risk is effectively diversified away, or at least reduced to minimal proportions.

SUMMARY

- The traditional concept of 'risk' is dead and should be given a decent burial. We need to arrive at a new definition of 'risk' and in order to do this we need to evolve a new understanding of what risk actually is.
- It is inaccurate and misleading to assume that volatility of returns, risk and uncertainty are all the same thing wrapped up in different terms. Risk will be different things in different situations and therefore any risk analysis can only be meaningful in the context of the individual circumstances of any individual investor.
- We must thus begin our attempt to define risk by viewing the real world circumstances of a real world investor. While these will of course be different in each case, the investor's concerns are likely to be the same.

- Any individual investor will be concerned to achieve the target rate of return over the period in question, and this should be his or her **ONLY** concern. Annual returns are irrelevant for this purpose. If the investor takes a train journey, he or she is not concerned with how fast the train may travel at any time, but only that it should reach its destination on schedule. Thus the only risk that is relevant to the investor is the risk that his or her portfolio as a whole might not achieve its target return over time. We can call this 'return risk'.

- The related concern as to loss of capital, either partial or total ('capital risk') may be viewed and calculated as a subset of return risk. In reality, low levels of capital risk can probably safely be ignored, assuming (1) a properly diversified portfolio and (2) that one need never be a forced seller of any particular asset class.

5

How to Calculate Risk

As I said at the close of Chapter 4, we are moving towards a position where we will measure risk using compound returns over time. We know, however, that the finance world does not currently evaluate risk on this basis, largely because of the widespread obsession with annual returns, and so it must be useful to point out that even if one were to use annual returns as an appropriate input then there are much better ways available of using these than simply plugging them into the CAPM, a model which, I hope, we have now thoroughly discredited.

To be fair, I am aware of work that is already being done in this direction by some investors (notably Yale) and some pension consultants, but please bear with me for I intend the following to be no more than a stepping stone on the path to our final destination.

PHI CALCULATIONS

Consider again the annual return figures for the S&P 100 that we used earlier. If you remember, I stated that there was a more sophisticated way to look at these statistically. As always, let us start with what we need in everyday terms and move from practice to theory, rather than vice versa. What do we need to know (or approximate)? We would like to know the probability of (1) an asset class allowing us to at least match our target rate of return (the 'return risk') and (2) an asset class resulting in some loss of capital (the 'capital risk').

Assuming for the sake of argument that our target rate of return is 13%, we need to calculate from our historic data (1) the probability of the annual return in any one year being equal to or greater than 13% and (2) the probability of the annual return in any one year being equal to or less than 0%. We can do this by using something called the normal distribution function, calculating the value Φ and then using the look-up tables (widely available in school textbooks) to give us the relevant probability (using $(1 - \Phi)$ if Φ is negative and Φ itself if positive).

We can calculate the probability of an annual return from Table 4.1 being equal to or greater than 13% by calculating the probability of it being less than 13% and then deducting this probability from 1. Thus:

$$z = \frac{x - \mu}{\sigma}$$

where z is the probability of a value occurring that is equal to or less than x, and is calculated by reference to Φ (the Greek letter phi).

$$z = (13 - 13.97)/17.07 \qquad z = 1 - \Phi(0.06)$$

Using the look-up tables we find that this equates to a probability of just over 52%. Therefore the probability of x being equal to or greater than 13% is $1 - 0.52$, or just under 48%. This is actually a fairly good match with our data set, since 13% was matched or exceeded in 11 out of 21 years. It is reasonable to assume that the larger our data set, the closer this approximation would become.

Now let us calculate the probability that x may be equal to or less than 0:

$$z = (0 - 13.97)/17.07 \qquad z = 1 - \Phi(0.82)$$

This time the look-up tables provide a probability of 21%. Again, this is a fair match as 4 out of our actual 21 values are negative.

So, using annual returns and applying standard statistical techniques we find that the S&P 100 seems to have return risk of about 50% and capital risk of just over 20%. Obviously the former figure would diminish with lower target rates of return, and increase with higher targets. We could accordingly calculate the return we might expect for any given level of return risk, should we feel so inclined. However, it would also seem logical to look at the extent to which the target return might be exceeded in any one year, and the relative level of capital risk when compared to other asset classes.

PHI AND BETA

Of course, all of this assumes that returns will exhibit normal distribution, and looking at some of the data sets with which we have to work this can sometimes seem to be a large assumption. This is a good argument for using vintage year returns, which necessarily has a smoothing effect, rather than annual returns. However, for the benefit of the unconvinced I would point out that the results generated by Φ seem generally consistent with the actual data set, even though they *may* depend on an assumption that may not be wholly reliable, whereas using the same returns within the CAPM *certainly* depends upon a number of assumptions that are known to be wholly artificial. There is also the little matter that Φ generates results that suggest answers to questions the investors actually care about in the real world, whereas the CAPM generates results that are of no validity to anyone save within the artificial world of 'the box'.

There is also a significant difference in the way in which these measures are put forward. Proponents of beta are forced to argue (since this is a fundamental assumption of the CAPM) that beta represents all the risk specific to any one asset or asset class. However, the only way to measure this is by reference to relative variation of returns. My submission is that (a) 'risk', whatever it may be, is far more than a product of historical variations in return, (b) the risk of the same asset or asset class will be different in the case of every individual investor according to his or her own particular circumstances, and (c) there is no one right way of measuring it.

However, there are various dials on the dashboard that can serve as guides to an experienced investor, and phi is one of them. Hopefully, we will never fall into the mistake made by the CAPM brigade of supposing that there is one universal measure of risk. For example, even phi based on annual returns may not be a good guide when analysing asset classes for which, as noted earlier, annual returns may not themselves provide a valid measure of relative attractiveness. We need a more flexible approach that can perhaps incorporate a number of different factors and will take specific account of our desire to achieve a target rate of compound return over a given period.

I am very reluctant to suggest a new risk model based on annual returns, precisely because this could be taken as some encouragement for the view that annual returns do of themselves constitute a valid measure of relative attractiveness. Similarly, it would encourage those in search of a universal 'fix' to adopt it and apply it blindly to any given situation. However, I am sadly aware that there will be many who will be slow to abandon the shibboleths to which they have clung blindly for so many years, and it must be better for them to apply a measure that may have some benefit rather than one that has none, and may well be actively misleading.

I am also acutely aware that it is not possible to construct a risk model that does not contain subjective elements – the way in which the figures are used, the underlying sensitivities, etc. – and my subjective viewpoint on these matters is no more valid than that of anyone else. Finally, it is of course impossible to construct any risk model that can be of universal application, unless all investors in the world adopted the same target rate of return, were subject to exactly the same personal circumstances, and agreed to use exactly the same subjective assumptions. That said, I would venture the following as a possible way in which any such measure might be constructed, if only on the basis that any change must be a change for the better.

As we noted above, phi only tells us part of the story. It must be appropriate to look at the extent to which outperformance can occur in any one year. Two asset classes might both have 50% return risk, but if one of them occasionally produces double the target rate of return while the other never outperforms by more than 10%, then clearly the former would seem more attractive on a classical risk/reward basis. I would propose that one might do this by looking at the degree of outperformance in any year in which the target return is exceeded, and then take the average of this over the period. In the above example, the average outperformance in those years which at least matched the target rate of return was about 14.5%. I would propose that we multiply this by the probability of the target return being exceeded, so it would become:

$$14.5\% \times 48\% = 6.9\%$$

Strictly speaking we have already taken capital return into account, since it forms part of the risk return. However I feel that there is understandably such a high sensitivity on the part of most investors to capital risk that they might wish to give this some additional weighting, perhaps by now multiplying the current figure by 1 minus the capital risk, thus:

$$6.9\% \times 79\% = 5.5\%$$

Thus the risk-adjusted return that we might expect for this asset class would be 18.5%, a super-return of 5.5% over our target of 13%.

Another approach might be to deduct the average underperformance in years when the return was less than zero, multiplied by the capital risk. This would produce:

$$6.9\% - (24.5\% \times 21\%)$$

$$6.9\% - 5.2\% = 1.7\%$$

which would bring the risk-adjusted return down to 14.7%.

Yet another approach might be to use only the average underperformance which lies below zero, rather than below the target rate of return (which would produce a risk-adjusted return of about 17.5%) . . .

I have touched upon this idea as lightly as I dare, and close this section by reiterating that I am in no way encouraging the adoption of it as a universal model, nor do I pretend that it is one. I present it simply as an illustration that if one *is* determined to use annual returns as an input, then there are undoubtedly better ways of doing so than the CAPM or any of its 'risk' related cousins. Phi is not a panacea, and it does not address the question of compound returns over time. It is, however, statistically valid and, used in the way I have suggested, it does address real world concerns.

Swensen is understandably coy about the precise analytical methods used at the Yale Endowment. Yet he does say that they employ 'mean variance analysis to estimate expected risk and return profiles of various asset allocation alternatives',[1] and 'mean variance analysis' is exactly what our phi workings do. As there is no indication that they use compound returns for their modelling rather than annual returns, then perhaps what they actually use is not a million miles away from what I have been outlining so far. However, we must now move on to what I actually advocate, which seems to me to do no more than take the final logical step along the path we have been travelling.

COMPOUND RETURN-BASED MODELLING

I used the image earlier of a passenger contemplating a train journey. Remember, he does not mind how quickly or slowly the train travels at any particular part of its journey, only that it should arrive on time. I hope that by now I will not need to labour the point that investment strategy can only (and indeed, must) be planned over a lengthy period and, it follows, that we are concerned only with the compound return that may be earned during this period, not the annual return of any one year. We must accordingly find a way of analysing the performance of different asset classes that pays due regard to compound rather than annual returns. This may sound a simple idea, but it is as profound as the difference between compound and simple interest.

---

[1] Yale Endowment Annual Report, 2004.

Fortunately the required inputs are readily to hand and in this regard private equity has been leading the way for many years. We can simply calculate the vintage year returns of different asset classes in the same way as we already do for private equity, and use these to assess (1) Return Risk and (2) Capital Risk. However, there is one obvious difference between compound and annual returns that we must first address.

An annual return, by definition, is the return earned within the space of a single calendar year. The period covered by a vintage year return will depend on which year we take: a 1988 vintage year return will cover every year from 1988 onwards, a 1996 vintage year return every year from 1996 onwards. I apologise for stating the obvious, but there is an important point here. If a vintage year return has been earned over 20 years it is clearly much more robust and reliable statistically than if it had been earned over two years. In other words, if we are to use vintage year returns, how are we to weight them relative to each other so that we give more credence to a 20-year return than to a two-year return?

A simple approach would be to multiply each vintage year return by the length of the period it covers, but there is something else to consider that may not be as obvious as the first point. Because of the time value of money, any vintage year return will be much more heavily influenced by what happens in its early years than what happens in, say, Year 20. In fact, what happens in Year 20 will have almost no impact regardless of how extreme it may be. For example, if you map out a series of 3% cashflows for 20 years it will of course give an IRR of 3%, but changing the return in Year 20 to 30% will only increase the 20-year IRR to 4%. In other words, increasing the return in one year (the twentieth) by 10 times will only increase the overall return by one third.

Are we comfortable with this? Well, it is a slightly absurd question. It is simply a manifestation of how vintage year returns work, and we are clearly happy with the general concept of vintage year returns, but it does raise something to consider. In a rapidly changing environment, vintage year returns will be slow to indicate the change, and will tend to understate the degree of change compared to annual returns. In theory, this may not matter very much as, from the various historical data with which we will be working, it would seem that most asset classes go through relatively short periods of turbulence (usually no more than about three years at a time) and then resume fairly consistent growth, so it could be argued that it is actually beneficial for vintage year returns to operate in this way since they discourage panic, short-termism and faddism. However, it is something that we need to take into account in constructing any statistical model, perhaps by cutting off any increased weighting after a certain period has elapsed. This will be of particular relevance to an asset class like private equity, where funds tend to have a typical life cycle and so reach a point (probably after about 10 years for a buy-out fund and about 12 years for a venture fund) where the return will be fully mature – indeed some of the funds within the population may already have been wound up by then.

Let us restate the S&P 100 figures on a vintage year basis assuming a dividend yield as before and run our statistical exercise again. You will see that I first take the vintage year returns and treat them exactly as before with the annual returns. Then I attempt a weighted exercise of the type just discussed, using a base factor of 5 and ceasing the weighting exercise after 10 years. (There is no magic in these particular figures and the reader should feel free to try others.)

You will see from Table 5.1 that considering compound returns rather than annual returns has a smoothing effect, and thus gives us a much tighter range of statistical possibilities. I would argue that the output is also inherently more reliable than in the earlier example (Table 4.1), as due to the time value of money the level of compound return becomes increasingly difficult to change the longer the period that one considers. See how, for the first 12 vintage years, there is almost no variation at all, whereas there is dramatic fluctuation in the last few years. The weighting process will of course give more effect to the former than the latter, but this is consistent with everything we have been saying about robustness of data and the time value of money.

We can now attempt exactly the same phi exercise as we did with our annual returns earlier. First the unweighted returns:

$$z = (13.00 - 9.44)/5.43 \qquad z = \Phi(0.66)$$

which gives a 75% probability that the vintage year return of any one year will be equal to or less than 13%, or a 25% probability that it will be at least 13%.

$$z = (0 - 9.44)/5.43 \qquad z = 1 - \Phi(1.74)$$

which gives a 4% probability that any vintage year return will be equal to or less than zero.

Table 5.1 Statistical exercise

	1984	1985	1986	1987	1988	1989	1990	1991	1992	1993
Vintage year return	13.16%	12.47%	12.35%	12.71%	12.63%	11.68%	12.82%	11.76%	12.29%	13.39%
Weighting	2.00	2.00	2.00	2.00	2.00	2.00	2.00	2.00	2.00	2.00
Weighted return	26.32%	24.95%	24.71%	25.42%	25.27%	23.36%	25.63%	23.52%	24.58%	26.78%
Mean	9.44%									
Standard deviation	5.43%									
Weighted mean	10.58%									
Weighted standard deviation	3.39%									

	1994	1995	1996	1997	1998	1999	2000	2001	2002	2003
Vintage year return	13.39%	10.78%	9.03%	6.24%	2.18%	−3.23%	−1.32%	2.48%	16.67%	7.36%
Weighting	2.00	1.80	1.60	1.40	1.20	1.00	0.80	0.60	0.40	0.20
Weighted return	26.78%	19.40%	14.44%	8.73%	2.62%	−3.23%	−1.05%	1.49%	6.67%	1.47%
Mean										
Standard deviation										
Weighted mean										
Weighted standard deviation										

Now let us repeat the same exercise but using the weighted returns:

$$z = (13 - 10.58)/3.39 \qquad z = \Phi(0.71)$$

which gives a 24% chance of returns at least equalling 13% in any one vintage year, or to put it more correctly, a return risk of 76%.

$$z = (0 - 10.58)/3.39 \qquad z = 1 - \Phi(3.12)$$

which gives a probability of 0.001%, just one chance in a thousand, of a vintage year return being less than zero.

So the effect of weighting our returns (and, at the risk of repeating myself, I am not suggesting that this is exactly the way the weighting should operate, just demonstrating the basic methodology) seems in this case to have made little difference to the output for return risk, but has emphasised the low level of capital risk.

THE FUTURE OF RISK ANALYSIS

I am convinced that the future of risk analysis lies in the use of compound returns. It seeks to analyse the very measure of performance that should form the basis of a real world investor's practical concerns, posing the question: How likely is it that this asset class will at least achieve my target rate of return over the period with which I am concerned? Surely it is only by working with compound returns that doubts over compound returns can be addressed?

Yet it does so without doing violence to common sense by trying to shoehorn annual returns into an artificial model that is not designed to meet these real world concerns. Nor does it ignore the fact that annual returns are probably not appropriate (and definitely not appropriate in the case of certain asset classes) as a performance guide to vintage year returns.

It also gets around the problem of excessive variation in annual return patterns. Interestingly, this is not an issue that seems to concern Yale, or, if it does and they have found a means to avoid it, then they are keeping very quiet about it. In their 2004 Annual Report they talk, for example, of domestic equities having an expected real return of 6% but with a standard deviation of 20%. So, unless I am missing something very fundamental about the way in which these figures are presented, all one could say with 95% certainty is that the annual return of any one year would be roughly (using $\pm 2\mu$ instead of $\pm 1.96\mu$) between 40% either side of the mean. With great respect to Yale, I cannot believe that such a figure is at all meaningful in planning investment strategy.

Even if the figure were meaningful, how does it actually assist our real world investor to know that there is a certain probability of a certain annual return occurring in any one year? There are obviously a few limited situations where this might be the case. For example, suppose you were faced with a target rate of return of 12% and your statistical analysis of annual returns showed that there was zero chance of a bond portfolio delivering that as an annual return. That would clearly suggest a fairly definitive conclusion that you need not consider bonds further as an asset class since, if they are incapable of delivering that as an annual return in *any* year, then it is logically impossible for them ever to deliver it as a vintage year return.

Another point of interest is that Yale are apparently not above tampering with annual returns data if they do not like what it says. Yes, I also experienced a double-take when I read about this, but see for yourself:

> Historical data provides a guide, but must be modified . . . to compensate for anomalous periods.[2]

I must confess that I have a real problem with this approach. If you choose to use annual returns as the inputs for your analysis process, then it seems to me that you are stuck with them and cannot simply change them if they do not suit your purposes or provide neat answers to your calculations. You have made your bed and you must lie on it. As for anomalous periods, these *do* occur, and so surely it is unrealistic to exclude them or to lessen their impact?

It may be that what Yale have in mind is that, looked at in isolation, the effect of an anomalous period appears too significant because in reality it would be but part of a long investment period, but that is the inevitable and logical outcome of using annual returns. Surely this is nothing more than another example of why compound returns should be used instead? To say nothing of a further extension to the world of the sterile box; yet one more convenient yet artificial assumption is being used to shore up a fragile apparatus that is likely to fall apart if roughly handled.

I am also advocating, as you will have seen in the course of this chapter, the simple idea of weighting vintage year returns relative to

---

[2] Yale Endowment Annual Report, 2004.

the length of time they cover. This seems logical to me since data is obviously more statistically reliable the longer the period it covers, and it is the compound return over a long period with which our risk perceptions should be concerned. I have chosen to impose a cut-off on the weighting process after 10 years for three reasons:

1. Given the effect of compounding, it becomes increasingly difficult to change a vintage year return as time goes by, since what happens in the early years will always have a greater mathematical impact.
2. In the case of one of our asset classes under discussion – hedge funds – it is difficult to obtain meaningful industry data that is much more than 10 years old.
3. In the case of private equity funds, the typical fund investment/divestment cycle is probably about 10 years (which may be more for a venture fund or less for a buy-out fund, so probably about 10 years on average).

However, I must stress that the weighting that I have chosen (1 year = 1x, 10 years = 10x, >10 years = 10x) is totally subjective and there is no particular reason why an investor should not substitute some other ratio, or indeed use totally unweighted vintage year returns, although I submit that this would give much less reliable results. Similarly, my 10-year cut-off period is also subjective (I will not say arbitrary because I have given my reasons above, and I think they are good ones) and so could be varied if desired.

There is another very important point that is well summarised by the Yale Annual Report[3]:

> Because investment management involves as much art as science, qualitative decisions play an extremely important role in portfolio decisions . . .

Such a statement will, of course, be anathema to the consultant with his slide rule, his risk model and his beta tables, yet it simply dares to say what any experienced investment manager already knows. Risk analysis (or, as I prefer to think of it, return analysis) can only take one so far and, frequently, instinct will then need to take over. I am not talking here about betting the ranch on a random hunch. The sort of instinct I have in mind could perhaps be better described as informed intuition; informed by many years' specialist experience of a particular asset class.

---

[3] Yale Endowment Annual Report, 2004.

Historic returns are all we have to work with, but what if, given the particular circumstances (structural change within a market, change of key personnel within a manager, etc.) they are not in fact a good guide to the future? Suppose you know that a depressed area has been zoned for intensive regeneration by government. What do you think is the best way of getting a feel for likely future property values in that area? Should you ask a consultant to spend a week analysing historic price data, or should you go to the area and have coffee with some local estate agents?

It is precisely this sort of opportunity set that the consultants, with their blinkered, 'risk-adjusted' view of the world, deny to their clients. Opportunities to outperform come through finding managers with different, often contrarian views of particular markets or market segments in which they have a demonstrable expertise, particularly if that asset class is illiquid and (perhaps because of this) has high return potential. Many such meetings will doubtless be wasted as the necessary confidence to proceed will not be generated, but every so often one will bear fruit. This failure to properly scout out the available pathways of opportunity is, of course, exacerbated by the tendency already referred to, and highlighted by Swensen, of investors to pick from that set of managers who already service their peer group, and from that set of assets in which their peer group already invests. Small wonder, then, that Yale talk about sound investment management being a 'combination of quantitative analysis and market judgement'.[4]

DIRECT COMPARISON OF DIFFERENT ASSET CLASSES

The really dramatic opportunity that is opened up by the use of vintage year returns, though, is the ability to compare, directly and validly, the returns of one asset class against those of another. This has been a major problem for investment consultants, particularly in the pension fund area, since an asset class such as private equity, for which annual returns are largely meaningless as a measure of performance, cannot be slotted conveniently into any traditional risk model.

In many cases this fact alone has been used as a reason (excuse?) not to consider an asset class further. In other cases, investors have adopted an attitude of 'let's just do it a little bit and then it doesn't really matter', setting an allocation of, say, 2%. Quite apart from the mistake

---

[4] Yale Endowment Annual Report, 2004.

of setting an allocation of less than about 15% to anything within the portfolio (which we consider elsewhere), I hope the illogicality of this approach will be obvious. If you are going to set your asset allocation on the basis of a risk model, then either something fits within the risk model or it does not. If it does, and you think that it can make a significant difference to your performance, then you should give it a sensible weighting. If it doesn't, then why do it at all?

With the use of vintage year returns for risk measurement purposes, however, we can leave such dilemmas behind. It affords us the opportunity to compare apples with apples; we are looking at returns prepared on exactly the same basis in each case. Now we can compare private equity directly against hedge funds, or property directly against quoted equities.

It is difficult to overstate just how liberating this technique is. If one ignores spurious excuses such as 'there are no proper benchmark figures available' (a myth which this book explodes – see the tables in Appendix 1), then the two main reasons given by investors for not having pursued a Multi Asset Class approach so far are the need for liquidity (to which I devote a separate chapter) and the inability to compare asset classes against each other on a risk-adjusted basis.

As with so many things, we need to be able to employ a little parallel thinking. The inability to fit some asset classes into a traditional risk model has been seen as the fault of the asset class rather than the model, whereas in fact the opposite is the case. If an asset class offers the opportunity for outperformance then the risk model must be able to accommodate it. The failure of the traditional model has been partly a symptom of a fixation with annual returns, and partly a failure to think outside the box. Once one accepts vintage year returns as a valid measure, and indeed as the most accurate possible measure of returns over a long period, then everything falls into place.

The idea of the train journey, with our only concern being that the train should arrive on time at the end of its journey, is a simple but effective image and will I trust allow the reader to see the force of my argument. If it is compound returns over time which are our only proper concern, then for goodness sake why not use them for all our analytic requirements?

The use of compound returns gives us a measurement of risk which is truly 'useful'. It directly relates to the investor's real life concerns (achieving a target rate of return), and it enables our investor to compare the relative risk of different asset classes directly against each other. In other words, it is relevant and it is universal.

Without wishing to become too cynical, I think that part of the problem has been a reluctance on the part of some consultants to adopt any measure of risk (or indeed of anything) that their clients might actually be able to understand. As in many other professions, complexity and obfuscation have often been deliberately employed to ensure that the client is left with the appropriate feeling of awe for the vastly superior intellect being deployed by those advising them; to suggest that risk is actually a relatively simple concept, and can be readily understood by any intelligent layman, may not prove popular in such quarters.

OTHER TYPES OF RISK

Before we leave the subject of risk (although we will be considering specific concepts such as alpha and portable alpha a little later) I would like to make one thing abundantly clear. Unlike the protagonists of the world of the box, I do not pretend that the method I have outlined captures *all* the risk attendant upon any particular investment or asset class. There are clearly all sorts of risk that need to be considered, which might include political risk, currency risk, and terrorism risk to name but three. The first two would be germane to any sort of overseas investment, while certain industries (airlines, hotels and the cruise business) may be dramatically affected by the third. However, I am not sure that there is any good way of measuring such risks arithmetically, nor am I sure that any method will in fact ever be discovered; the levels of uncertainty are simply too great, and an assessment of them is too subjective.

However, I do suggest very strongly that while we should bear these in mind we should probably ignore them if we have no choice but to incur them; what we cannot measure or assess cannot really be allowed to influence our decision-making. However, where we *do* have a choice, then clearly the situation is different. For example, if we have a choice between two asset classes that seem to offer the same level of return risk, but one carries currency risk and the other does not, then the logical outcome must be to choose the less risky option. If they offer different return risks then we would need to consider what a suitable risk premium might be. This may seem an obvious point to make, but you will see when we come to look at Yale's exposure to non-US quoted equities that this is something they do not seem to have appreciated. Their foreign equities carry greater risk, but have consistently produced lower returns.

To extend the train journey analogy, we have focused on the risk of the train not arriving on time and also on the risk of it being involved in an accident, but there is also the risk that we might contract food poisoning from eating a sandwich from the buffet car, or that we may have our wallet stolen by a pickpocket while on the train, or that we might be attacked by football hooligans on their way home from an away match. If we have a choice between incurring this risk or not, then we exercise it (we might, for example, choose to travel on a train with no buffet car or eat before we leave home) but if we do not have any choice then we simply accept it and hope that things turn out for the best.

What we have done in these last two chapters is to isolate any risk that is (1) material and (2) measurable, and we have suggested the best possible way of doing this from the point of view of a long-term investor. This in turn allows us to have a better view of other types of risk. In the example of two asset classes, only one of which carries currency risk, had we not been able to measure the return risk of each asset class then we should not be in a position to think about what a suitable risk premium might be in anything but an unscientific, instinctive manner.

So, as we proceed further with our look at MAC investment strategy, and with some particular asset classes, let us bear in mind that:

- The only measures of risk with which we are concerned should be return risk and capital risk.
- These relate directly to the practical concerns of a real life investor: (1) Is this asset class likely to achieve my target rate of investment return? (2) Is this asset class likely actually to lose me money?
- We can measure both these probabilities by using phi analysis of weighted vintage year returns.
- We will, however, bear in mind the place for informed professional judgement, particularly if it appears there may be a possibility that historic returns are not necessarily a good guide to future performance.

When considering any measure of risk I find myself turning again and again to Holton's question of 'is it useful?'. Surely this is the crux of the matter? One of my favourite writers, Von Clausewitz, summed this up in a different context:

The probabilities of real life take the place of the conceptions of the extreme and the absolute.[5]

SUMMARY

- If one is determined to use annual returns for risk measurement purposes, then there are better ways of doing so than by plugging them into the CAPM. A more valid technique is to use phi calculations (a form of mean variance analysis). However, such calculations can lead to seemingly absurd results and this should alert us to the fact that a better approach is available.
- Instead of annual returns, we should be looking to use compound returns as suggested in the previous chapter. It is submitted that vintage year returns are the most convenient form of compound returns available.
- Return risk can be calculated by stating the returns of any asset class on a vintage year basis, time weighting the results, and then performing phi analysis using the normal distribution function. It is understood that this in its turn requires the use of certain assumptions, but it is submitted that these are kept to a minimum and, unlike the traditional method, it is a measure of risk that addresses the real world concerns of real world investors. Capital risk can be calculated in the same way.
- This enables an investor for the first time to compare the returns of any asset class directly and validly against those of any other asset class. In other words, we now have a risk model that is universal in its application, thus facilitating a Multi Asset Class approach.
- It is important to remember that any risk figures produced in this way are a guideline only (though a very powerful guideline in the absence of any conflicting evidence) and that they can never hope to capture **ALL** of the risk inherent in a particular investment. There should always be room for informed intuition where specialist expertise is available. In particular, there are occasionally situations where historic returns are not necessarily a good guide to future performance, for example if some structural change has occurred in the relevant market.

---

[5] Carl Von Clausewitz, *On War*, London, Penguin Books, 1982 (but published originally, and posthumously, in 1832).

6
Quoted Equity

Quoted equities have traditionally formed the core of most investors' portfolios; indeed, when coupled with bonds they still represent in many cases effectively the whole of the portfolio. It is worth remembering, however, that outside the USA and the UK investing in equities was a relatively recent phenomenon, due partly to legal restrictions to which various classes of investors were subject, but more often to blinkered thinking and asset class prejudice.

While domestic quoted equities form the backbone of most investors' holdings, portfolios have become increasingly international in flavour. For example, Local Authority pension funds in the UK had just 3.5% of their assets in North American equities in 1995, but this had doubled to about 7% by 2004. Currently, overseas equities represent about 28% of their total assets, plus about 42% for UK equities.[1] Contrast this latter figure with Yale's target allocation of just 15% to each.

Yale has traditionally viewed domestic and foreign equities as distinct asset classes, and this chapter will be examining whether this is a valid policy, or whether certain equity indices are in fact so highly correlated that this is not advisable. Also, does this change as between, say, dollar- and sterling-based investors?

We will also be looking at the debate between the devotees of active versus passive equities management; in other words, whether or not to index the portfolio. One quick point of terminology here: I am aware that there are various 'index' funds where all that is meant is that the manager has discretion to choose stocks from within that particular index. When I talk of 'indexing' I am of course using it in the sense of tracking the index; in other words, the manager would have no discretion whatever, but would be obliged simply to reproduce the index by selecting its constituent stocks pro rata to their weighting within the index.

Other issues will include whether quoted securities can deliver the sort of returns which a modern investor will be seeking. What is the

---

[1] All figures from the *WM Annual Review 2004*.

return risk? Is there any capital risk? Are there any ways in which we can increase that return? In this context we will discuss the possible use of leverage, and examine the levels of gearing that might be prudently accepted.

We will take these points slightly out of order, since the way in which we resolve the active versus passive debate may condition exactly how we should view the available benchmarks for our purposes of analysis later. Accordingly, let us deal with that first.

ACTIVE VERSUS PASSIVE EQUITIES MANAGEMENT

This debate is hardly hot news, since it has been raging for many years, and so much has already been written about it that I enter upon it with some diffidence. Briefly, the question is whether an actively managed portfolio will outperform the index over a sustainable period on a cost-adjusted approach, or whether an indexed approach is to be preferred.

Before we begin, let me enter an important caveat that may not have affected some earlier deliberations. The MAC investing approach is conditioned by long-term compound returns (vintage year returns) and not by short-term gains or annual returns as an input for analysis (except in certain special situations where they *are* appropriate, such as correlation analysis). Therefore, we are concerned with what happens over the long term (and, if possible, the very long term) and it is to long-term considerations that we will give the benefit of the doubt, should any such doubt need to be resolved.

I want to be completely open and state this up front because I am aware that it does impose an element of bias. Perhaps without realising it, investors often choose managers on short-term criteria; but sometimes this is unavoidable, for example, where the manager is newly formed and does not have a long track record. Nobody should want to exclude promising managers from an investment programme simply because they are newly formed; they may have good individual track records at other firms, or they may have some startling new insight into a particular market, but this can sit rather unhappily with a long-term investment strategy. Changes of manager (i.e. firing as well as hiring) are frequently driven by short-term performance, particularly very poor performance, and these can be disruptive to the process, taking up much investor time that could be better employed elsewhere.

However, when looking at the long-term prospects for an active manager other factors come into play. If a manager specialises in a particular strategy or 'tilt', will that continue to be valid over a long period? What changes in key personnel may take place? Can compound performance over time keep pace with the compounding of the extra cost burden associated with active management?

Why would an investor choose to have an equity portfolio actively managed? Clearly for one reason only: he or she must believe that it is possible to outperform the benchmark index consistently, and that the particular manager who has been selected has the ability to do so. We will examine in a moment the various ways in which such outperformance may be achieved. However, they can only be driven by one or both of two factors: first, the active manager may have information that is not available to the market as a whole; second, the active manager may have a better method of analysing the available information.

The first factor is one of the many that are excluded from the operation of the Capital Asset Pricing Model by way of an artificial assumption. I have no doubt from having worked for 20 years in close proximity to public equity markets that this was once a major issue and could indeed confer a very significant advantage. However, public markets around the world are steadily tightening their definition of what constitutes 'insider information', and so not only is the advantage that can be gained by an analyst being more astute or persistent than the pack being progressively squeezed, but investors are also having to be more and more careful in the way they use such information.

As to the second factor, I have sat in many meetings with quoted managers and they have all claimed to have a better 'black box' than their competition. In recognition of the clear importance that their marketing effort attaches to such things, long-haired mathematical geniuses with scary eyes and poor personal hygiene are frequently showcased alongside their slick and sophisticated institutional sales colleagues. However, can it logically be the case that, with so many financial gurus at work in so many investment houses around the world, there can really be any unique advantage that can be conferred on the analysis process? And, even if there is, how long would it be before it would be copied by the opposition, if necessary simply by poaching some key staff?

Be that as it may, let us look at the ways in which an active manager can attempt to outperform the index.

Firstly, she can, from within the index try to select shares that she thinks are likely to outperform in the short term (the 'stock picking' approach). This is all fine and dandy, but what method is she using to do this, and can it really confer a lasting advantage (see above)? And how can it be assessed? To what extent can you distinguish between investment insight and luck?

Secondly, she might use an event-driven approach, trying to predict how certain shares might react to particular external stimuli – for example, a major movement in the price of oil, or the result of a particular election. If allowed by the terms of her mandate, she might even use derivative instruments to leverage such positions.

Thirdly, she may believe in a particular approach, perhaps highlighting stocks that have a low ratio of market capitalisation to net asset value, or have a high exposure to a particular market. This is known as a 'tilt'. Again, this is all fine and dandy but what happens when that tilt becomes no longer effective, even if it was the correct one to choose in the first place?

All this may give the impression that I am sceptical about the ability of any active manager to outperform the index consistently over a long period – which is true, but let me explain a little more of the background issues that I believe work against the active manager.

Firstly, there is the question of costs. I do not wish to labour this point as it is raised so often by the proponents of passive management that it has become almost a knee-jerk reaction, but I believe it is relevant and that its impact on the annual compounding of returns is often not fully appreciated. A truly passive portfolio may be managed for less than 50 basis points. Depending on the circumstances, an actively managed portfolio may well cost four or five times as much.

A sum of $100 discounted by 2% a year will decline to $82 over 10 years and $67 over 20 years. That is the extent of the burden of the extra costs of active management. Put more simplistically, it means that an actively managed portfolio will need to outperform the index consistently by 2% every year just to stand still. In other words, if the total return of the passive portfolio was 4% in one year, then the active manager would have to outperform by 50%. How likely is it that this can be done consistently every year for 20 or 30 years?

Secondly, one must touch on the question of taxes. Although many institutional investors (pension funds, endowments, foundations) are tax exempt, some (insurance companies, banks, family offices) are not. A passively managed portfolio needs to be changed only when companies move into or out of the relevant index. An actively managed portfolio may well change frequently (at its extreme, this practice is known as 'churning'). In some jurisdictions this can give rise to more (and earlier) exposure to tax as gains are realised. Where this is the case, the returns of any active manager need to be calculated not just net of costs but also net of tax.

The most important consideration of all, however, was pointed out by Sharpe as long ago as 1991.[2] The total return earned by the whole universe of actively managed portfolios based on a particular index must, when reckoned before taking the extra management costs into account, equal the return earned on the index itself. In other words, for every active manager who has made a gain, there is a notional active manager who has made a corresponding loss. Of course, the situation is complicated slightly where a manager may have been allowed to use derivative instruments, or to gear the position with debt, or to remain partially uninvested, but the basic logic, as one would expect from someone of Sharpe's stature, is impeccable. He expresses it as two principles:

(1) before costs, the return on the average actively managed dollar will equal the return on the average passively managed dollar, and
(2) after costs, the return on the average actively managed dollar will be less than the return on the average passively managed dollar.

Let us consider what this means for active returns. We are really just restating the earlier principle that any active manager needs to outperform the index by the amount of the extra costs involved just to stand still. This is bad news when coupled with Sharpe's principles. If, on average, 50% of managers by market capitalisation weighting will underperform the index before costs, and 50% will outperform, then this is changed radically by the burden that the extra costs impose. Now the only managers who will outperform the index will be that segment of the 'winning' 50% who have 'won' by more than, say, 2%. Therefore, significantly less than half of the actively managed dollar will beat the index in any one year, and with less than a 50% chance of outperforming in any one year the chances of outperforming in every year over a 20-year period are almost non-existent (try calculating it on the basis of even a 40% chance each year – it's a very small number!).

So in terms of financial theory, the odds seem well and truly stacked against the active fund manager. It may well be that individual active managers can outperform the index by more than the amount of the extra costs and taxes in any one year. It may well be that there is even a small number who can do so over a three- or five-year period, but the probability of anyone doing so every year for 20 years is remote – less than 1%.

The actual studies that have been published must on occasions be treated with caution. For example, some analysis does not necessarily look at the situation on a market capitalisation-weighted basis and, as pointed out above, not all 'index' funds are fully passive. However, Sharpe is adamant that the theory works:

> Properly measured, the average actively managed dollar must underperform the average passively managed dollar, net of costs. Empirical analyses that appear to refute this principle are guilty of improper measurement.

When viewed over a long period, the evidence appears to support this view. For example, one commentator,[3] claims to have analysed the returns of the average equity fund against those of the Vanguard 500 Index fund on a compound basis over a 20-year period and found that the actively managed approach had produced only 57% of the value of the index fund before taxes, 41% after taxes and just 34% after both taxes and inflation. In fairness, it should be pointed out that the commentator in question was Chairman of the Vanguard Group, but the numbers do point out the enormous drag that underperformance net of costs can have on a portfolio's returns when compounded over time.

This 'long term' element, which is so crucial in the case of MAC investing, may work against an active management approach. In the short term, a small team of managers with great market insight may well be able to produce truly superior returns, but what happens when one or more of the team is poached by competitors or (more likely these days) a hedge fund? And any competitive advantage that is conferred by insight must logically erode rapidly over time as successful investment strategies will inevitably be copied by others.

I must also touch upon something that has become known as Dunn's Law, which suggests that an indexed portfolio will outperform an actively managed one in good times (i.e. when the index rises in any given year) but will underperform when the index falls. At first glance this seems counter-intuitive, since one would expect the actively managed portfolio, carrying relatively more specific risk of relatively

---

[3] John C. Bogle, *The Relentless Rules of Humble Arithmetic*, Bogle Financial Markets Research Center, February 2005.

fewer companies (and therefore being less well diversified) to have a higher beta than the index and thus both rise and fall to a greater extent than it does itself (i.e. to have a beta greater than 1).

Two main reasons are given to support Dunn's Law. The first is that many active managers are in fact given permission to hold some of their portfolio in stocks that do not form part of the benchmark index. The second is that active managers are generally allowed to hold some of their portfolio in cash if they wish, while passive managers are generally required to be fully invested. Both these factors would tend to cushion a portfolio from the movement of the index, giving rise to the phenomenon described in Dunn's Law.

Empirical evidence seems to suggest that this is indeed the case. For example, a *Morningstar* article in 2000[4] (which of course was towards the end of a long bull market, and so a period of steadily rising indices) demonstrated that where five-year return figures were available, index funds had predominantly outperformed their active counterparts. This also squares with the figures put forward in Bogle's (Vanguard) article referred to above.

Now, one thing becomes very apparent when looking at historic investment returns – as one has to do in the preparation of this sort of book – and it is so universal that I may safely state it as a principle. Generally speaking, the return on most asset classes is positive in most years. Of course there have been some years of heavily negative returns, particularly in public markets, but the fact remains that over the last 20 years or so we have seen many more positive annual returns than negative ones. Indeed, this is what one would expect even if only from the natural operation of inflation. If Dunn's Law is valid, then it must follow that, even ignoring the cost implications, the passive dollar should do better than the active dollar more often than vice versa.

We began our consideration of MAC investing by looking at the Yale Endowment, and an obvious flag for the 'active' lobby to wave is the outperformance by Yale's domestic equities portfolio over a number of years relative to its index. However, while I am extremely reluctant to advance any observation that may seem at all critical of their approach, given the huge success they have achieved, I must point out that the passive benchmark that they adopt is almost certainly not an appropriate one for them to use.

---

[4] Dan Culloten, "It's an Active Manager's Market – at first glance", *Morningstar* 12th July 2000.

In order for any comparison between the active dollar and the passive dollar to be valid, the active portfolio must be selected from the universe represented by the constituent companies of the underlying index. In the text of their annual report Yale make it clear that they favour small cap stocks, yet their benchmark index is the Wilshire 5000. Now it is quite true that this is a very broad index; indeed, it claims to be the broadest US index in existence. Yet it is weighted by market cap, so that large cap stocks will be disproportionately and heavily represented within it. How can this be an appropriate passive counterpart to an active portfolio which is tilted away from large cap stocks towards small cap stocks? Surely a much better solution would have been to adopt the Dow Jones Wilshire Small-Cap Index, which was specifically designed to act as a benchmark for active managers using this tilt?

It may well be that even if this index were to be used, then Yale's managers would still have outperformed over time. I do not know, because they have not presented those figures. Yet Yale admit that it is difficult for active managers to outperform the market on a consistent basis. Why do they say this when they could equally well say something like 'our active managers have consistently outperformed the market, so yah boo sucks to all you indexed investors . . .'?

The Yale report could also be misleading in a different way. They state their overall return (which, let me say yet again lest there be any misunderstanding, is outstanding) net of fees, but the report is silent on whether the returns of the individual asset classes are also stated net of fees. As we have seen, this could make a huge difference. If the domestic equities return is stated before fees rather than after them, given the effect of compounding the cost burden, their return could be much closer to the appropriate passive counterpart (whatever that may be) than seems the case. Again, it may be that I am completely mistaken about this. It may be that the returns *are* stated net of all fees, but if they are then the report does not say so, and the omission seems strange, since such a statement would be a very strong point in their favour.

It is for all these reasons that I cannot accept the active management proposition. I have an open mind and am willing to be persuaded, but nothing that I have seen, either by way of theory or by way of practical evidence, convinces me. We will see from our look at portable alpha that it is generally acknowledged that an active management approach involves more 'risk' ('alpha') than a passive approach, and even if one does not necessarily agree with the nature of the risk, or how it should be calculated, it must be significant. For example, we have demonstrated above that more than 50% of the actively managed dollar will carry return risk relative to the passively managed dollar. A risk premium is valid when an acceptable level of extra return may reasonably be anticipated, but why should we voluntarily accept extra return risk when no extra long-term return is in fact guaranteed, or even likely?

We will accordingly continue our look at quoted equities on the basis of index returns. However, it is more correct to say 'the return of the index portfolio' since we will be looking at the total return, i.e. the capital gain (or loss) represented by the movement of the index itself, as well as the relevant dividend yield. The one exception to this is when we consider the NASDAQ index, since the dividend yield is so negligible that it may safely be ignored.

WHICH INDICES SHALL WE EXAMINE?

Sadly it is not possible within the confines of this book to examine quoted returns around the world. In any event there are already many fine publications available that do this, and all relevant figures are in the public domain and readily available on the internet and in the back copies of financial newspapers in reference libraries.

I have chosen the FTSE 100 since it is the most likely benchmark index for a sterling investor (although I am aware that MSCI benchmarks are increasingly used), and the S&P 100 since it is obviously the closest in nature to the FTSE 100 from among the various indices that might be a natural benchmark for a dollar investor. There is a further relationship, of course. The thoughts of a sterling investor will probably, and instinctively, turn first to the USA when considering foreign quoted equities, just as the thoughts of a dollar investor will probably turn first to the UK when looking outside the USA.

I am aware that this is probably less true in the case of a dollar investor. US investors, in particular seem to feel irresistibly and instinctively drawn to Asia. (We should not lose sight of the fact that there are many investors around the world for whom the dollar is essentially the currency of investment, even though they may not be situated in the USA, or even necessarily American, since so many currencies are linked to the dollar, and so many global businesses are effectively dollar denominated.) However, the use of these two indices provides a useful means of demonstrating how we might look at correlation within the confines of a MAC model, and given the highly probably coexistence of at least some of their constituents in just about every dollar or sterling investment portfolio, not just in an illustrative capacity.

While recognising that these two indices do probably represent the most useful with which to demonstrate the basic analysis technique for selecting quoted equity indices for use within a MAC portfolio, let us also look briefly at some other possibilities. It might be very useful, for example, to look also at the NASDAQ, DAX and Nikkei indices and see how the five indices move relative to each other.[5]

WHAT CORRELATION IS THERE BETWEEN QUOTED MARKETS?

Anyone embarking upon research for a book of this nature is naturally subject to various preconceptions. I must confess that one of mine was that quoted indices, and particularly comparable ones in the USA and the UK, generally march in lockstep with each other, and at first sight this does indeed appear to be borne out by Table 6.1. Note in particular how not only the S&P and FTSE indices, but also the DAX and the NASDAQ, appear to exhibit near-perfect correlation with each other. Only the Nikkei sticks out like a sore thumb, exhibiting negative correlation with all of its fellows.

At first sight the Nikkei seems to be an ideal candidate for a MAC portfolio as it would provide perfect diversification for either the FTSE or the S&P depending on whether one was a dollar or sterling investor. Remember, however, our observation that most asset classes have positive returns most of the time, and tend to increase in value. Thus any asset class that exhibits negative correlation would tend to have a preponderance of negative returns and/or to diminish in value over time.

Looking again at the Nikkei, returns have been negative in less than half the years under consideration (but still 9 out of 21 compared with 4 out of 21 for the S&P) but the second part of this hypothesis certainly holds true. The S&P was trading at the end of 2004 at mid-1998 levels, whereas the Nikkei was still slightly below 1984 levels. In other words, this is an asset class that has actually lost money even in nominal terms (i.e. even before adjusting for inflation to arrive at a real return) over

---

[5] Due to the differences in the relevant data sets, correlation with the DAX is measured from 1990, whereas the others are generally measured from 1984, but this is still a long enough period to give a valid result.

Table 6.1 Correlation between quoted indices

	S&P 100	FTSE 100	NASDAQ	Nikkei 225	DAX
S&P 100		97%	97%	−46%	97%
FTSE 100	97%		94%	−39%	98%
NASDAQ	97%	94%		−38%	94%
Nikkei 225	−46%	−39%	−38%		−48%
DAX	97%	98%	94%	−48%	

Source: Own workings from public data.

a 20-year period. Now of course historic returns are not always a good guide to future performance and there is no reason why the Nikkei might not rebound dramatically in the future, but we are looking for asset classes that ideally exhibit low levels of return risk and capital risk, and both of these would appear to be unacceptably high (probably close to 100%) when looking at this data. Thus, while I would be the last one to restrain anyone from taking a contrarian approach I would say that, in the absence of some informed market insight as to (for example) major structural changes in the Japanese economy, the figures simply do not justify further consideration of this asset class and we will accordingly not be mentioning it again.

As pointed out in an earlier chapter, the generalisation that most asset classes will tend to have positive returns most of the time (if only because of the impact of inflation) strongly suggests that we should moderate the strict logic of the MAC investment model and instead of seeking asset classes that exhibit negative correlation with each other, we should seek those that exhibit positive correlation, but not too much. In practice, it may be that those that have something like 60% positive correlation can in fact be perfectly acceptable.

Does this pose us a problem, given that the various quoted indices seem to have very high levels of correlation? Actually, no, or, at least, not as much as might at first appear. What we have been looking at so far is the extent to which the various indices move up and down relative to each other. A real life investor, however, is not concerned with this but with the total return that can be achieved by investing in the index. This is partly the annual percentage change in the index itself, and partly the income stream the investor receives by way of dividend yield from holding shares in the constituent companies.

This can make quite a significant difference to the analysis shown in Table 6.1. Take a look at Table 6.2 and observe the changes.

Table 6.2 Correlation of total returns earned on quoted indices

	S&P 100	FTSE 100	NASDAQ	DAX
S&P 100		86%	88%	76%
FTSE 100	86%		71%	87%
NASDAQ	88%	71%		70%
DAX	76%	87%	70%	

Source: Own workings based on public data.

There is still quite high correlation, but it is less than before and in one case it is as low as 70%. There are two main reasons for this. The first is that the correlation coefficient is now being calculated on the annual change in the index value rather than on the index values themselves. This alone brings down the correlation between the S&P and the FTSE, for example, from 97% to 85%. The other difference is that companies listed on the London Stock Exchange have traditionally paid higher dividends than their counterparts in either Germany or the USA. However, this seems to have little overall effect, since the resulting figure for the same relationship (FTSE against S&P) is only about 40 basis points higher than that which looks at the index return alone.

What assistance can we derive from these figures in thinking about the way in which we could mix and match quoted indices?

Correlation and the Dollar Investor

Let us first look at the case of a dollar investor. Her foreign index of choice would probably be the FTSE, but in fact this does not make a lot of sense within the context of a MAC portfolio as it exhibits a high correlation of total returns (86%) with the S&P, and we are assuming that she would already be using this as her domestic index. She would be better off looking at the DAX as a foreign index in which to invest since this is still high, but not as high (76%). Of course, in reality this decision would not be taken in isolation but against a backdrop of advice on the relative strength of the UK and German economies and how sterling and the euro might be likely to move against the dollar. Also, in practice it is unlikely that these will be the only two indices to be considered.

It may be that a dollar investor, having gone through the exercise of considering different indices around the world against which to set the S&P 100 as a separate asset class, comes to the conclusion that there simply is not a sufficiently attractive answer to justify taking this course, particularly not given the very high degree of uncertainty (economic, currency, political, etc.) hanging over any possible choice. It would certainly be my instinct, based simply upon the fairly limited research and analysis appropriate to a single chapter within a book of this nature, that it may be mistaken to think about using an S&P index based approach to US equities as one asset class, and any major index (FTSE, Nikkei, DAX) based approach to foreign equities as another asset class.

As I stated at the outset, it is in fact slightly uncertain whether Yale think in terms of foreign equities being a separate asset class or not. The body of their most recent annual report is slightly ambiguous, saying:

> The definition of an asset class is quite subjective, requiring precise distinctions where none exist.[6]

However, in both the tables and the charts foreign and domestic equities are shown as separate asset classes, and the fact that they have identical target allocations (15%) strengthens my impression that this is in fact how they are viewed.

Yale are understandably coy about revealing too much of their precise analysis of different asset classes, but it is apparent from their description of their domestic equities allocation that they favour an actively managed approach (another point on which I would probably differ) and small cap stocks. It may therefore be slightly unfair to comment on their approach from a different perspective (i.e. a passive approach based on a large cap index), not least because, as we have seen, their benchmark index is the Wilshire 5000, which obviously has a much broader constituency than the S&P 100. However, it is weighted by market cap and almost 80% of its companies by value are quoted on the New York Stock Exchange.

Similarly, without knowing Yale's precise allocation to foreign stocks it is impossible to attempt any meaningful analysis of the actual correlation of the underlying indices,[7] although we are told that half

---

[6] Yale Endowment Annual Report 2004.

[7] It is clear that the passive benchmark is 50% MSCI EM and 50% MSCI EAFE, but it is also clear that this does not mirror the actual content of the portfolio.

the allocation is to emerging markets and half to developed countries. There is a risk premium of 2% in real terms for the 'emerging' allocation as against the 'developed' (which is the same as domestic equities at 6%). In theory this means that Yale are expecting the return on foreign equities to be 1% more than domestic after inflation.

However, this conflicts with their actual experience, whereby foreign equities have dramatically underperformed domestic equities over the last decade. This point is frankly just fudged in the Yale annual report. It is claimed, correctly, that the foreign equities portfolio has substantially outperformed its benchmark, but this benchmark is very much lower than the corresponding one for domestic equities (less than 5% as against more than 10%). Nowhere does it explain why an endowment should accept a much lower benchmark for an asset class that one would have expected, by any commonsense view, to exhibit more 'risk' than domestic equities, and whether a risk premium of just 1% in real terms would actually be sufficient.

In reality, Yale have earned only about 10% on foreign equities over the last decade, as opposed to 17% on domestic equities. My hypothesis would be that Yale have fallen prey, in common with many US investors, to a powerful yet irrational attraction to Asia, and have effectively lost quite a lot of money in relative returns in consequence. Against this backdrop of huge underperformance, the fact that the target allocation to foreign equities has risen from 9% to 15% over the last five years seems puzzling to say the least.

However, let us leave Yale to one side and consider the position in more general terms. Table 6.2 points to an intriguing possibility for any dollar investor willing to trust the pure logic of MAC investing. Why not use the NASDAQ rather than the S&P 100 as one's domestic index? Its correlation with the S&P is so high (88%) that one would risk losing very little by making the switch (we must, however, examine the relative return risk before being able to state this with certainty), and it would then be possible to put together a passive portfolio of foreign equities based 50% on the FTSE and 50% on the DAX, which would have a positive correlation with the passive domestic portfolio of 70%. Purely from a correlation point of view (and specifically subject to analysing the relative return risk) this would seem a near-perfect solution for a dollar investor. Were an investor prepared to take this approach then the selection of both domestic and foreign equities as separate asset classes could indeed be justified.

Correlation and the Sterling Investor

Things are also a little complicated for the sterling investor where correlation is concerned. As we have seen, the FTSE and the S&P indices appear to move very similarly in lockstep. As I wondered whether the slight difference between them could be due to changes in the dollar/sterling exchange rate, I experimented with re-indexing the S&P 100 into sterling values at the correct prevailing exchange rates for the periods in question. To my surprise, this returned a lower correlation figure than before (93.4% as against 96.2%).

This would suggest either that currency differences tend to be ignored, or that people are seeking to adjust for them and are over-compensating (perhaps due to the presence of currency rate/index value arbitrageurs playing around with derivatives). However, neither of these explanations seems particularly compelling to me. Having had an opportunity to think about it at length, it occurs to me that many of the constituent companies in the FTSE 100 have a high proportion of dollar-denominated earnings and so currency changes will, to a large extent, be accommodated in the earnings multiple applied in London, at least on a year end basis. Whatever the case, there does not appear to be any justification for a sterling investor to incur currency risk simply in order to invest in the S&P 100. Indeed, the very high level of correlation on a total earnings basis (86%) probably makes this a totally unsuitable additional asset class for a sterling investor. Nor does the DAX offer an acceptable alternative, since the correlation figure is marginally higher than the S&P 100.

The figures appear to show very clearly that the appropriate US index that a sterling investor should choose is the NASDAQ, exhibiting, as we have discussed above, a correlation of just over 70% with the FTSE 100. This would in principle appear to be justified as a separate asset class. My one reservation is that when we later examine private equity as an asset class I will be discussing the possible use of the NASDAQ index as a formalised 'money box' for money that has been allocated to private equity (perhaps even committed to private equity funds) but not yet invested. Let us leave this point for the moment, but bear it in mind as an issue when we later consider exactly how our MAC portfolio should be structured.

RETURN RISK OF QUOTED EQUITIES

As we have seen, return risk is best calculated by using phi analysis on vintage year returns. In this way we can not only address the real world concerns of individual investors, regardless of their particular circumstances, but can also use as inputs the data that most closely approximates to the way in which they are likely to be investing and viewing their investment objectives. We can then calculate the risk of any asset class not achieving any given rate of return.

Table 6.3 shows the return risk of the S&P 100 on both a vintage year and a weighted vintage year basis. The former is simply for illustrative purposes to see how great an effect weighting the results can have. In this case there is a significant uplift since the returns of the index in the early years of the period were positive. It can be argued that weighting the returns simply adds to the uncertainty rather than diminishing it, since one's entry timing is random. However, I believe that this most closely approximates to the way in which an investor should view her strategic framework. She is investing for a 20-year period but will also be investing over that period to a certain extent since she will need to reinvest both when rebalancing and when recycling cashflows (though I agree that these will be of lesser impact than the initial investment).

The analysis shows us just how difficult it has been to achieve high compound returns from quoted equities in recent years. There is only a 44% chance of achieving even 10%, and this drops away rapidly to only just over a 1 in 10 chance of achieving 15%. In fact, one has to go down to 9% as a target before it becomes more likely than not that the rate will be achieved. At least capital risk is low, even on an unweighted basis; certainly well within acceptable limits.

Table 6.4 shows the same figures for the FTSE 100 index and shows at once how unreliable a measure it is if we simply look at the way in which respective indices have moved against each other over time. As we saw earlier, looking simply at the indices themselves would produce a correlation coefficient of about 97%, whereas in reality the actual total returns produced by each have been significantly different. This is due partly to different dividend yields, but not wholly. The arithmetic way in which the correlation coefficient works means that a relatively small

Table 6.3 Return risk of S&P 100 on vintage year basis

	1984	1985	1986	1987	1988	1989	1990	1991	1992	1993
Vintage year return (%)	12.55	11.80	11.61	11.88	11.71	10.69	11.70	10.60	11.06	11.10
Mean (%)	8.26									
Standard deviation (%)	5.51									
Target return (%)	10	11	12	13	14	15				
Return risk (%)	62.5	69.1	75.2	80.5	85.1	88.9				
Capital risk (%)	6.7									
Weighted mean (%)	9.38									
Weighted SD (%)	4.45									
Target return (%)	10	11	12	13	14	15				
Return risk (%)	55.6	61.8	72.2	79.1	85.1	89.6				
Capital risk (%)	1.8									

	1994	1995	1996	1997	1998	1999	2000	2001	2002	2003
Vintage year return (%)	11.99	9.34	7.56	4.78	0.76	-4.58	-2.55	1.40	15.55	6.32
Mean (%)										
Standard deviation (%)										
Target return (%)										
Return risk (%)										
Capital risk (%)										
Weighted mean (%)										
Weighted SD (%)										
Target return (%)										
Return risk (%)										
Capital risk (%)										

Table 6.4 Return risk of FTSE 100 on vintage year basis

	1984	1985	1986	1987	1988	1989	1990	1991	1992	1993
Vintage year return (%)	10.56	10.83	10.40	9.74	9.93	9.94	8.22	9.32	8.46	7.66
Mean (%)	6.21									
Standard deviation (%)	4.97									
Target return (%)	10	11	12	13	14	15				
Return risk (%)	77.6	83.2	87.7	91.5	94.2	96.2				
Capital risk (%)	10.6									
Weighted mean (%)	7.50									
Weighted SD (%)	3.69									
Target return (%)	10	11	12	13	14	15				
Return risk (%)	75.1	82.9	88.9	93.2	96.1	97.8				
Capital risk (%)	2.1									

	1994	1995	1996	1997	1998	1999	2000	2001	2002	2003
Vintage year return (%)	6.32	7.65	5.95	4.81	1.87	-0.44	-4.06	-3.04	0.75	13.72
Mean (%)										
Standard deviation (%)										
Target return (%)										
Return risk (%)										
Capital risk (%)										
Weighted mean (%)										
Weighted SD (%)										
Target return (%)										
Return risk (%)										
Capital risk (%)										

fall compared to a small rise will be given greater weighting than, say, a large rise compared to a more moderate rise. In other words, the coefficient is more concerned with whether two series of numbers have moved in the same direction than with the relative extent to which they have moved in the same direction.

You will see that, despite UK shares having generally produced a higher dividend yield, it is their US blue chip counterparts that have consistently produced a higher total return. With the S&P 100 it is more likely than not that a 9% compound return can be achieved. With the FTSE 100 one has to come down as low as 7% before the same statement is true.

I apologise for labouring this point, but it is one that most institutional investors, obsessed as they are with annual returns, simply do not realise. I have lost count of the number of times that I have shown quoted returns restated on a vintage year basis to pension fund investors and been met with looks of blank incomprehension. The truth is very stark, I am afraid. At no time since about 1992 has it been possible to invest in the FTSE 100 index with any realistic expectation of being able to earn even 9% over a number of years. This has in fact occurred only in 2 out of the last 14 years, and one of those covers only a very short period.

See what happens, for example, if one charts the FTSE 100 vintage year return against even the capital-weighted private equity vintage year return (Figure 6.1).

The difference is dramatic, but again, many people do not realise just how dramatic, since the very powerful effects of compounding seem to pass them by. Let me put some numbers to it: $10 invested in the FTSE 100 index in 1994 would have grown 10 years' later to just over $18. The same $10 invested in private equity the same year would have grown over the same period to over $90 – in other words, five orders of magnitude. Tragically, however, investors in many parts of the world, with the UK being an obvious example, had no exposure at all to private equity during this period, but dramatic overexposure to their own domestic quoted market.

Bearing in mind the requirements of a pension plan in deficit (whose plans should logically include the reduction and eventual elimination of that deficit), these figures seem to throw into debate whether quoted equities might even be a questionable asset class within a MAC portfolio, but we will examine a little later some ways in which these returns might be rendered more palatable.

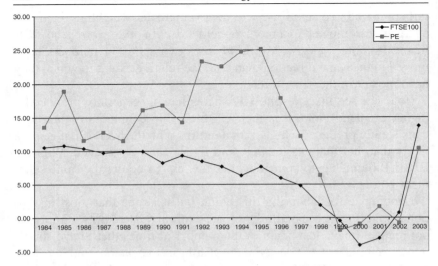

Figure 6.1   Vintage year returns for FTSE 100 versus upper quartile CWA private equity

Before we leave considerations of return risk, let us look at the NASDAQ in Table 6.5, particularly since we seem to be moving towards using this as an index of choice in many situations.

Although there have only been three negative vintage year returns during the whole period covered by our data set, likely returns pay a heavy price for the volatility that has been experienced. In our first two examples – the S&P 100 and the FTSE 100 – the weighted standard deviation is only about half of the mean; here, it is over two-thirds. This inevitably flows through the analysis process as extra uncertainty, which in turn leads to higher probability of not attaining any particular target rate of return. We have looked already at the danger of relying too unquestioningly on analysis of data sets with high variances (and thus high standard deviations, since the one is simply the square of the other), and my instinct is that, because of this, these figures probably slightly understate the likely returns of the NASDAQ.

HOW TO IMPROVE QUOTED EQUITY RETURNS

As was stated at the beginning of the book, the new world of pension fund deficits requires trustees and managers alike to target much higher rates of investment return than would have been necessary for their old

Table 6.5 Return risk of NASDAQ index on vintage year basis

	1984	1985	1986	1987	1988	1989	1990	1991	1992	1993
Vintage year return (%)	11.4	10.52	10.70	11.71	11.50	10.99	13.40	10.61	10.21	9.81
Mean (%)	8.35									
Standard deviation (%)	7.65									
Target return (%)	10	11	12	13	14	15				
Return risk (%)	58.7	63.7	68.4	72.9	77.1	80.1				
Capital risk (%)	13.8									
Weighted mean (%)	8.73									
Weighted SD (%)	6.00									
Target return (%)	10	11	12	13	14	15				
Return risk (%)	58.3	64.8	70.8	76.1	81.1	85.3				
Capital risk (%)	7.8									

	1994	1995	1996	1997	1998	1999	2000	2001	2002	2003
Vintage year return (%)	11.20	8.40	6.74	4.77	-0.14	-11.77	-3.13	3.71	27.64	8.59
Mean (%)										
Standard deviation (%)										
Target return (%)										
Return risk (%)										
Capital risk (%)										
Weighted mean (%)										
Weighted SD (%)										
Target return (%)										
Return risk (%)										
Capital risk (%)										

world counterparts (although they may in many cases be the same people). It is for this reason that we have been looking at return risk in the context of double digit returns, and (thus far, at least) quoted returns seem to have been found wanting. In not a single case have we been able to identify a quoted index whose probability of achieving even a 10% compound return over time can be calculated as better than even.

We need then to examine whether there may be ways of improving quoted returns, and in so doing we also need to question the way in which institutional investors have treated their quoted portfolios. Hedge funds, portable alpha, stock lending, the use of derivatives, and many other tactics have been used to try to boost the returns of a quoted port-folio, yet the most obvious of all – simple leverage – has been largely ignored.

It seems ironic that whereas investors seem content to be drawn into the rarefied atmosphere of complex concepts such as Monte Carlo analysis and portable alpha, they seem to find two of the simplest aspects of finance theory – compounding and leverage – difficult to grasp. Investment strategy is like anything else. If you know the basics and apply them well you will be successful, whereas if you attempt to build a highly elaborate edifice on shaky foundations it will collapse.

If we buy a house, we are routinely prepared to enter into very high levels of debt (at least 90% asset value, and sometimes as much as 100%) in order to do so. Of course, in practice we often have little choice since very few people have the necessary financial strength to be able to buy a house for cash. However, the fact remains that in respect of our own home, about which surely we should be more sensitive and protective than any mere business asset, we do not lie awake at night worrying about the percentage loan to value.

This is in part due to the phenomenon that we have already stated several times; our expectation, based on empirical observation, is that the value of most assets will increase most of the time, if only because of inflation, and therefore that loan to value percentage will drop steadily over time. When it comes to investment, this phenomenon should actually be a logical driver of our decisions rather than simply a retrospective comfort factor.

This expectation of rising asset values over time means that funding the purchase of any asset, partly with debt, where possible, is not only prudent but positively sensible. As a lawyer might say, it raises a presumption in favour of the use of debt. Of course, it is all a matter of degree, and that degree must be judged from a commonsense point of view. If debt is only available on wildly unattractive terms, then this would clearly rebut the presumption. A proposal to leverage a share portfolio with 75% debt is clearly not the same as seeking to leverage a property portfolio with 75% debt, and so on.

Thus, in considering the possibility of using debt to gear up our equity position we need to think about the levels of debt that are prudent in relation to all known circumstances, i.e. can be shown so far as possible by analysis to carry effectively little risk in practical terms. We can do this by looking at two things: asset cover and interest cover.

Asset cover is straightforward. We can simply take the net asset value (NAV) of the quoted portfolio at the end of the year, and express the amount of borrowing as a percentage of it. Forgive me for stating the obvious, but one basic point is often overlooked here. The asset value that we need to take for our calculations is the original value of the unleveraged portfolio plus the value of the additional shares that we have been able to buy with the debt. Thus if we were to borrow 30% of NAV at the end of one year, the debt to value percentage would be 23% (30/130), not 30%. Of course, if one was thinking from the viewpoint of a lending banker, one would probably be concerned to look for security purposes at the assets of the pension fund as a whole, and therefore the loan to value percentage would be calculated on the net asset value of the fund as a whole, but for the sake of simplicity and ease of analysis I propose to limit consideration of this issue to the equity portfolio itself.

What level of asset cover might be appropriate? Well, lending bankers are generally happy with relatively high levels of borrowing secured against real assets, and we will be considering that separately when we later look at property as an asset class, but what about less liquid (and yes, that is how they are viewed) assets such as shares? My instinct is that most lenders would be content as long as the loan to value percentage never fell below about 50%. This is not quite as simple as it sounds, however. Suppose that we borrow 50% of our equity portfolio value at the beginning of the year and the relevant index then falls during the course of the year, thus taking the percentage above 50%. Of course, we could simply sell some shares to repay debt until the percentage came back to 50%, but would we really want to do that? We would be selling into a falling market and thus would not necessarily get the best price. Also, if the index continued to fall we would have to sell progressively more and more of our portfolio in an attempt to keep the percentage at 50% since the value of the loan would be constant but the value of the shares would not. In other words, we would be the victim of compounding now working against us rather than in our favour. I would suggest, therefore, that we need to set our borrowing at a sufficiently prudent level that this should not happen.

Let us take the FTSE index by way of example. The largest one-year fall during the period we have considered was about 24.5% in 2002. Assuming we were readjusting our gearing every year, this would mean that we could have been 37% geared at the beginning of the year and still not have breached the 50% loan to value limit. However, there are two things we need to consider. The first is that we are attempting to fix a prudent rate of borrowing, not merely a possible rate, and so we would probably need to build in some sort of contingency. This might suggest a level of, say, 30% which would provide plenty of safety margin (the index would need to fall 40% in a single year before we would be in trouble) or even 25% (in which case we could survive even a fall of 50% in a single year).

The second is the possibility of the index falling in two or more successive years, as it did, for example, between 2000 and 2002, for if we are not to be a forced seller of stocks then we need to be able to ride out any prolonged downturn. The compound fall across those three years was 44% – that is, before taking dividend yield into account, which would soften the impact of this considerably. Thus, the figure of 25% gearing would have comfortably survived even the worst period of historic index movements. In order to arrive at a loan to value percentage of 25%, we have to borrow no more than about 33% of our asset value at the beginning of the year, since:

$$\frac{33}{133} = 24.8\%$$

Let us take this figure and see how it stacks up in terms of interest cover. Let us first look at the dividend yield available on the FTSE index over the period and see, in respect of each year, how much borrowing this could support by way of interest service. We will use the 12-month LIBOR+1% as at January of the year in question as our interest rate. We also need to see what the loan to value ratio would be at the end of each year, and what vintage year returns could be obtained relative to the unleveraged FTSE 100 index portfolio.

I have already referred to various preconceptions with which I started the process of preparing this book, and which have subsequently been

Table 6.6 Vintage year returns from leveraging the FTSE 100 index

	1985	1986	1987	1988	1989	1990	1991	1992	1993	1994
Vintage year return (%)	10.83	10.40	9.74	9.93	9.94	8.22	9.32	8.46	7.66	6.32
Mean (%)	6.21									
Standard deviation (%)	4.97									
Leveraged VY return	10.21	9.71	8.95	9.33	9.54	7.47	9.10	7.87	6.96	5.22
Mean (%)	4.95									
Standard deviation (%)	6.33									
Interest cover	1.12	1.00	1.00	1.00	1.00	1.50	2.11	1.16	1.35	2.13
Loan/value (at year end)	0.22	0.19	0.21	0.23	0.17	0.28	0.21	0.22	0.21	0.28

	1995	1996	1997	1998	1999	2000	2001	2002	2003
Vintage year return (%)	7.65	5.95	4.81	1.87	−0.44	−4.06	−3.04	0.75	13.72
Mean (%)									
Standard deviation (%)									
Leveraged VY return	6.79	4.64	3.12	−0.59	−3.45	−8.12	−6.86	−1.58	15.77
Mean (%)									
Standard deviation (%)									
Interest cover	1.31	1.68	1.20	1.00	1.03	1.00	1.12	2.15	1.94
Loan/value (at year end)	0.21	0.22	0.20	0.18	0.21	0.24	0.30	0.33	0.22

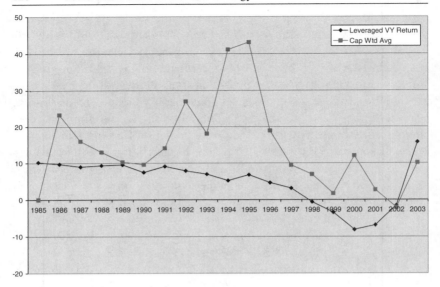

Figure 6.2 Leveraged FTSE 100 vintage year returns versus CWA private equity

shattered; here I must admit to another. It had always been my instinct that a prudently leveraged quoted index would comfortably outperform an unleveraged one, but here is clear proof that this would not in fact have been the case. In the period covered by Table 6.6 there are no less than nine years in which the leveraged portfolio delivers an annual return of more than 20%, compared to six for the unleveraged return, but of course gearing operates equally on both positive and negative returns, so that, for example, an annual return of −13.4% in 2001 becomes a return of −21%, and so on.

I believe these results should be of particular interest to those working in the buy-out business, since they all hear the question 'but wouldn't simply leveraging the quoted index give us just as good a return?' from investors on a regular basis. As Figure 6.2 shows, the answer is a resounding 'no'. This strongly suggests that the outperformance achieved by the buy-out industry is not a simple product of leverage, and that an investor would certainly not be better off leveraging a quoted index as an alternative to investing in private equity.

The figures will also be of interest to those who work within the hedge fund industry, since there are many who view a hedge fund's return as simply analogous to a geared equity return, and ignore the complexities of market timing, financial arbitrage, etc., which make up

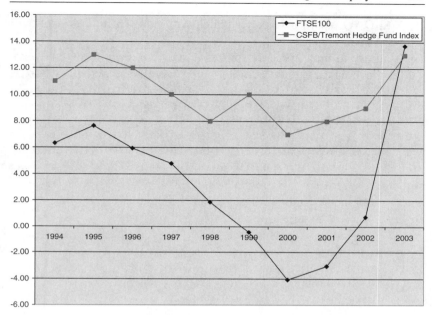

Figure 6.3   Leveraged FTSE 100 versus CSFB/Tremont vintage year returns

the armoury of a hedge fund manager's skills. Figure 6.3 shows the leveraged FTSE 100 return against the CSFB/Tremont composite index, again on a vintage year basis.

SUMMARY

- Quoted equities comprise the bulk of most institutional portfolios. Indeed, most institutional investors around the world are grossly overexposed to quoted equities in general and domestic equities in particular.
- Quoted equities will continue to form the bedrock of most port-folios but it is important to understand how they should be deployed as part of a properly diversified investment programme.
- There is little evidence that active management can deliver con-sistent cost-adjusted outperformance over any lengthy period, and so a passive approach should be preferred.
- Close attention should be paid to levels of correlation between different quoted indices. For example, the figures suggest that the

NASDAQ would be a better match with non-US indices than the S&P 100.

- Contrary to many preconceptions it does not seem to be the case that leveraging quoted equities will generally be beneficial for a pension fund or other non-taxpayer investor. Nor do leveraged quoted equity returns rival those of private equity or hedge funds. Therefore the outperformance of these two asset classes cannot be explained simply by the use of leverage.

7

Hedge Funds

WHAT IS A HEDGE FUND?

The phrase 'hedge fund' can be a trifle misleading, in that hedging has been around for a long time, but is not strictly speaking what hedge funds do at all! Investors have for many years used derivative products to hedge assets that they own, or cashflows that they anticipate receiving at a fixed time in the future, against movements in the equity markets, against fluctuations in foreign exchange, and even against changes in interest rates. Depending on the investor's circumstances and the tactics employed, this activity can range from effectively doubling up a market bet at one extreme to prudently laying off some potential upside to buy a more certain outcome at the other.

Hedge funds also utilise derivative products, and while some do hedge against market downturns in the manner just described, many do not. Indeed, a bewildering number of investment strategies are pursued, some of which I will attempt to summarise. It is also important to understand from the outset that, in addition to using derivative products such as options, futures, swaps, etc., hedge funds also use short selling and leverage their positions with debt. To my mind it is this ability to gear their positions by borrowing that really sets hedge funds apart from anything their investors might attempt for themselves, and from the other asset classes I consider in this book. Quoted equity investors such as pension funds do not generally borrow against their positions as a matter of course while private equity and property investors typically 'ring-fence' any borrowing exposure within the context of an individual investee legal vehicle, or by security granted solely against one individual asset. This exposure to debt of a whole fund vehicle is perhaps unique to hedge funds and is a factor that I am not sure is always fully understood or taken into account when considering their riskiness and attractiveness relative to other asset classes.

Some attempts are in fact made to ring-fence borrowings, both by fund managers who may create an umbrella fund structure (but there are still circumstances where so-called 'contagion', i.e. cross-defaults affecting different sub-funds may occur) and by regulators. Guernsey has introduced 'protected cell company' legislation, although it remains to be seen to what extent (if any) effect would be given to this by courts in other jurisdictions. Luxembourg and Bermuda now provide something with a similar intent, whereby liabilities can be ring-fenced by reference to different assets owned by the same company. The fact remains that having leverage present within a fund structure, where the manager is pursuing an investment strategy that is dependent upon movement in prices quoted by public markets, must perforce carry a much higher level of perceived risk in the eyes of investors than is the case typically with the other asset classes we consider in this book.

Having mentioned regulators, it is also worth pointing out that many hedge funds are entirely unregulated (though in some cases the management entity may itself be so) and this is facilitated by them being located in some fairly exotic global locations, although, to be fair, there are often valid tax planning reasons for these choices. 'Should hedge funds be regulated?' is currently a hot conference topic and something that various regulators (the FSA in the UK and the SEC in the USA, for example) are known to be considering. I know that various mutual fund managers do feel that this lack of regulation (which apart from anything else has serious cost-saving implications) may give hedge fund managers an unfair advantage (see below).

I understand that about 40% of the largest hedge fund managers in the USA are regulated, and that some fund of hedge funds use the fact of registration as a criterion in selecting managers. This is a particular issue in the USA where (strangely, since one thinks of it as being the most sophisticated financial environment in the world) there are loopholes through which registration can be avoided, even by managers who are resident in the USA. The loopholes are based, among other things, on the number of US investors in a fund, the size of the fund and the length of lock-up period.

I am often asked to differentiate between a hedge fund and a typical US mutual fund. I believe that it is the use of such tactics as short selling, leverage and derivatives that set hedge funds apart. Mutual funds are subject to strict SEC disclosure and reporting requirements and, generally speaking, are not allowed to use these products or tactics. In particular, hedge funds often use something called 'concentrated investment' whereby they may attempt to gain control over a large number of a company's securities, or class of securities (e.g. a convertible debt issue), which a mutual fund would not be able to do because they are subject to strict rules about the maximum exposure they may have to any one company.

In terms of typical legal status, hedge funds take a wide variety of different forms. For European investors, companies are a common route to take, but can be incorporated in a number of different jurisdictions (the Channel Islands, Cayman Islands, British Virgin Islands and Bermuda have been jurisdictions of choice, but others that are currently being pushed include Malta and Italy) and can be either open-ended (with investors subscribing for and redeeming shares) or closed ended. US and Japanese investors will usually prefer a Limited Partnership structure[1] and sometimes a hybrid is evolved with a partnership feeder structure sitting on top of a company (or number of companies), or vice versa.[2] In such cases somewhere like the Luxembourg or Irish stock exchanges can be used to provide a nominal quote for the feeder vehicle.

As one might guess from my comments about regulation, the question of the jurisdiction both of the fund vehicle (or vehicles) and for the investment manager (and possibly investment adviser, investment sub-manager, carry vehicle, general partner vehicle, etc!) will be driven by both tax planning and what may be called cosmetic reasons. If a fund is to be domiciled in, for example, the Cayman Islands, then it may be thought useful from a profile point of view to have an 'investment adviser' vehicle located somewhere like London. However, even where this is the case there is no guarantee (depending on the precise legal structure that may be adopted) that the activities of even the London-based vehicle are subject to scrutiny by a public regulator and, as I have mentioned already, this lack of widespread regulation (at least at the fund level) is another feature largely unique to hedge funds so far as the coverage of this book is concerned.

It should also be noted that some US managers run both a US and an 'offshore' fund (this is still overwhelmingly a US-based industry, so that 'offshore' means 'non-US') and, as we will see later, it is very

---

[1] However, a limited partnership structure can pose problems for non-Japanese investors in non-Japanese hedge funds which seek to invest in the Japanese government bond market.

[2] Such complicated structures are not unique to hedge funds. Private equity funds, particularly in the early days when the legal constraints of many investors were less sophisticated than they are today, frequently employed an 'umbrella' structure, which might include a bewildering variety of different vehicle types. At one time, for example, Japanese insurance companies could only invest in unquoted investments through unit trust type structures.

important that you perform your due diligence on both funds even if you are only looking to invest in one of them (as will usually be the case). The establishment of offshore funds was initially driven partly by a tax break whereby the US tax payable on the fund performance fee by the manager could be delayed by astute tax planning. However, as we will see later when we discuss liquidity, other practical issues also came into play resulting in some significant differences in lock-up periods.

HEDGE FUND INVESTMENT STRATEGIES

The manager of a hedge fund will normally be tied to a particular investment approach by the legal documentation creating the fund structure. There is now a seemingly huge number of officially recognised strategies and substrategies. The following is not an exhaustive list, but covers most of the main variants. As we will see a little later, we will be paying particular attention to various strategy indices produced by Hedge Fund Research, and I will attempt to cover all those to which I refer later, plus a few others.

Convertible Arbitrage

This is analogous to the traditional hedging activity of a conventional equity investor as outlined above. A typical strategy is to be long in the convertible bond and short in the ordinary share (common stock) of the same company at the same time. The difference is that whereas the conventional investor will be seeking to protect from unexpected market movement a position that he is holding for some particular reason, the hedge fund investor will have entered into the position solely with the intention to make money, if possible, on both the bond and the share. A further difference is that the hedge fund investor will frequently leverage his position with debt.

Distressed

This strategy was originally called 'distressed securities' since the idea was largely to invest in, and quite possibly to sell short, the shares of a company where the price of the shares had been adversely affected by one or more distress events, such as corporate reorganisation, insolvency, credit rerating, etc. Hedge fund investors may try to take advantage of the company's capital structure, for example by buying debt and selling shares at the same time (or vice versa) in the hope of shifting the market's relative pricing of each. A well-known example of this activity was trading in the debt and shares of Eurotunnel in the mid to late 1990s. The reason why the strategy is now generally just called 'distressed' is that hedge fund investors have become more imaginative and may now seek to buy not only securities issued by the company but assets, trade claims and other assignable third-party rights.

Emerging Markets

It does what it says on the tin. HFR, for example, offer a number of substrategy indices covering areas such as Asia, Eastern Europe and Latin America. An interesting variation here is that the stock exchanges of many emerging market nations do not permit the sort of short selling usually engaged in by hedge funds, nor is there usually such a rich profusion of derivative instruments available. Therefore such funds are typically 'long only'.

Equity Hedge

Equity hedge managers combine a core portfolio of long equities mixed with short sales of shares, or share options, or even options on a related index such as the FTSE 100 or S&P 100. The more aggressive managers may maintain more than 100% market exposure, and while this obviously increases the upside potential it also increases capital risk.

Equity Market Neutral

A market neutral portfolio will endeavour to eliminate beta (the risk of holding any individual stock) as far as possible. Leverage may be used to enhance returns.

Equity Non-Hedge

As the name suggests, these funds may not always have a hedge in place against any position they may take. They are more inclined to be individual stock-pickers, and may in particular look to short individual stocks, although they are predominantly long only.

Event Driven

The description 'Special Situation' is also sometimes applied to this category. It can be related to events such as corporate reconstructions and spin-offs, in which case it can be known as 'corporate life cycle' investing. It can also extend to merger arbitrage (which I consider separately below). There is a specialist area known as 'regulation D' which refers to shares or convertible instruments issued by small US companies that are not publicly tradable until registered later with the SEC.

Fixed Interest

In the interests of simplifying the situation as much as possible, the index that I have chosen to demonstrate is Fixed Income (Total), which, as the name suggests, covers a selection from the whole fixed income field. However, this category covers a range of strategies with respect to fixed income instruments. Arbitrage seeks to exploit pricing differences between related types of instrument, e.g. corporate versus treasury bonds. Other managers specialise in areas such as mortgage-backed securities, high-yield bonds and convertible instruments.

Macro

These are the so-called 'big picture' or 'top down' investors who take positions in the world's major markets based on macro events such as economic shifts or political developments. Most of these funds invest globally not only in developed markets but also in emerging markets.

Market Timing

These are the 'trend' investors who specialise in technical analysis, i.e. analysis of the movement of prices rather than analysis of the financial fundamental underlying a company. Frequently managers will switch between equities and cash, with the aim of being in cash during downward trends and in equities during upward trends.

Merger Arbitrage

Sometimes called 'risk arbitrage', this involves taking positions against specific events such as corporate mergers, although increasingly this will also include the activities of private equity houses making leveraged acquisitions of public companies or their subsidiaries. This is perhaps the most sensitive of all hedge fund strategies, since there is a fine line between brilliant prediction and the use of inside information, and in many cases a different department of an investment bank advising on such a transaction may be earning large fees from a merger arbitrage hedge fund.

Relative Value Arbitrage

This is probably the most arithmetically complicated of all hedge fund strategies, with very complex analysis being used in an attempt to unearth pricing discrepancies between, for example, a convertible instrument and the underlying security. Relative value managers tend to use such arcane concepts as pairs trading and yield curve trading.

Sector Strategies

There are any number of these. I have chosen to highlight the Financial and Real Estate (Property) sectors, but indices exist for several including Energy, Technology, etc.

Short Selling

Short selling is simply the opposite of being long in a share. Believing that the price of a share will fall, you sell shares that you do not have (borrowing them from someone else if necessary – stock lending is a lucrative source of income for some pension funds and insurance companies) and then buy them in the market later. This was once a mainstream hedge fund strategy until the prolonged bull market of the 1990s made it increasingly difficult to exercise. Indeed, the indices suggest that this has been perhaps the most volatile (and least successful?) of all hedge fund strategies.

A little later we will look at the returns of various hedge fund strategies against each other and, in particular, examine the level of correlation they may exhibit, but for the moment let us consider the benchmarks that might exist for us to use in our analysis of hedge fund returns generally.

WHAT BENCHMARKS ARE AVAILABLE AND WHICH SHOULD WE USE?

When setting out to evaluate hedge fund performance, the choice of benchmark can seem bewildering. Unlike private equity, where one benchmark provider is long-established and universally recognised, the hedge fund community supports a large number of indices. Four of the main families are S&P, Hedge Fund Reseach (HFR), CSFB/Tremont and Edhec, all of whose indices are in the public domain by courtesy of the internet. Thus, unlike private equity, where the debate is not so much over which benchmark to select as over the quality and appropriateness of the data in certain situations, with hedge funds one is presented at the outset with a basic question of which index (or group of indices) to use.

Also, when attempting to assess hedge fund performance, there is one issue to consider that is not really relevant to an analysis of the other asset classes covered in this book, and this is the difference between an index and an 'investable' index. This distinction springs from a recognition that an index can be used in two ways: either as (1) a benchmark for measuring the performance of assets within that class against the performance of other asset classes, or as (2) effectively an investment vehicle designed to capture the performance of that asset class with minimal levels of asset-specific risk. We did not have to consider this question when looking at quoted equities, for example, since any public market index can be duplicated very easily in practice by simply buying the constituent shares on a pro rata basis.

Why this becomes a problem with hedge funds is that each index will have far too many single funds as constituents for this duplication process to be practicable, or even possible. Thus, while it may be fine to use a particular index as a benchmark against which to measure the performance of any hedge fund in which you decide to invest, it is not valid to assume that one can simply 'buy the index' in the same way that one can with any of the public market indices that we considered earlier. By the autumn of 2005 there were already well over 8000 active hedge funds totalling nearly $900 billion[3] and so it will be obvious that attempts to select the constituents of any performance index, while well-meaning, are likely to result in considerable diversity.

---

[3] *Source:* The Hedge Fund Association.

We therefore need to look at the question 'which benchmark should we choose?' not once but twice, and by definition the answer should be different each time since, in the first case, we are looking for the best way to analyse historic performance and, in the second, we are looking for the optimum way to invest in the asset class.

Of course this distinction itself leads to further uncertainty, since there is no one obvious way to adapt any hedge fund index into an investable index (i.e. something that *can* be used as an investment proxy), and so it is quite possible that different index providers will choose different selection criteria and different strategy weightings, thus meaning that further elements of non-uniformity must creep into the equation.

Edhec, for example, use a sample of funds that use Lyxor (the Société Générale managed accounts system), restrict these to five strategy-specific subgroups and do not offer an overall Fund of Funds/strategy neutral product. S&P offer an investable strategy neutral index which is made up of 42 individual funds employing nine different strategies, all of which are equally weighted. CSFB/Tremont offer an investable index made up of about 60 funds selected from 10 different strategies, and so on.

The indices also cover different periods. Edhec, for example, map data only from 1997 and others are younger still. Given that it must be right that we want data from a significant period this probably rules out such contenders for our purposes although that is not to imply that they are in any way unworthy of everyday use by investors. Variation of time period thus adds yet another layer of confusion to the situation.

However, let us deal with the first question before venturing into these rather muddy waters. Which index (or family of indices) would it be best to use as a measure of historic performance? Again, this is far from a simple question as different index families have different constituents. As an exercise let us see what correlation is present between, say, the main HFRI and CSFB/Tremont indices and thus how much statistical 'noise' we may be introducing into the system by choosing any particular one.

We can of course only compare the period that is covered jointly by both indices, that is to say from 1994 to 2004. The relevant figures are shown in Table 7.1, giving the annual return as a percentage in each case. You will see that the correlation between the two sets of annual returns is only 0.86, which is disappointing. This does indeed suggest that some significant differences in purported returns from this asset

Table 7.1 CSFB/Tremont versus HFRI (1)

CSFB/Tremont hedge fund index

Year ending	Dec. 1994	Dec. 1995	Dec. 1996	Dec. 1997	Dec. 1998	Dec. 1999	Dec. 2000	Dec. 2001	Dec. 2002	Dec. 2003	Dec. 2004
Annual return (%)	−4.36	21.69	22.22	25.94	−0.36	23.43	4.85	4.42	3.04	15.44	9.64

HFRI fund-weighted composite

Year ending	Dec. 1994	Dec. 1995	Dec. 1996	Dec. 1997	Dec. 1998	Dec. 1999	Dec. 2000	Dec. 2001	Dec. 2002	Dec. 2003	Dec. 2004
Annual return (%)	4.1	21.5	21.1	16.8	2.6	31.3	5	4.6	−1.5	19.6	9

Correlation coefficient: 0.86.

Table 7.2 CSFB/Tremont versus HFRI (2)

CSFB/Tremont hedge fund index

Vintage year	1994	1995	1996	1997	1998	1999	2000	2001	2002	2003
IRR (%)	11%	13%	12%	10%	8%	10%	7%	8%	9%	13%

HFRI fund-weighted composite

Vintage year	1994	1995	1996	1997	1998	1999	2000	2001	2002	2003
IRR (%)	12%	13%	12%	10%	10%	11%	7%	8%	9%	14%

Correlation coefficient: 0.95.

class can be attributed simply to the choice of benchmark. In 1997, for example, the CSFB/Tremont index showed a return of nearly 26% while the HFRI index returned less than 17%. In 1999 the reverse is true, with the CSFB Tremont showing just over 23% while the HFRI 'equivalent' returned over 31%.

Table 7.2 shows the vintage year returns[4] produced by each index, again solely for the period they have in common. As one would expect, there is much less variance here, the two series producing a correlation coefficient of 0.95. Since, as already explained, it is compound returns over a long period with which an institutional investor (particularly a pension fund or life insurance company) should be concerned, rather than short-term periodic returns, then this is clearly of comfort though it remains undeniable that the current situation surrounding hedge fund benchmark data is very unsatisfactory and it must be a matter of regret that the various data providers have not found some way of combining (or at least aligning) their figures.

In the end I was unable to draw any great distinction between these two, but happily the decision was made for me in practical terms by CSFB/Tremont kindly granting me a copyright waiver to use their data in this publication, for which I am sincerely grateful. This may sound a slightly negative thing to say, but where there is no clear candidate as a universal benchmark then it probably does not matter very much which is taken as long as the data it contains is robust and is professionally prepared and managed, which is obviously the case here. It remains a source of mystery to me, however, how institutional investors and their advisers are able to draw valid comparisons between hedge fund assets in different hands since no standard performance benchmark exists. Perhaps this is an argument for looking at any hedge fund, hedge fund strategy, or hedge fund manager in terms of the absolute (rather than relative) return that is capable of being produced, since this at least will be clear. However, we should of course still be looking to compare that return to our own target rate of return, which is not only valid but very necessary.

How do the Various Hedge Fund Strategies Compare?

Table 7.3 shows the annual returns of the CSFB/Tremont strategy indices for the period from 1994 (except in the case of 'multi-strategy,' for which data is only available from 1995).

---

[4] Calculated to December 2004.

Table 7.3 Annual returns of hedge fund strategies

	1994	1995	1996	1997	1998	1999	2000	2001	2002	2003	2004
Dedicated Short Bias	14.91	-7.35	-5.48	0.42	-6.00	-0.42	15.76	-3.58	18.14	-32.59	-7.72
Convertible Arbitrage	-8.07	16.57	17.87	14.48	-4.41	16.04	25.64	14.58	4.05	12.90	1.98
Emerging Markets	12.51	-16.91	34.5	26.59	-37.66	44.82	-5.52	5.84	7.36	28.75	12.49
Equity Market Neutral	-2.00	11.04	16.6	14.83	13.31	15.33	14.99	9.31	7.42	7.07	6.48
Event Driven	0.75	18.34	23.06	19.96	-4.87	22.26	7.26	11.5	0.16	20.02	14.47
Fixed Income Arbitrage	0.31	12.5	15.93	9.34	-8.16	12.11	6.29	8.04	5.75	7.97	6.86
Global Macro	-5.72	30.67	25.58	37.11	-3.64	5.81	11.67	18.38	14.66	17.99	8.49
Long/Short Equity	-8.10	23.03	17.12	21.46	17.18	47.23	2.08	-3.65	-1.60	17.27	11.56
Managed Futures	11.95	-7.10	11.97	3.12	20.64	-4.69	4.24	1.90	18.33	14.13	5.97
Multi-Strategy		11.87	14.06	18.28	7.68	9.38	11.18	5.50	6.31	15.04	7.53
Composite Index	-4.36	21.69	22.22	25.94	-0.36	23.43	4.85	4.42	3.04	15.44	9.64

The most obvious thing that strikes one from these figures is the impossibility of seeing any real pattern of returns between the various strategies. There are one or two 'blips' in the same place, but these are few and appear random. For example, 'emerging markets' and 'long/short equity' both had very high returns in 1999 and yet we know that many emerging financial markets do not allow short selling, so it is difficult to ascribe any common causative factor.

If we look at correlation between the various sets of annual returns then the scattered nature of the data becomes explicit (see Table 7.4). Of the individual strategies, only 'event driven' and 'fixed income arbitrage' are at all highly correlated, yet even this is not straightforward, since 'event driven' is highly correlated with the composite index (91%) and yet 'fixed income arbitrage' only moderately so (78%). There are two particular points that struck me about these figures, however.

Firstly, before I performed this analysis I had assumed, perhaps simplistically, that a multi-strategy approach would approximate most closely to the composite index but, as you can see, this is not the case. In fact, of the 10 strategies reviewed, the multi-strategy approach comes a poor equal fifth.

Secondly, just look at the extent to which 'managed futures' exhibit negative correlation with just about every other approach, including the composite index itself. This seems to be the classic contrarian investment and, subject to return risk, could be an interesting one to hold alongside the composite index.

What Return Risk is Present in Hedge Funds?

We can use the CSFB/Tremont composite index annual return figures to perform phi analysis, from which we will see that there is nearly a 58% probability of the return of any individual year being equal to or less than 13%. However, there is a lot of variation – the mean is 11.45 and the standard deviation almost as much at 10.71.

As we have already seen, it is however much more meaningful to look at the vintage year returns of the index as our inputs for this analysis (Table 7.5). The difference in this case is telling indeed. See how one could be completely misled by looking only at the annual returns. This is a classic example of just how misguided an approach it is to try to predict in advance how fast the train may be travelling at any particular time rather than at what time it is likely to arrive. These figures

Table 7.4 Annual return correlation of hedge fund strategies

	DSB	CA	EM	EMN	ED	FIA	GM	LSE	MF	MS
Dedicated short bias		-0.12	-0.15	-0.10	-0.53	-0.18	-0.25	-0.43	0.03	-0.34
Convertible arbitrage	-0.12		0.30	0.69	0.66	0.73	0.65	0.33	-0.58	0.46
Emerging markets	-0.15	0.30		0.06	0.69	0.66	0.25	0.34	-0.21	0.40
Equity market neutral	-0.10	0.69	0.06		0.42	0.36	0.45	0.60	-0.28	0.41
Event driven	-0.53	0.66	0.69	0.42		0.88	0.66	0.62	-0.61	0.61
Fixed income arbitrage	-0.18	0.73	0.66	0.36	0.88		0.71	0.37	-0.61	0.41
Global Macro	-0.25	0.65	0.25	0.45	0.66	0.71		0.21	-0.41	0.67
Long/short equity	-0.43	0.33	0.34	0.60	0.62	0.37	0.21		-0.44	0.36
Managed futures	0.03	-0.58	-0.21	-0.28	-0.61	-0.61	-0.41	-0.44		-0.13
Multi-strategy	-0.34	0.46	0.40	0.41	0.61	0.41	0.67	0.36	-0.13	
Composite index	-0.42	0.62	0.54	0.60	0.91	0.78	0.74	0.77	-0.56	0.74

Table 7.5   Return risk of CSFB/Tremont composite index

	10%	11%	12%	13%	14%	15%
Annual return	47.6%	51.2%	54.4%	57.9%	61.4%	64.4%
Vintage year return	48.0%	69.9%	86.0%	95.0%	98.6%	99.7%

appear to show convincingly that while there is a moderate chance of hedge funds as an asset class delivering, say, 13% in any one year (although there is still a 58% chance that they may not) it is almost impossible (only a 5% chance) that they can deliver such a return on a compound basis over a lengthy period.

I say 'appears to show' because I think we must treat this analysis with caution for two reasons. Firstly, we are dealing here with a relatively short series of data; the CSFB/Tremont index runs only from 1994, whereas we are using data from 1984 for our analysis of other asset classes. I have attempted to compensate for this by making sure that we calculate the standard deviation for $n - 1$, but even so I am uneasy about extrapolating a run of only about 10 years' data for the purposes of predicting possible future returns.

Secondly, the returns shown by the index do not conform to what I have heard at first hand from those in the hedge fund industry; in fact, I was surprised at just how low they turned out to be. I have heard consistently about hedge funds and funds of funds delivering IRRs in the high 20s, but there are only three years in the data set when this actually occurs, and the most recent example was as long ago as 1997. While, of course, I accept the very real possibility of those trying to sell a particular asset class over-egging its returns, it does ring warning bells in my mind when there is such a huge discrepancy between the expectations of those working in the industry at first hand and the official performance measure. It would be interesting to know if, as is the case with Private Equity, there is a large variance between the median fund and the top performers, or even between the upper quartile and the top performers. However, if so, that would itself be of concern since it would argue against any attempt to invest in the index.

This of course raises another issue, for we would not be investing in the index but in the investable index, and we must therefore test this as well as the composite index. Unfortunately we run into some very real statistical problems here as well. Let us take a look at how the investable index is prepared.

It comprises approximately 60 named funds whereas the index itself includes every fund with more than $50 million assets under management and at least a one-year track record. Also it excludes US-domiciled funds, whereas there is no mention of such a requirement in the construction rules of the main index. Given all this, it is perhaps hardly surprising that the investable index thus far should have a correlation with the full index of only just over 31%, but it does raise significant questions about the validity of assessing historic returns based on one index and investing on the basis of that analysis in another index which may be radically different. It is more worrying still that when the returns are calculated on a vintage year rather than an annual basis there actually appears to be negative correlation (−25%).

However, I feel that these results, particularly those in respect of vintage year returns, are probably largely valueless. The investable index runs only from 2000 and thus it has not had a chance to build a proper head of steam behind any vintage year result, apart from possibly 2000 itself. (The vintage year returns are tightly clustered between 6.6% and 7.5% − hardly returns to get excited about.)

Unfortunately, there is yet another layer of potential statistical confusion to explain. The investable index is based upon the actual performance of its constituent funds only from August 2003. All figures in respect of the period before that date are based on presumed prior performance rolled backwards from the asset values of 1 August 2003. To place yet one more piece of grit in the machinery, not all of the constituent funds have a track record going back to the beginning of 2000, in which case yet more assumptions come into play. I should state for the record that all of this is openly disclosed by CSFB/Tremont, who recognise the scale of the task they are undertaking, and deserve praise for the intellectual courage with which they are pursuing it.

Does the Index Properly Show Potential Portfolio Returns?

Clearly any index is better than none but, if reports of 8000 hedge funds are correct (and the SEC is said to believe that there may actually be more than 10000 hedge fund managers in existence), I do think there must be a question mark over whether the full composite index does indeed capture the bulk of the institutional grade investment opportunities. (The CSFB/Tremont database tracks over 4000 funds, of which only about a quarter are included in the index. Presumably the remaining 3000 either do not satisfy the size filter or the reporting requirements, but what about the other 4000 that are said to be in existence?) However, even an index of approximately 1000 constituent funds is clearly going to mask the performance of any that stand out (no one fund, or even several funds, can possibly move the needle on the index as a whole). For both these reasons, it may be quite possible for the apocryphal remarks I have heard concerning the returns of individual funds to be true, despite appearing to be in conflict with the index.

If this is in fact the case, then manager selection will be able to make a radical difference to the performance of any hedge fund portfolio. This in turn would argue strongly in favour of investing through professional fund of fund managers who should logically have a much higher chance than a generalist investor of consistently making upper quartile fund picks. Yet the CSFB/Tremont index specifically excludes funds of funds, presumably because they already capture the underlying funds and to repeat these perhaps many times in the portfolios of funds of funds would be not just double counting but perhaps serial multiplication. This is another reason for my caution in adopting the index unthinkingly as a proxy for actual performance, since there may be many fund of funds managers whose portfolios (each representing only a tiny fraction of the index) do in fact exhibit very high returns.

Why I think the investable index also fails to capture this is that the index providers have very professionally done everything possible to exclude subjectivity from the selection process, and yet I suspect that it is precisely such subjectivity that will help to select the stand-out funds. For example, it takes broadly the top six funds in each sector, ranked by assets under management. In other words, it is choosing the largest funds from each strategy rather than the best performing. Once a fund is selected then generally any other fund managed by the same firm becomes ineligible. In practice, both these rules strike me as unrealistic. One would surely select funds (at least in large part) on historic track record rather than size, and one would not be averse to having different funds from the same manager; indeed, this actually makes sense in logistical terms.

The other big issue is that of strategy selection. Given the very different returns produced by different strategies, then I am not sure that an indexing approach is appropriate since, by definition, one is then stuck with the strategy allocation methodology of the index provider which may or may not reflect the performance and relative risk of each for the individual investor. We looked earlier at the annual returns recorded for each strategy, but when looking at the performance of the index as a whole we also saw that these returns could be very misleading when thinking of compound performance over a period, so let us have a look at them again, restated on a vintage year basis.

In Table 7.6 you will see that there are some strategies that have outperformed the others and thus also the full index; Global Macro is a good example, having outperformed the index consistently. Just look at the relative return risk in Table 7.7.

Even the unweighted vintage year returns show a huge difference, but when one calculates them on a weighted basis (with a cut-off at 10 years as usual) then the difference becomes really dramatic. You will see that one would have been infinitely better off in a Global Macro strategy-specific portfolio than in the index as a whole. At a target rate of investment return of 13% the Global Macro index would have been a good investment, while tracking the full index would have been disastrous (a 33% return risk compared with 94%).

HEDGE FUNDS WITHIN THE YALE PORTFOLIO

It may be interesting to view Yale's hedge fund (which they call 'absolute return') approach. Yale claim to have been the first institutional investor to begin investing in hedge funds as a distinct asset class, with an initial allocation (in 1990) of 15%. Over the last five years the amount allocated to hedge funds has risen steadily from 19.5% to a present target of 25%, which makes it significantly the biggest of Yale's asset classes. By implication, this must mean that they expect it to be the best performer of all going forward, but we will examine their return experience with this asset class in a moment.

Yale's strategy for hedge fund investment has been to put 50% of their allocation into 'event-driven' strategies and the remaining 50% into 'value driven'. They select as their passive benchmark the one-year treasury rate plus 6%, which sets their historic expectations for the asset class at about 11%. I have no problem with this. However, once we turn to the question of their active benchmark I believe that significant problems arise. They use the CSFB composite index, and one has to ask 'why?' given that this does not match their actual portfolio. To go back to our discussion of the active dollar versus the passive dollar, valid comparisons can only be made against a benchmark index if the

Table 7.6 Vintage year returns of hedge fund strategies

	1994	1995	1996	1997	1998	1999	2000	2001	2002	2003	2004
Dedicated Short Bias	−2.28%	−3.85%	−3.45%	−3.20%	−3.70%	−3.32%	0.57%	−8.25%	−9.76%	−21.13%	−7.72%
Convertible Arbitrage	9.69%	11.65%	11.11%	10.29%	9.71%	12.26%	16.27%	8.24%	6.21%	7.30%	1.98%
Emerging Markets	7.58%	7.10%	10.17%	7.45%	4.96%	14.49%	5.48%	13.26%	15.85%	20.35%	12.49%
Equity Market Neutral	10.27%	11.58%	11.64%	11.03%	10.50%	10.04%	10.70%	7.56%	6.99%	6.77%	6.48%
Event Driven	11.67%	12.83%	12.23%	10.95%	9.72%	12.36%	9.05%	11.30%	11.23%	17.21%	14.47%
Fixed Income Arbitrage	6.81%	7.48%	6.94%	5.86%	5.37%	7.82%	6.86%	7.15%	6.86%	7.41%	6.86%
Global Macro	13.93%	16.10%	14.59%	13.28%	10.24%	12.74%	14.84%	14.81%	13.64%	13.14%	8.49%
Long/Short Equity	12.10%	14.35%	13.43%	12.97%	11.81%	10.94%	2.99%	5.53%	8.78%	14.38%	11.56%
Managed Futures	6.97%	6.49%	8.11%	7.64%	8.30%	6.37%	8.38%	9.89%	12.69%	9.97%	5.97%
Multi-Strategy		9.60%	9.38%	8.87%	7.75%	7.76%	7.49%	7.92%	7.09%	7.35%	3.70%
Composite Index	11%	13%	12%	10%	8%	10%	7%	8%	9%	13%	9.64%

Table 7.7   Return risk of CSFB/Tremont composite index versus Global Macro

Unweighted vintage year return	10%	11%	12%	13%	14%	15%
Full index	47.6%	51.2%	54.4%	57.9%	61.4%	64.4%
Global Macro	6.8%	15.1%	28.4%	45.6%	63.3%	78.8%
Weighted vintage year return	10%	11%	12%	13%	14%	15%
Full index	42.1%	65.5%	83.9%	94.3%	98.5%	99.7%
Global Macro	1.6%	5.5%	15.1%	32.6%	55.2%	95.6%

constituents of that index actually match the population from which the active manager is making selections. Yet the CSFB/Tremont composite comprises less than one quarter event-driven funds, whereas we know that Yale have about a half. This may seem a rather petty point to take, but in fact it is not.

If you look back at Tables 7.3 and 7.6 you will see that event-driven strategies have consistently enjoyed much higher returns than the composite index, particularly since about 1998. So a mix of, say, 50% of the event-driven index and 50% of the composite would provide a much more valid comparison with what Yale are actually doing, and would of course also give a higher figure. This may be significant given that Yale's portfolio has in fact only just matched the CSFB/Tremont composite index, which means that its historic returns within the Yale portfolio have been lower than any of our five asset classes, except foreign equities.

Given that we can assume the event-driven managers to have outperformed the composite index, this can only mean that the value-driven managers must have underperformed. Thus, we would have two interesting questions to pose to Yale:

1. Why are they persisting with a 50% value-driven tilt when we assume this to have underperformed?
2. Why are they increasing rather than decreasing their exposure to an asset class that has underperformed the rest of their portfolio?

So, although this is an unsatisfactory conclusion in the sense that there is little one can put forward with confidence based on statistical analysis as with the other asset classes we are considering, I think the returns data is sufficiently variable that one has to say that it would depend very considerably on the strategy weighting you chose to adopt, and the actual fund managers whom you selected. To extend the above example, a 33% return risk would seem very attractive based on comparable levels for quoted equity and would almost certainly represent a 'go' decision, while 94% would certainly not.

It would, however, be possible to run such analysis based on the actual historic returns of the funds one selected and I feel this would give a much more valid result, provided always that due consideration was given to any periods that were particularly short (less than 10 years?). It is of course also the case that different investors will have different target rates of investment return and, as the examples I have used illustrate, the risk can change quite quickly with relatively small changes in the target rate.

WHAT CAPITAL RISK IS PRESENT IN HEDGE FUNDS AS AN ASSET CLASS?

Given that I am fairly confident that the available figures probably have the effect of understating hedge fund performance, then we can probably use them with confidence in assessing the capital risk. As we know by now, this is simply a subset of the return risk and can be calculated in exactly the same way (Table 7.8). You will see that there is no capital risk at all inherent in investing in the index over a period, although there is some small chance (less than one in five) of suffering a negative return in any one year.

That is what the figures say, and subject to the usual provisos (the reliability of the data, the period covered by the data series, and whether historic returns are a good guide to future performance) we may seek to rely upon them. However, there is a practical issue that impinges on the question of capital risk which is unique to hedge funds among the asset classes we are considering, and although I am reluctant to mention it, since it is an emotive and contentious area, I feel I must.

Table 7.8   Capital risk of CSFB/Tremont composite index

	$x \leq 0\%$
Annual return	17.4%
Vintage year return	0%
Weighted vintage year return	0%

That issue is manager fraud. Sadly, this is far from uncommon in the industry, but I must stress that with possibly more than 10000 managers in the business your chance of being involved in anything unpleasant is very low indeed. Not so low that it can be totally disregarded, but probably low enough that provided adequate due diligence is done, and known danger areas avoided, it can be disregarded for practical purposes.

Adequate due diligence includes matching audited financial statements against marketing claims and interim figures, as well as exhaustive background checks on the individual owners of the management firm and connected persons. Known danger areas include funds that are not regulated, do not use an independent administrator, and use their own in-house broker/dealer (unless they are a large, internationally recognised financial organisation).

Fraud ranges from the straightforward black and white case where money is simply stolen from the fund by passing phoney trades through the administrator and broker/dealer, or where assets are bought by the fund from connected individuals, to greyer areas such as running an overseas (non-US) and a US fund at the same time and settling the most advantageous deals through one fund or the other in order to boost their performance (because the manager wishes to attract more money into that fund) at the expense of the other. (Incidentally, CSFB/Tremont use both US and offshore funds in their indices, including both the standard composite and the composite investable.)

In another case, a manager gradually bought up virtually all the free float of a small internet company. This was a disaster from an investment point of view, since the fund ended up being dramatically exposed to the shares of just one company (many of which, it turned out, were in any event subject to lock-up). From the manager's point of view, however, it was great, since the company's share price rocketed, as did the NAV of the fund, and the manager pocketed large amounts of performance fee.

I hesitated to touch on this because it is an issue about which the whole of the hedge fund industry is understandably sensitive, and while I think I would be failing in my duty if I did not give you the whole picture, please let us keep all this in proportion. There have been a few, highly publicised instances in what is a very large industry. This is unfortunate, but should not deter anyone from investing in the asset class. It does however argue in favour of very detailed due diligence and monitoring. I would also mention that various insurance products are available to indemnify investors against manager negligence, and even fraud, and a useful precaution might be to establish whether your potential manager carries such insurance before deciding to invest.

HOW ARE HEDGE FUND RETURNS CORRELATED WITH THOSE FOR QUOTED EQUITY?

We can show this easily using the annual returns of the CSFB/Tremont index and investable index against those of the S&P 100 and FTSE 100 indices (Table 7.9). Once again we see the uncorrelated nature of the hedge fund index and its investable offshoot. However, that is not important for present purposes. You will see that even the index exhibits a level of correlation that is quite satisfactory for our purposes, although correlation with the FTSE index is perhaps a little too high to be ideal. Again, since I do not believe that the index is necessarily a good guide to what the return pattern of our actual portfolio of hedge funds is likely to be, I am relaxed about this, particularly as the investable index shows very low correlation indeed. Of course, this is open to the same sort of objection as the full index, but the fact that it shows correlation falling sharply when only a very limited number (less than 6%) of funds is included suggests very strongly that this would be likely to happen regardless of which individual funds they might be.

It is also worth noting that Yale claim that their hedge fund investments over the last decade have shown effectively no correlation at all with their quoted returns. This would also tend to strengthen the hypothesis we have just advanced, since clearly they will be investing in an even smaller number of funds than those comprising the investable index. Yet this does again raise the question of why they are using the CSFB/Tremont composite index as a benchmark, since this does in fact exhibit quite high correlation (about 65%) with the S&P 100 according to my analysis. It does, however, demonstrate why Yale

Table 7.9 Correlation coefficient for hedge fund returns versus quoted equity

Annual returns	S&P 100	FTSE 100
Composite CSFB/Tremont index	64.67%	74.30%
CSFB/Tremont investable index	31.37%	25.38%

consider hedge funds to be an ideal component of a Multi Asset Class portfolio.

SUMMARY

- Hedge funds differ from the hedging activities that investors may already carry out for themselves since they are not seeking to protect an existing position. Their market dealings (which may not be 'hedging' at all in the strict sense of the word) represent not a peripheral activity but their core business.
- For this reason it may be more sensible to refer to them (as Yale do) as 'absolute return funds'.
- A hedge fund will specialise in one of a growing number of 'strategies', though these are not really 'strategies' in the sense that we have defined earlier and may be more accurately described as 'tilts'.
- A number of benchmark indices exist although there is not as yet one universally recognised industry standard. For hedge funds, unlike other asset classes, it is necessary to distinguish between an index and an investable index. The latter is one that an investor can easily reproduce, or is linked to a related investment product. The former may comprise several thousand different funds.
- Hedge funds exhibit acceptable levels of correlation with other asset classes and are an appropriate choice for inclusion in a MAC portfolio.
- However, there has been significant variation in the returns of different hedge fund strategies, and an investor may wish to weight his or her hedge fund exposure in particular directions rather than simply buying the composite index.
- Sadly there have been some isolated instances of fraud in the hedge fund industry and while the overall risk is very low, it is most important that investors should exercise prudence by carrying out, or commissioning, proper due diligence and monitoring.

8
Private Equity

Private equity has a long history as an asset class. The predecessor of what today is 3i began investing in the UK just after the Second World War and, according to the NVCA,[1] professional private equity firms have been active in North America since the early 1960s.

What do we mean by 'private equity'? Perhaps in no other asset class is one so bedevilled by conflicting terminology. In North America the whole asset class is sometimes referred to as 'venture capital' with what Europeans call 'large buy-out' being referred to as 'private equity'. Others refer to the whole asset class as 'private equity', with venture and buy-out being subasset classes within it,[2] As will be apparent from the title of this chapter, I have chosen to adopt the latter approach.

Private equity may best be understood as meaning an investment of an equity nature (though this may take the form of, say, a convertible debt instrument) in any company that is not listed on a stock exchange. This is not actually a totally exhaustive definition, since there are transactions (usually called PIPEs in the USA) in which a private equity firm will invest in a quoted company, though the particular instrument in which they invest may not be quoted. There are also situations where a private equity firm may invest in a public company with a view to making it private once they gain control of it.[3] However, for general purposes it will serve us very well.

Perhaps it would be helpful if at the outset I explained what I mean by 'venture' and 'buy-out'. These represent the two broad subclasses into which private equity is notionally divided, though there are a number of important differences that create further categories within each.[4]

---

[1] National Venture Capital Association (of the USA).

[2] The meaning of 'mezzanine' can also be different. In the USA it commonly refers to pre-flotation funding of venture companies. In Europe it usually refers to convertible debt funding of buy-out companies.

[3] Publicly quoted shares may also be found within private equity funds where an IPO (flotation) has been used as an exit mechanism and shares are still in 'lock up' and cannot presently be distributed.

[4] Given the limitations of having to discuss a huge subject within the scope of a single chapter I have chosen not to discuss secondary funds and transactions in any detail, although in truth they form an important part of the market, and are becoming more so with every year that passes.

VENTURE CAPITAL

There are two basic differences that distinguish venture from buy-out and let us note these now. Venture capital firms invest in young companies, perhaps even raw start-ups, whereas buy-out firms invest in developed (and generally profitable) businesses. Venture investments will usually take the form of pure equity (since there is rarely any cashflow available to service loan interest) whereas buy-out investments will almost always include, or be accompanied by, a large element of debt. Thus we have already learned two things about venture capital: it takes the form of *equity* investing in *young* companies.

Strictly speaking these do not have to be technology companies in order to satisfy our definition of venture capital. Historically, for example, a lot of venture investing took place in the retail sector (particularly branded clothing products and fast food outlets), and even today some venture companies may properly be classified as offering a service (though usually technology related). It has, however, come to be expected, at least as part of the everyday concept of 'venture capital', that the companies concerned will be developing new technology.

Sadly, since these expectations lead to many unfortunate misunderstandings and uninformed prejudice about the asset class, this is not actually the case. It is comparatively rare for a venture-backed company to be developing a new technology in the sense of 'when I switch it on will it work?'. There are few venture capitalists around who would be prepared to finance genuine technology risk of this nature. It is much more the norm for companies to be developing some new application of an existing, usually tried and tested technology to meet a particular commercial need. The risk involved is therefore usually more a marketing risk ('will they buy it?') than a technology risk ('will it work?').

This is such an important point to grasp that I make no apology for labouring it. The ideal venture company, from an investor's point of view, is one where the team has experience of a particular industry and a particular technology and have identified a genuine commercial need for which they think they can develop a specific application of the existing technology. A team of bright university researchers with no business experience who think they can invent a completely new type of computer are, by contrast, likely to find it very hard to attract professional venture funding.

The one exception to this comes in the world of healthcare, where drug discovery projects can and do obtain venture funding. However,

I would hedge even this example with a couple of qualifications. Firstly, few of these projects are genuinely ground-breaking – many being, for example, work on particular protein or DNA combinations that have already been noted in some context. Secondly, given the large amounts of time and money required, there is a growing school of thought that such projects are probably best left to the large drug companies and public funding (e.g. university research grants) rather than forming part of the portfolio of a venture fund.

Venture can itself be subdivided by, *stage*, *sector* and *geography*.

Stage

All venture companies are young, but some are younger than others. As with other terminology, there is some confusion in people's classification of investment stage, and no hard and fast criteria that are universally accepted. What follows is therefore something of a generalisation, but, like most generalisations, is generally true.

Seed

This is the earliest stage of all and refers to what is sometimes called a 'naked' start-up. However, even this is flexible and is used by many to refer to the first 'institutional' round of financing (i.e. the first round in which a professional venture firm participates). A start-up can vary in size and complexity from the traditional 'two guys in a garage' concept to a large team of software engineers renting space, and the amount of financing required to get off the ground obviously varies accordingly.

In Europe, for reasons we will discuss later, start-up funding is usually provided by business 'angels', with venture firms investing later, whereas in the USA venture firms are much readier to invest at the seed stage themselves.[5] There is also a big difference between the sort of person who constitutes an angel investor in the USA. In Europe an angel will perhaps have built up and sold a small engineering business. He may well have a net worth of less than $10 million, and he will be intending to invest about $100 000 in any one company, usually as a passive investor. In the USA it may be someone who has sold

---

[5] Again this is necessarily a generalisation. There are a small but growing number of European venture firms who are happy to be seed stage investors.

several successful venture companies. His net worth may run to several hundred million dollars and he will number several leading venture capitalists among his acquaintances. He will typically be looking to be an active co-founder of a business, helping to build it up with ideas and introductions.

This has implications for venture firms when they invest in an angel-backed company. In Europe, the company's capital structure may already be quite congested, with a large number of relatively small investors, none of whom has the means or inclination to follow-on pro rata in later funding rounds, yet none of whom is happy at the prospect of being diluted! Such situations can become difficult, to say the least. In the USA there will be much more alignment of interest between angel and professional investors.

Early Stage

A judge once famously remarked that it was impossible to define what an elephant was, although we would all recognise one when we saw it. He might well have been describing the somewhat ambiguous terminology of venture capital. Hence 'early stage' has slightly different connotations depending on your audience. A late stage investor will often lump everything that occurs before his own involvement as 'early stage', whereas a seed investor will often refer to what she does as 'early stage'. I would prefer to put forward the idea that it is usually the stage at which at least one institutional investor invests for the first time, and this will often be (particularly in Europe) the first round of financing that is composed entirely of professional investors. This is typically called 'the A round', with everything that has gone before being called 'seed rounds'. Another way of thinking of it might be 'all seed investors are early stage investors but not all early stage investors are seed investors'.

Mid-Stage

With inescapable logic, the progress of venture funding proceeds inexorably from the A round to the B and C rounds and it is these that I would classify as mid-stage investing properly so-called. Depending on the type of company, these may be quite small (perhaps no more than $5 million) or very large (during the internet bubble mid-stage rounds of $80 or even $100 million were not unknown). It is at this stage that the lead venture firm will consider exactly which investors may be able to add most value to the company and might seek to attract, for example, a large technology company who may be a key customer or even potential acquirer, or a venture firm in a different geographic area to help with rolling out the business. In particular, it is at this stage that a non-US venture company might first start trying to attract the attention of a high-quality US venture firm to help it to relocate its business (or at least the sales and marketing functions) to the USA.

Late Stage

To my mind this probably covers everything from the D round onwards. Naturally, funds that specialise in late stage investment tend to be rather larger than those that invest for the first time earlier in the game, since the value of the company increases with each round and so proportionally more money is required to acquire a meaningful equity stake. There are even some specialist pre-IPO firms who aim to invest at high valuations but hopefully shortly before an exit, thus realising a high IRR, but this approach is obviously heavily contingent on the exit window staying open for the foreseeable future, and there were many burnt fingers when the IPO euphoria of the dot com bubble burst.

Sector

There are three main sectoral divisions within venture capital: Life Sciences (often called Healthcare), Telecommunications and Information Technology (although the distinction between the last two is becoming increasingly blurred). Thus the combination of stage and sector may be thought of as creating a grid, as shown in Table 8.1. In fact, this is not an exhaustive description since, as I pointed out above, venture capital can also embrace retail and service companies, but I am deliberately cutting a few corners here in order to confuse the reader

Table 8.1

Life sciences	Telecoms	IT
Seed	Seed	Seed
Early	Early	Early
Mid	Mid	Mid
Late	Late	Late

no more than is absolutely necessary. Also, it is of course actually a cube rather than a grid because geography imposes a further division. This is broadly into North America and Europe. However, North America is so dominated in terms of size by the USA that it can be convenient simply to think of US and non-US. This is a somewhat simplistic classification, though, since there is increasing interest in Asian venture capital, and Israel – long a sizeable and exciting venture market – hovers uneasily in the middle. It can be variously classified as US (since virtually all Israeli venture companies actually start life as US corporations), Europe or Asia according to which seems most convenient at the time! I will have some more to say below about differences in the way in which venture is practised in Europe as opposed to the USA, but for now let us focus on differences of technology.

The Life Sciences sector covers a number of different areas. The one that would probably suggest itself immediately to the intelligent layman would be drug discovery, but in fact this is quite a small part of the sector (at least by number of deals, but each drug discovery business tends to absorb much more capital than other types of company) and, as already noted, there is an increasing body of opinion that questions whether this is actually a good use of venture capital. Other areas include devices, services, diagnostics, DNA and protein research, wound dressings, and healthcare-specific applications of information technology (and even then I have probably overlooked a few).

The most widely known type of medical device is the stent (a tube which creates in effect an artificial artery) but there are many others, ranging from the mundane (artificial joints) to the highly complex (heart valves). This is an exciting area and has the great advantage over various other healthcare applications in that it requires relatively short trial and approval periods. The others speak for themselves, but I would single out for special attention the enormous difference that has been made to this sector by the human genome project. As one venture capitalist said to me at the time 'from today onwards everyone is playing with a new deck of cards'. Not only is it the potential of isolating particular genetic features that condition particular ailments (asthma, epilepsy and haemophilia are among the more commonplace examples) which is exciting, but also the enormous strides that have been made in specialist software applications that can dramatically speed up and improve the isolation process.

Telecommunications has been the scene of much technical innovation in recent years, so much so that technology advanced beyond the readiness of people (particularly the incumbent telecom carriers) to deploy it. The optical sector, in particular, was particularly hard hit by this phenomenon which was perhaps in retrospect inevitable given that, both in the USA and in Europe, governments allowed the existing providers to maintain effective monopolies of supply, and thus shut out the newcomers. Challenges abound, as things such as broadband and VOIP (voice over internet protocol) have become seen as commodities, and priced accordingly. My instinct is that the telecom companies that will be the big winners of the future will either be producing a very focused solution to a particular technical problem, or the much-vaunted 'killer application' such as Skype produced in their ability to link VOIP with conventional telephony.

Information Technology has changed significantly over the years. Originally it was quite common to find companies such as Apple creating a new type of computer or Microsoft effectively creating a new basic operating system, but it is unlikely that such a project would get funded now. Venture capitalists today are looking for specific solutions to particular business problems, the resolution of which will have a very real commercial advantage for those involved. This point is important, since many IT scientists are product-focused. The chairman of a European software association told me some time ago, 'every year I see hundreds of solutions in search of a problem'.

As I have already mentioned, with the growth of the internet and digital communication generally, the dividing line between telecoms and IT is becoming increasingly blurred and it can be difficult to classify a company with any certainty. Computers have been seen increasingly as communication devices, in many cases as part of extended telecoms networks.

Geography

The United States represents an overwhelming proportion of global venture capital. Amounts raised vary enormously from year to year and the figures are not always clear, but it is obvious from Table 8.2 that it is an overwhelmingly larger pool of capital, especially given that the economies of the United States and the European Union are roughly equal. In fact, so large did the pot of capital become in the USA during the late 1990s that it brought major problems in its wake. The industry expanded in size, both in terms of the number of funds raised each year (less than 100 in 1993, more than 500 in 2000) and in the average

Table 8.2 US venture capital fund vintage year performance

Year	Fund #1	Upper quartile
1990	74.9	25.3
1991	61.4	25.7
1992	102.3	31.7
1993	116.4	39.8
1994	113.0	39.8
1995	247.8	63.5
1996	454.9	95.9
1997	296.0	60.8
1998	721.0	12.2
1999	140.7	−0.9

Source: Thomson Financial Venture Xpert.

fund size ($55 million in 1993, $193 million in 2000), with a monster $101 billion being raised in 2000 (the figure was originally even more than this – about $120 billion I believe – but has been adjusted downwards to take account of subsequent fund size reductions).

Investors ignored the essential effect of a huge stream of money flowing into any asset class and, even without the bursting of the internet bubble, US venture returns would necessarily have plummeted as larger fund sizes drove higher entry valuations, and pushed many firms towards later stages of investment in order to be able to deploy more money in each deal. As we will see, this herd mentality, and an unwillingness to accept that the returns of any asset class must inevitably be affected (for good or ill) by the amount of money seeking to access it, is a recurrent theme in the story of asset allocation, and nowhere more so than in private equity.

It must also be understood, however, that it is in the USA that the very best of venture capital practice has been found, and where the very best venture returns have been recorded. It is hardly surprising, therefore, that so many investors from around the world should have clamoured for entry to this exciting market. However, what does not seem to be widely understood (although there is ample evidence available, particularly from those fund of funds managers who have been in the industry a long time) is that venture returns are hugely binary, both at the company level and at the fund level.

Venture returns are driven by a very small number of very big winners ('home runs' in venture parlance); it is now generally accepted that if you have invested with the very best US venture firms then you can expect about 5% of your companies by cost to generate as much as 80% of your final value. To be brutally realistic, what happens to the remainder is largely irrelevant. It is in fact one of the main differences between the US venture model and the traditional European venture model (please note that I say 'traditional' – this has changed dramatically in recent years) that Europeans were uncomfortable with a return model that was so starkly binary and clung to the (mistaken) idea that one could generate returns more or less equally across their portfolio.

However, the key phrase here is 'if you have invested with the very best US venture firms', since this is where the second binary element comes into play. The very high returns that have indeed been earned in this market have been produced by a very small number of firms. According to the NVCA, there are approximately 700 venture firms in the USA yet the truly outstanding returns of the late 1990s were in fact produced by a very small number of firms – certainly no more than 25 and possibly as few as 15 (opinions vary). We will discuss this in more detail later when we consider private equity returns, but for the moment let us simply note the stark truth which is that unless you can gain access consistently to the funds of this very small handful of firms then you will not achieve anything like the best benchmark returns and you may well struggle to earn any sort of decent return at all compared to what may be available from other private equity categories.

Before we move on to consider buy-out, it may be instructive to dig a little deeper into the different ways in which venture capital has been practised in the USA and Europe. In fact, as you will see, those ways are so different that it is probably misleading to call what has happened historically in Europe 'venture capital' at all.

I must enter two huge caveats at this point, one of which I have touched on already. The first is that I can only possibly deal with such a huge topic within the confines of a few paragraphs by way of generalisations, some of which may appear sweeping (this is really a subject that could take up a whole book just by itself). The second is that I am talking about the historical situation, not the current. There have been huge changes in European venture in recent years, with many firms openly espousing the US model. Equally, the huge influx of new personnel into the US venture industry (the number at least doubled during the dot com boom, with many of the new entrants coming from an investment banking background) means that my comments about the entrepreneurial background of US venture capitalists are no longer of nearly such general application as might have been the case in the mid 1990s.

The difference starts with the sort of people who practise venture capital. Traditionally if you were an entrepreneur in the USA and you approached a venture firm for their backing, you were not going to them primarily for money. That may seem a very strange thing to the ears of someone accustomed to the cash-strapped venture market in Europe where 'getting funded' is usually the only objective, so let me explain what I mean. Traditionally if you went to a top US firm it was because the two people on the other side of the table had probably both had at least one start-up themselves in your area while they were entrepreneurs themselves. You were looking for them to come into the company, work with you and help you to build it. They would take a leading role in hiring key executives (many of whom would be personally known to them) and approaching key customers (many of whom would have been their key customers previously). Because of this hands-on approach (often called 'value add' in the USA) they were happy to target the seed stage, both because entry valuations were lower and because they saw it as an area of opportunity, a chance to build the company in the right way from day one.

In Europe the opposite was generally true. Most venture capitalists had a background in management consultancy or investment banking. Because of this they were unable to provide 'value add' and had to be content with what the Americans call a 'just money' approach. Also because of this they were disinclined to invest at the seed stage, seeing it as an area of risk rather than of opportunity.

The other big difference, as we have already noted, was in the absence of a home-run mentality in Europe. This was exacerbated by most European venture firms being parochial in outlook (often politically motivated: local financial institutions funded local venture firms which were, in their turn, expected to support local companies) with little cross-border co-investment. The temptation was to grow medium size companies in relatively small local markets (imagine being number one in Belgium . . .) rather than growing companies globally and relocating them to other countries where necessary. In Israel, by contrast, venture capitalists recognised from the outset that they had little option but to be global in their approach and made a virtue out of necessity by forming all their companies as US corporations and leaving only the R&D function in Israel. Suffice it to say that many European venture capitalists were openly dismissive of a home-run approach, even going so far as to suggest that there were serious structural differences in Europe that made such a strategy impossible to implement.

Happily these folk are now in the decided minority thanks to a real sea change in European venture. There are many, most notably the smaller and more recently formed firms, who recognise that venture capital has been done best (indeed dramatically better) in the USA and that it is logical to look there for their role models. Accordingly, we now see a small but growing number of European firms adopting the US venture model and there seems no logical reason why it should not in future produce returns at least as good as those available, not least since entry valuations are dramatically lower in Europe. This is not an easy story to sell to people, since there is no empirical evidence for it, at least not in the shape of available benchmark returns (nor will there be for some years, for obvious reasons). It is a classic example of where a sophisticated investor should be prepared to respect the opinion of someone like a fund of funds manager who has been informed by many years of first-hand experience and, by so doing, gain a significant first mover advantage. Similar situations arose in the world of hedge funds a few years ago, but hedge funds had then suddenly become fashionable, whereas European venture is currently unfashionable.

It also points to an important difference between investing in venture and buy-out funds. With buy-out, you can gain a great deal of insight by objective quantitative analysis. With venture, the process is more qualitative and subjective (particularly so in Europe where the industry is younger and few venture firms have long track records) and there is no substitute for the intimacy afforded by close personal relationships with the individual venture capitalists themselves.

Buy-out

After discussion of so many complicated issues, some of them rather nebulous, it comes almost as a relief to turn to the world of buy-outs, which is comparatively straightforward by contrast.

Buy-out investments are widespread both in the USA and in Europe as well as (to a lesser extent as yet) other places around the world such as Asia. However this is a distinction without a difference as the way in which these investments are made and structured is essentially the same wherever buy-out firms are to be found.

Buy-out investing is 'control' investing where the firm will take a majority stake (frequently all the equity apart from that which is earmarked for the company's key management) and fund the purchase of that ownership position partly with equity (purchased out of their fund) but also with debt (and sometimes lots of it!). The debt is classically supplied by third party banks but the situation is usually more complex than that, with different tranches of senior debt and different layers of subordinated debt (usually with a 'kicker' – some equity conversion rights – attached). Some of this subordinated debt may at times be supplied by the buy-out fund although the intention is usually to retire it at some stage as part of a recapitalisation. There are in fact specialist funds that have sprung up to supply this 'mezzanine' funding and they themselves occupy a discrete position in the private equity world.

It was not always like this, particularly in Europe, but this is more a question of definition than of substance. In continental Europe control investing was traditionally frowned upon for a whole host of reasons (mostly cultural) and so many firms who described themselves as buy-out investors actually took minority stakes, and frequently encountered all too predictable problems in trying to force an exit. This is simply not buy-out investing, but development capital or some such genre and the confusion arose only because in many cases they chose to wrap themselves in the buy-out cloak with a view to facilitating fundraising.

The three main drivers of buy-out performance at the company level are (1) gearing, i.e. the level of debt within the transaction, (2) earnings growth over the period the company holds the business and (3) multiple expansion, i.e. hopefully being able to sell the company on a higher earnings multiple than was paid for it. If you look at any period of dramatically good buy-out returns, for example the Nordic region during the mid-1990s, then it is a racing certainty that at least two of these factors were working in their favour to produce them. However, the situation has changed dramatically with much larger fund sizes forcing firms to target public companies, or their subsidiaries, which suggests that (1) they will already have high levels of operating debt, (2) they will have been well managed, thus reducing the potential for significant earnings growth and (3) they will presumably have to be bought at a premium over the quoted multiple. Thus, while I believe that good returns will continue to be made by the best buy-out managers, everyone would probably agree that the 'happy hunting time' is over and that return expectations of mid-teens IRRs may now be more realistic than the mid-twenties of yesteryear.

These three drivers can be quite easily modelled on a simple spreadsheet and an experienced investor who has a historical base of data from which to work can readily see who is using high levels of debt, who has been successful at growing the profits of their businesses, and who may have been paying unacceptably high multiples for their companies. As mentioned above, this is a big advantage that a buy-out fund investor has over a venture fund investor: the comparative ease of analysis.

Benchmarks

We are fortunate indeed that for private equity a widely accepted and respected set of benchmarks exists, namely the Thomson Financial Venture Xpert system (formerly known as, and still frequently referred to colloquially as, Venture Economics). It is a source of constant puzzlement to me that so many pension consultants, particularly in the UK, say that 'there are no proper benchmark returns' or 'the data is much too young to be reliable' when this is manifestly not the case. It is even stranger to find these same consultants happily recommending investment in hedge funds where arguably these same objections do in fact have some force.

Thomson Financial are a long-established and highly professional organisation and the data within their system goes back to 1969 (in the case of US venture, for example) although it is probably fair to say that it does not become truly meaningful until about 1988 for any of the private equity subsectors. However, this is a period of nearly 20 years and the figures are universally accepted as an industry benchmark. Other measures do exist, including some published by specialist consultants, but these do not have the same constituent funds; some, for example, only include the funds invested in by their own clients. Compare and contrast this with the situation described in the previous chapter and you will hopefully be able to share my perplexity.

Thomson Financial have generously agreed to make their data available to me for the purposes of this book and I am very happy to make use of it. However, before we proceed further there is one very important aspect of private equity returns that we must discuss and digest, since it is a fundamental difference that sets private equity apart from all other asset classes but, paradoxically, also points the way ahead to how the returns of other asset classes should properly be assessed.

VINTAGE YEAR VERSUS ANNUAL RETURNS

We discussed earlier why it was not appropriate in general terms to use annual returns when looking at target investment returns over a long period; I do not care how quickly or how slowly my train travels at different times during my journey, only that it should arrive on time. We should bear in mind, however, that annual returns are used for two different purposes. They are used as a target for future returns, and we have seen (as in the train journey example) that this is not relevant when what we are really concerned with is the totality of future performance over a significant period.

They are also used to analyse the historic performance of an asset class (with disastrous results when coupled with the assumption that variance of return and risk are the same thing), and you will remember that I accepted earlier, though with very significant reservations, that they could indeed perform a useful function in this regard provided always that the 'variance equals risk' assumption was first taken outside and shot. With private equity, however, there are specific reasons why annual returns may not even be used as an appropriate measure of historic performance.

Private equity is a cashflow game. Money is drawn down into private equity funds where it is used partly to pay fees and expenses and partly to make investments. In the fullness of time money flows back to the investor by way of distributions from the fund as companies are exited (sold or floated). Thus the only proper measure of the performance of any individual fund is to take the cashflows across the whole period of the fund's life and see what IRR (compound return) they have produced. It is the IRR to date (or to the date when the fund was finally wound up) from the year in which the fund was formed that gives us the 'vintage year' return.

Because expenses will be payable in respect of each investment as it is made, and fees are payable from the very beginning of the fund's life, this means that if this exercise were to be attempted in the early years of the fund's life, then it would show a heavily negative return. Remember the 'J-curve' from Chapter 3 (see Figure 8.1). While the actual position of the J-curve may vary from fund to fund, its basic shape will always be the same. Thus, if a private equity fund were to be valued in, say, Year 2, whether on a vintage year or an annual basis, it would show the same sort of negative return regardless of whether it was the best private equity fund in history or the worst. In fact it is

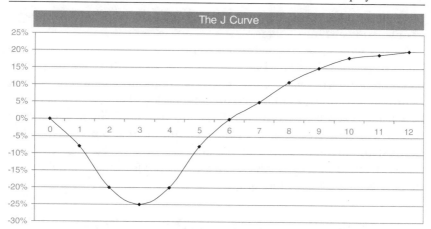

Figure 8.1   The J-curve

almost impossible in anything like 'normal' conditions (i.e. excluding the dot com period in the case of venture) to gain any meaningful insight into the performance of a fund until it is at least five years old in the case of a buy-out fund, or about eight years old in the case of a venture fund – and even then this will only be an indication, not a guaranteed outcome.

Within the portfolio of a private equity fund investor the situation will be further complicated as each fund will represent a different J-curve, all of which overlie each other and form one large, combined J-curve representing the investor's cashflow forecasts. Thus, if an investor had a fully mature private equity programme, say about 10 years old, you could argue that the annual return of that programme as a whole was indeed a valid measure of its performance. However, we immediately encounter two practical problems.

Firstly, there are very few investors who do in fact have a fully mature programme. Most current investors came into the asset class only within the last six years or so, and many of them have either (1) already exited in panic or (2) did not diversify their portfolio over time so that their J-curve would not be a valid example of a mature portfolio. Even if one ignores these points, however, there is the added requirement that one should not have significantly increased the amount (the amount, not the percentage) of the private equity allocation, since if one begins to commit larger amounts as one proceeds with the programme, then the J-curve will be perpetually skewed towards its younger (lower return) stage.

This is what poses problems that some pension consultants seem to find insuperable. It is possible that when they say 'there are no proper benchmark returns' they really mean 'there are no meaningful annual return figures for me to plug into my risk model'. The reality, of course, is that there is a huge body of reliable historic performance data, and that the challenge is to find a replacement for the traditional risk model, not just for private equity but for all asset classes. Perhaps it is the inherent threat posed to their cosy way of doing things by this challenge that they resent most of all.

FURTHER COMPLEXITIES OF PRIVATE EQUITY RETURNS

Before performing any calculations it is only right that I should touch upon some controversy that exists about the correct type of returns to use when evaluating private equity as an asset class. Again, I will try to be as brief as possible, but this topic almost deserves a book to itself rather than a few paragraphs.

It is traditional when evaluating private equity funds, and the returns of the asset class as a whole, to use the upper quartile vintage year return. This seems very strange to those accustomed to other asset classes and they are not slow to point it out. Surely it confers an obvious and unfair advantage if one takes only the top performing 25% of the population?

The answer is actually 'no', but understanding exactly why it is 'no' requires a deep understanding of the private equity industry and of the way in which the Venture Xpert figures are collected and presented. Very briefly, there are three main reasons.

Firstly, there is a huge variation in terms of quality between private equity firms, and there is an art to discerning these. Like most arts, once learned it works very well. As a result, most experienced investors, such as funds of funds, are able to pick mainly upper quartile funds consistently. I worked for a leading example of such a firm for many years, and over about a 20-year period the performance of their fund picks were collectively upper quartile in every single vintage year. Given the huge variation in results, even within the upper quartile (see below) this can be achieved probably with no more than about 60% upper quartile picks by number. In my experience it is possible for an experienced fund of funds actually to get above 70% upper quartile picks by number over a period of many years. Therefore, if one is attempting to mimic the effect of investing with an experienced fund of funds, then the upper quartile is an appropriate measure to take.

Secondly, it is frequently overlooked that the 'upper quartile' return referred to is not the pooled IRR of all the funds in the upper quartile, but the IRR of the individual fund that stands at the boundary of the upper quartile. Thus, if the population for any one year was 32 funds, we would be looking at the return on fund number 8. Within the upper quartile itself there is a huge variation (see Table 8.2, p. 162).

As you can see from the table, the difference in a typical year can be dramatic. $10 invested in the upper quartile 1990 US venture fund would have grown to just over $95 10 years later, while the same $10 invested in the top performing US venture fund formed in 1990 would have grown to nearly $2700 in the same period – 28 times as much! Thus the 'upper quartile' figure that we use is not really any true indication of the returns that can actually be earned from choosing from the top few funds and, if anything, actually understates the case.

Thirdly, many of the funds included in the Venture Xpert for the sake of completeness are not institutional investment grade. Indeed many, particularly in Europe, are very small local and regional development or seed funds. In a typical year as much as half of the population of the European venture funds, for example, can quite simply be excluded on grounds of size. Thus the Venture Xpert population is put together with the worthy aim of capturing as much private equity activity as possible, but does not necessarily represent the actual population from which institutional investors can choose their commitments. The median and average figures (eagerly touted by most consultants) are therefore even more unrealistic as valid industry benchmarks since the effect of this overpopulation is artificially to depress them.

Unfortunately, however, I have learned from bitter personal experience that there are many people to whom you can explain all this until you are blue in the face, but they are simply not prepared to listen. They have jumped to the conclusion that this is all some huge confidence trick perpetrated by the private equity industry, and have closed their mind to any valid explanation. I will therefore, when possible, base my calculations not just on the upper quartile fund performance but also on the capital-weighted average, but I must stress that this latter measure may significantly understate private equity return expectations, and I base this opinion on 20 years of practical experience. The truth is that the upper quartile fund should form the floor of any return expectations.

What Return Risk is Present in Private Equity?

We can deal with this question mercifully quickly since private equity has been perhaps the best performing asset class of all over the last two decades.

However, since, as I have pointed out above, this is an asset class whose returns attract a great deal of ill-informed controversy, let me first state very clearly what my methodology will be, since I hope this will satisfy everyone, including those who do not accept the upper quartile as a valid performance benchmark. I will be performing analysis not just on the upper quartile fund figure but also, as I stated above, on the capital-weighted average so that the sceptics can use these outcomes if they prefer.

Equally, since there are those who do not understand the asset class and insist on using annual return figures even though these will at best provide a proxy for the return of a fully mature private equity programme of unchanging amount, I am also going to use these figures; they are available from Venture Xpert from 1986 for US private equity and 1987 for European.

If we were going to look at private equity allocation in depth then we would need to differentiate between the returns of buy-out and venture in both the USA and Europe and decide how best to allocate our resources between these four market segments, particularly having regard to issues of access, as well as looking at Asia, Eastern Europe, etc. However, since I feel that this level of detail lies beyond the scope of this book, I have created figures for all private equity on a global basis so that we can simply evaluate the asset class as a whole against other asset classes. I have done this by weighting according to annual fundraising. Interestingly, the process points up how private equity has become increasingly global over the past 20 years. The US share of the market declined from over 90% in 1984 to 65% in 2004 and actually dipped below 50% at one stage during the intervening period (Table 8.3).

We can now use the resulting figures (see Table 8.4) for phi analysis in exactly the same way as for other asset classes. However, we must make one small change that is specific to private equity. Given the effect of the J-curve, we will ignore any vintage year returns later

Table 8.3 Venture capital fundraising by year

Vintage Year	1984 $ bn	1985 $ bn	1986 $ bn	1987 $ bn	1988 $ bn	1989 $ bn	1990 $ bn	1991 $ bn	1992 $ bn	1993 $ bn	1994 $ bn
United States	3.6	3.8	3.8	4.3	4.8	5.2	3.0	1.9	5.1	4.9	9.0
Europe	0.8	0.7	1.0	0.9	1.6	1.4	1.2	1.0	0.6	3.3	1.2

Vintage Year	1995 $ bn	1996 $ bn	1997 $ bn	1998 $ bn	1999 $ bn	2000 $ bn	2001 $ bn	2002 $ bn	2003 $ bn	2004 $ bn	2005 $ bn
United States	10.0	12.1	20.7	30.7	61.1	101.4	38.0	10.7	10.4	18.6	25.0
Europe	3.4	3.4	4.7	6.8	13.2	36.1	16.2	3.6	2.7	4.2	3.0

Source: Own workings from Thomson Financial Venture Xpert data.

Notes

1. 2005 figures are approximate in each case.
2. For reasons that lie beyond the scope of this book, the European figures are artificially inflated – the real figures for 2004 and 2005, for example, may be as low as $1 billion and $1.3 billion respectively.

Table 8.4 Global private equity returns

	1984	1985	1986	1987	1988	1989	1990	1991	1992	1993	1994
Vintage year											
Upper quartile	11.85	15.28	12.51	16.74	16.59	19.13	19.58	21.54	24.64	28.06	26.98
Mean	15.23										
Standard deviation	11.32										
Weighted average	13.59	18.96	11.61	12.79	11.54	16.11	16.80	14.28	23.31	22.57	24.74
Mean	10.99										
Standard deviation	11.73										
Annual returns											
Upper quartile			13.90	11.22	9.96	13.80	10.71	19.02	16.83	27.63	25.13
Mean		25.02									
Standard deviation		19.97									
Weighted average			15.00	−25.26	13.58	30.45	2.04	10.83	3.97	18.11	16.29
Mean		13.86									
Standard deviation		17.97									

	1995	1996	1997	1998	1999	2000	2001	2002	2003	2004
Vintage year										
Upper quartile	31.90	35.05	18.78	10.44	2.90	1.04	8.07	3.34	7.79	−12.43
Mean										
Standard deviation										
Weighted average	25.11	17.88	12.22	6.36	−1.86	−0.93	1.65	−0.75	10.38	−25.48
Mean										
Standard deviation										
Annual returns										
Upper quartile	44.25	49.32	39.07	31.07	83.88	40.62	2.17	−0.62	14.26	23.22
Mean										
Standard deviation										
Weighted average	24.65	35.29	34.32	8.72	53.58	14.78	−6.76	−11.89	8.06	17.60
Mean										
Standard deviation										

Source: Own workings from Thomson Financial Venture Xpert data.

Table 8.5 Private equity return risk

	10%	11%	12%	13%	14%	15%
Upper quartile vintage year[a]	18.2%	21.2%	24.5%	28.1%	31.6%	35.6%
Weighted average vintage year[a]	28.8%	33.4%	37.8%	42.9%	47.6%	52.8%
Upper quartile annual	22.7%	24.2%	25.8%	27.4%	29.2%	30.8%
Weighted average annual	41.7%	43.6%	46.0%	48.0%	50.4%	52.4%

[a] Because of the effect of the J-curve, vintage years less than five years old have been ignored.

than 2000. As we have already agreed that, in general, we must give much more weight to vintage year returns of any asset classes that cover a long period, and correspondingly little to those that cover only a few years, this is in any event hardly a radical proposition. (This gives a new mean and standard deviation of 18.41 and 9.27 for the upper quartile, and 14.41 and 7.89 for the capital-weighted average to be substituted for those shown in Table 8.4 as having been calculated for the total period.)

Having done so, we find in Table 8.5 that for a target rate of return of 13% the upper quartile vintage year figures give a probability of just 28% of failing to meet a target return of 13%, while using the unrealistic capital weighted average figures gives a probability of 43% – still more likely than not that the target rate will be achieved.

This is without assigning any greater weight to the results of earlier years. Given that the upper quartile figure exceeded 13% in eight out of the first 10 years, and seven out of 10 in the case of the capital-weighted average, then we may safely assume that the resulting figures would have been much lower had we done so, as demonstrated in an earlier chapter. In fact, the upper quartile return risk would come down from 28% to 16.6%, and the weighted average capital risk would come down from 43% to 27.8%.

Note also that even the annual return figures suggest that a fully mature private equity programme will fail to return 13% only in one out of every four years (if using the upper quartile) or in less than two out of every four (even if using the weighted average). I have had my say on the inappropriateness of using annual returns in this way for private equity, but even the worst case annual return scenario is hardly disastrous; there is a 50% chance of making at least 14% in any one year.

Whatever the case, given these figures, we may safely assume that private equity exhibits a sufficiently low degree of return risk for us to accept it as one of our asset classes.

What Capital Risk is Present in Private Equity?

Investing properly in private equity funds involves planning a commitment programme over about eight vintage years. This is because experience shows that it is absolutely vital to have diversification by time, and this is achieved by committing an equal amount every year to funds formed in that year. Actually, sufficient diversification could almost certainly be achieved over five or six years, but one cannot guarantee that after just six years there will be enough money coming back from the earliest funds in the programme to fund drawdowns to the later ones. After eight years, one can safely assume that a private equity programme will be self-funding; indeed, the problem usually lies in deciding what to do with the excess cashflows.

It is for this reason that it is essential to over-commit. In other words, the amount that you have notionally committed to funds will be greater than your official allocation to the asset class. Depending on their degree of conservatism, most sophisticated investors reckon on committing anywhere between about 1.5 and 1.8 times their allocation figure.

It is also for this reason that, in reckoning capital risk within private equity as an asset class, one has to look at the potential for capital loss across a whole commitment cycle. If you commit equal amounts for eight years, then logically the only way in which you can suffer a capital loss is if the cumulative return is negative when calculated across a continuous eight-year period. As you can see from looking at the figures, there has never been a time when this has been the case and nor, frankly, is there ever likely to be. Thus in practical terms the capital risk of investing in private equity funds on a properly diversified basis is zero.

However, for those who are simply never going to believe this no matter how logical it may be, we can perform phi analysis to see what the notional capital risk may be.

The figures in Table 8.6 speak for themselves. There is some risk of the annual return of a fully mature private equity programme being negative in any one year of its existence, but there is effectively no risk at all of it being negative on a cumulative (or, rather, compound) basis over its full term. We can therefore conclude that private equity as an asset class effectively exhibits no capital risk whatever if investment is conducted through a programme of investing in private equity funds on a properly planned and implemented basis.

Table 8.6 Capital risk of Private Equity: probability of a return being equal to or less than zero

Input figures	
Upper quartile vintage year (unweighted)	2.4%
Upper quartile vintage year (weighted)	0.2%
Capital-weighted average vintage year (unweighted)	3.4%
Capital-weighted average vintage year (weighted)	0.2%
Upper quartile annual return	10.6%
Capital-weighted average annual return	22.1%

Source: Own workings based on data from Thomson Financial Venture Xpert.

Table 8.7 Correlation between Private Equity annual returns and quoted equities

Upper quartile correlation with S&P 100	52.63%
Upper quartile correlation with FTSE 100	34.59%
Capital-weighted average correlation with S&P 100	62.31%
Capital-weighted average correlation with FTSE 100	57.80%

What Degree of Correlation does it Exhibit with Quoted Equity Markets?

We have seen that private equity appears to satisfy all our requirements from a returns point of view. Let us now see if we can accept it also on the basis of low correlation with quoted equities. Here we clearly have no option but to use annual returns, despite my reservations about their validity. In this context, however, their use is perhaps less objectionable since at some stage of the period to be covered by our investment strategy our private equity programme will become mature, even though we will presumably have to increase the amount of our allocation steadily as the value of our whole portfolio grows.

As you can see from Table 8.7, private equity exhibits positive correlation with quoted markets, but at a fairly low level; in fact at exactly the sort of levels we considered to be ideal to target when we discussed this issue in an earlier chapter. It would seem, therefore, that private equity is an ideal asset class for our purposes.

How do we Address the Slow Capital Take-up Issue?

We have seen that it is necessary to plan one's commitments to private equity over several years. While this is eminently sensible from a cashflow and diversification point of view it causes a major problem in terms of putting money to work in the early years of a programme. I know one pension plan that committed all its allocation on the first year (a terrible practice) and was complaining three years later that they were only about 10% invested. This struck me as betraying a complete lack of understanding of the asset class, in terms both of what they had done and of their complaints. However, the situation that they describe is entirely possible. In fact, it is not just possible but highly probable, in which case why had they not planned for it and done something about it?

Even within a well-planned private equity programme this is an issue that will constantly resurface, since it is almost impossible to predict, even within a mature fund portfolio, exactly when cashflows will arise. There is thus essentially a paradox about cash efficiency in these circumstances; one needs to have as much money as possible at work in the chosen asset class, yet it is difficult to access: there are a limited number of high-quality managers, they only raise money every three years, and the timing of cashflows both in and out of your fund are very difficult to anticipate.

Unfortunately, the approach that I encounter in practice is that these issues are rarely considered at all, and they are of course compounded if the investor has not even worked out that their level of commitments needs to be much higher than the amount of their allocation. (If it is not, then you can almost guarantee that you will *never* be more than about 60% invested.) I have come across many situations, for example, where money that is earmarked as part of a private equity allocation is being held at money market rates by the treasury department; in some cases this can be 90% or more of the allocation.

One technique that has been tried by various pension schemes is to invest the surplus in publicly quoted private equity vehicles. This is definitely a step in the right direction, but it is flawed. Firstly, these vehicles are themselves heavily cash rich for all sorts of reasons that lie outside the scope of this book, and so one is often simply replicating the problem on a different level. Secondly, such vehicles may, from time to time, be able to offer returns that are competitive with quoted equities, but will never (again, for various good reasons that lie outside the scope of this book) be able to act as a proxy for private equity returns, certainly not over any sort of significant period.

There are two ways in which I would look at tackling this problem.

The first would be by committing as much as possible to secondary funds in the first few years of the programme, additional to the existing commitment programme that I have already planned out. Secondary funds specialise in buying the interests in private equity funds of investors who suddenly have an unanticipated need for liquidity, or who have perhaps made a mess of their private equity investments and want to exit the asset class. (Incidentally, this is why in practical terms private equity fund investments should not be regarded as illiquid.) Because they are buying interests that have already been partly or even fully funded, the investment cycle is much shorter and one can reasonably expect to have cash coming back within two or three years. Of course, the price you pay is the need to accept a much lower cash multiple but this really does not matter since (1) you will have at least some of your private equity allocation at work earning private equity IRRs, and (2) the alternative may be having it sitting in a money market account.

The second might be to hold any uninvested capital in the NASDAQ index. I make this suggestion with some diffidence since it is borne more from instinct and personal experience than from science. I have heard various people suggest that a very high correlation exists between NASDAQ and private equity (and specifically venture capital) returns. All I can say is that although I have tried to replicate such an outcome (since it would suit my purposes!) I have been unable to do so. Using annual returns it is possible to find a correlation of about 70% with US venture. Using vintage year returns one can get this figure up to about 76% for the capital-weighted average of private equity as a whole. This is well below the sort of figures I had been led to believe. To place them in context, NASDAQ has a correlation over the same period of about 88% with the S&P 100 (and it is probably very slightly higher than this as the NASDAQ dividend yield is so minimal that I have not taken it into account).

Whatever the outcome of the calculations, perhaps this is one of those occasions where an element of 'subjective probability' may be allowed. Of the various options available, investing money that is earmarked for private equity fund commitments in the NASDAQ index seems to me the least objectionable of those available. The NASDAQ operates as one of the two exit channels for US venture company investments, as well as a thriving after-market for those companies which, while technically 'public', still exhibit many of the exciting growth characteristics of venture investments. For these reasons, it seems logical to me to expect it to influence and, in turn, be influenced by the US venture capital sector, and to be likely to produce returns that will share the same pattern. (It is clear to any venture capital observer, for example, that the collapse of the NASDAQ in 2000, the collapse in venture valuations, and reduction in venture fund sizes, in 2001 and 2002 were all clearly interrelated, and that the first probably sparked off the whole downward cycle.) It is also my instinct that, of all other asset classes, NASDAQ is the only one capable of producing anything like the level of returns that private equity has enjoyed. Indeed, it is almost certainly the case that if one had been unable to invest with the so-called 'golden circle' venture groups during the 1990s then one would probably have done at least as well by investing in the NASDAQ index as by investing in second or third quartile US venture funds.

SUMMARY

- There are problems of terminology and definition in this asset class. It is best to think of 'private equity' being the asset class as a whole, subdivided into a number of subclasses of which the two most important are buy-out and venture capital. Other significant areas include mezzanine and secondary transactions.
- Buy-out activity focuses on acquiring established businesses, and the transaction will almost always involve an element of debt – hence the term 'leveraged buy-out' or 'LBO'. Venture activity focuses on early stage companies (even start-up in the case of seed stage venture capital) and will almost never involve debt. Venture companies are invariably looking to develop new applications of existing technology.
- Private equity activity is also segmented by geography, mainly into the USA and Europe, although other areas such as Central Europe and Asia are becoming more important.
- Private equity funds are subject to the J-curve, which means (1) that all will appear to have heavily negative returns in their early years and (2) that annual returns are not a valid measure of performance. This in turn means that traditional risk models cannot be applied to private equity.
- Investors have felt challenged by any comparison of private equity returns with those of other asset classes. In fact this is simplicity itself once the returns of other asset classes are converted into vintage year returns.

- The direct comparison that is made possible shows that private equity has consistently (and often dramatically) outperformed all other asset classes. Yale announced a compound return of 35% on their private equity programme in the 10 years to 2004, and other US investors have done even better.
- Access to high-quality private equity managers (particularly US venture managers) has become a significant issue, particularly for newcomers to the asset class. There is dramatic variation in performance between the very best private equity managers and the rest of the pack (even within the upper quartile) and it is vital that proper attention is paid to how the private equity allocation should be dispersed by geography and sector, and to the selection of individual managers. A fund of funds approach is a logical alternative but may lead to a suboptimal portfolio if large amounts have to be put to work.
- A private equity programme must be put together over time as it is essential to gain proper diversification by vintage year. The programme may take anything up to 10 years to become fully invested.
- Investors must accept that (because of the J-curve) by launching a private equity programme they may experience slightly lower annual returns in the short term as the price of much higher compound returns in the long term.

9
Property

Property (or real estate, or real assets) is the one so-called alternative asset class into which pension funds around the world have been prepared to venture for some time. Public pension funds in the UK, for example, currently have about 6.5% of their assets allocated to property, compared to less than 1% in both hedge funds and private equity put together.[1]

In this chapter, we will examine the different ways in which a pension fund may invest in property, analyse the levels of return risk and capital risk, and see the extent to which property returns exhibit correlation with quoted returns. We will also look at the issue of leverage.

INVESTING IN PROPERTY

There are two broad strands here: direct and indirect. Investing directly in property is done by retaining one or more managers to find, buy, and manage individual property assets on your behalf. Many will have a particular specialty either by sector or geography. Investing indirectly means investing not in individual properties themselves, but in a fund or other vehicle that will in turn invest in property.

Many investors who refer to this part of their portfolio as 'real assets' will be buying into more than this. Specifically, they may be buying oil or gas royalties, or streams of rental payments. Effectively they are just buying future cashflows at discounted present values. This is an area in which US endowments (not just Yale – the University of Rochester, for example, was doing it over 25 years ago) have led the way, but it is a specialist area and while I mention it here for the sake of completeness I do not intend to discuss it in any detail. Similarly, forestry, which some investors may be surprised to hear, was once viewed by some as a competitor to private equity.

---

[1] All numbers from the WM Annual Review, 2004.

INVESTING IN PROPERTY
(REAL ESTATE) DIRECTLY

Property lives in its own little eco-system of legal requirements and practical and technical issues, and for this reason expert guidance will clearly be essential to any successful property investment and management programme. Most modern legal systems draw a distinction between 'real' and 'personal' property. Real property is freehold land out of which other (lesser) interests may be created. The owner of a freehold may grant a 999-year lease to somebody who may in turn grant a lease of 99 years (or 1 year, or 999 years less one day) to somebody else, and so on. All these leases, regardless of their length, are personal property strictly speaking although a long lease is in many respects difficult to distinguish from a freehold, and in most countries leases of more than a certain length (and third party interests in respect of them) are capable of registration.

Direct investment in property is divided both by geography and by sector.

Geography

The typical investor will favour the property market in his or her own country. This makes sense from the point of view of both avoiding unnecessary currency risk and general familiarity with local conditions. Surprisingly little cross-border property investment goes on compared to other asset classes, although very large investors may have exposure to two or more markets (the UK and the USA, for example). It is also worth bearing in mind that some markets are inaccessible for legal reasons (in the UAE, for example, foreign nationals may not own property, so Dubai and Abu Dhabi are currently off the radar screen – although this is rumoured to be due for a change, driven by a huge explosion of residential property development in Dubai).

Special mention should be made of Central Europe (how quickly nomenclature changes – until recently these countries were referred to as Eastern Europe) where investors have been sniffing around for bargains for the last decade or so. These include some of the earliest private institutional property funds, together with some US-based funds that could be described as operating more like hedge funds, seeking opportunities to buy and hold undervalued property, often on a fairly short-term basis.

Asia has also featured as a possible destination for European and American property investment dollars (there is at least one REIT which specialises in the Hong Kong office market, for example) but such exposure is not for the faint-hearted as Asian property markets generally have exhibited much higher levels of volatility than their western counterparts.

Property investment will be driven by the same issues in any country, but the local market conditions will obviously fluctuate against each other. In a sense, this does not really matter very much since most investors will as a matter of practice already have allocated their property exposure to their own home market. Also, of course, property assets cannot be traded and swapped at very short notice to take advantage of different market conditions around the world in the same way that a trader or arbitrageur may seek to do with, say, quoted securities or derivatives. In fact, by the time you realise that a trend is occurring in a property market, it is probably too late to take advantage of it anyway.

There is generally reckoned to be a natural cycle of property development for new investment based on the swings of supply and demand, and with many developments being planned three years in advance, the potential for a repeated self-fuelled 'boom and bust' pattern is clearly present. In fact, given these uncertainties (depending upon things as intangible as, say, the level of corporate mergers and acquisitions (M&A) activity in any one year) it is perhaps surprising that most of the major property markets around the world have exhibited such robust returns as they have.

It is clearly impossible in the scope of a single chapter to attempt a review of all the world's major property markets. I have accordingly chosen the UK property market as my example, but most of my comments will apply *pari passu* to the property market in any investor's home country.

Sector

The three main sectors are *Commercial, Retail* and *Industrial and Residential*.

Commercial property comprises office accommodation, and institutional investment grade offices will usually be found in upmarket city centre locations (Mayfair in London would be a good example). The general impression of what comprises institutional investment grade property is nowhere formally defined, but is widely understood and accepted (a British judge once said that you cannot define an elephant but you recognise one when you see it) and very little falls outside these areas. For example, in London it is only really the West End, Mayfair, the City, Midtown (the area between the West End and the City) and Docklands. Other areas are sometimes contemptuously dismissed as 'commercial tat' and would certainly not be found in pension fund portfolios.

The main reason for this is not snobbishness but what is referred to as 'the tenant's covenant' or even just 'the covenant'. Confusingly, this can mean, in legal terms, the individual obligations that the tenant is required to perform under the terms of the lease (e.g. a covenant to repair, or to pay rent), but in investment terms it means the financial quality of the tenant, and how likely they are to pay rent promptly and not get into financial difficulty. Property agents or managers will often talk of a 'strong covenant' or a 'good covenant'. Thus, while there is nothing wrong from an investment point of view with owning an office over a sweet shop in some obscure part of town, this would definitely not attract the sort of tenant whose covenant would be acceptable for institutional purposes.

In the UK, average commercial lease lengths are becoming progressively shorter (now only about 13 years compared with over 18 years a decade ago[2]), so that from a security of income point of view the market might be seen as less attractive than it once was, but prime London commercial property will probably always remain the backbone of the UK pension fund property portfolio. Apart from any other consideration, London consistently figures at the top of any poll for location of choice for the European office of global companies.

Investors will often develop a site in conjunction with a development and/or construction company. Depending on the terms agreed, the investor will usually end up with the freehold, but occasionally this will stay with the developer and the investor will instead be granted a (very) long lease. Large professional property managers are adept at arranging this sort of transaction. While many pension funds and insurance companies are active in these joint ventures, the transaction should really be seen as a means to an end (owning a brand new high-grade investment property), since in many cases there may be a shortage of these on the open market.

---

[2] ING Research.

Retail property, as the name suggests, comprises shop properties. The covenant here is the main stumbling block for institutional investors (in fact, most institutional investment occurs in the commercial space for this reason) but large new shopping centres can and do form part of their portfolios. Again, 'new build' deals may well be entered into in conjunction with a developer, and/or a large retail company, who will be the anchor tenant. For obvious practical reasons such developments will rarely be in city centre locations while some of them are 'out of town' altogether, perhaps by a particular motorway junction, for example.

Industrial property was traditionally factory property but given the decline of the UK's manufacturing base, and its concentration in areas with traditionally low property values, there is little of interest here today for the institutional investor. However, some attention has focused on the 'light industrial' sector which usually consists of large modular warehouse type premises. Some of this constitutes a sort of hybrid sector with retail as it may include one or more discount warehouse. An exciting growth area in recent years has been the need for large enclosed spaces by businesses in the field of logistics, driven partly by the rise in 'just in time' manufacturing and assembly processes, partly by a growth in outsourcing and partly by online shopping.

Residential property has generally not been part of the investment plans of large institutions, although in the UK some investors, such as the Church Commissioners and Eton College, have large residential freehold holdings for historical reasons. This does differ a little in other parts of the world, where high-quality residential developments may be considered, but given the traditional leaning towards home ownership rather than home rental in the UK (home rental tends to be a transitory state, with few tenants staying longer than a year or two) I do not feel we need discuss this further.

Recent years have also seen increasing diversification into specialist areas such as leisure centres, marinas and hotels as institutions become bolder (and, a cynic would argue, competition increases for more mainstream sectors). These new areas are really sectors with their own specialist professionals, who often have operating experience within the sector itself, i.e. a hotel investment specialist will often have been a general manager of a five-star hotel at some stage.

INVESTING IN PROPERTY INDIRECTLY

The investor has three main choices: quoted property companies, specialist quoted vehicles and private institutional funds.

Quoted Property Companies

The problem with the shares of most quoted property companies (in the UK, at least) is that they are not really a proxy for holding property itself. Most of the so-called 'property' companies are actually house-builders, or perform other sorts of building and development activity. While they do hold a land-bank for future development, their share price can often be driven as much by their level of development activity as by the analysts' views of the property market. It is also the case, of course, that these are quoted equities and will therefore duplicate exposure that the investor will already have through his or her quoted portfolio, which is not good news for correlation.

There is also the fact that these companies pay tax on the same basis as any other business, which is very disadvantageous to a tax-exempt investor, such as a pension fund, and is one reason why the shares of most quoted property companies trade at a discount to Net Asset Value. What is required is a vehicle which is tax neutral (i.e. where tax is collected from the individual investor rather than from the vehicle itself – sometimes called tax transparency) but if what you are looking for is a UK quoted tax-neutral vehicle through which to invest in UK property, then I am afraid you are in for a long and fruitless search.

Specialist Quoted Vehicles

Investors in the USA have for a considerable time been able to invest in REITs (Real Estate Investment Trusts) which can offer a good proxy for holding property directly. These are available to both retail and institutional investors and frequently have some sort of specialty coverage, whether by geography, sector, or both. Apart from the USA, REITs have also been a significant feature of the investment landscape in places such as Australia, Singapore and Japan. The lack of something similar in the UK has been a glaring omission for many years, due mainly to the Treasury's reluctance to allow property investors the sort of tax breaks that investment trusts traditionally enjoy, but a consultation document was issued on the back of the 2004 budget which purported to desire 'a savings and investment vehicle that would provide a liquid market in property investment'. It is as yet unclear exactly where this process is going to end up; what Government gives with one hand it traditionally takes away with the other and there is a rumour that the Treasury does not want the overall tax yield to fall, and may impose an initial 'conversion charge' that would presumably be calculated with reference to the tax that would otherwise have been payable in the future. Interestingly, the French seem well ahead here, with property companies being offered a substantial tax discount as an incentive to convert into SIICs (the French equivalent of REITs).

Be that as it may, there is currently no REIT option available in the UK. The reason I have spent some time discussing it, however, is that at the time of the 2005 budget the Government announced its intention of bringing in legislation creating UK REITs some time in 2006, so by the time this book is published the REIT option may actually be available in the UK, or at least imminent.

The tax treatment finally decided upon will clearly be crucial (perhaps ominously, there does not appear to be any mention of tax transparency in the Government's utterances) and swingeing conversion charges would be prohibitive and probably kill the idea stone dead for many potential participants, but if the Government does actually get something right for once then a REIT programme would offer an attractive alternative (or complement) to direct property investment.

Concerns might focus on the Government's previously expressed intentions that any such vehicle should be used to boost the residential property sector, although they do now seem to be saying that a REIT could invest at least partly in commercial property. Other concerns might be how such vehicles might perform on a cost-adjusted basis, and whether a sudden influx of money from new investors could drive up property prices (and drive down rental yields) in the UK property market generally.

A more viable option presently in use by pension funds is the Property Unit Trust (PUT). While this is not actually 'listed' in the strict legal sense of the word, for practical purposes it is listed and regarded as liquid. The distinction may be subtle, but is nonetheless important. Like any other form of unit trust, it is not possible to buy and sell units on the open market (although see below) but prices are quoted on a daily basis at which the unit trust manager is prepared to issue and redeem units. Most PUTs invest directly in property, but some have fund of fund characteristics, investing in other property vehicles.

PUTs can be classified into (1) authorised and unauthorised and (2) offshore and onshore. A PUT must be authorised to be offered to retail investors, but this obviously does not affect institutional investors. The vital distinction is that an authorised PUT must be onshore, and both the PUT and its manager are regulated by the FSA. An unauthorised PUT may be offshore (thus providing a completely tax-neutral vehicle for the tax-exempt investor) and while its manager will be regulated, the PUT itself will not.

There are a couple of caveats to this brief general description. Firstly, it is now possible for authorised PUTs to become formally 'listed', although none has sought to do so to date. Secondly, a secondary market is developing to facilitate the sale and purchase of units from one investor to another. This was originally operated by some managers themselves, but HSBC have recently offered a matched bargain service and it seems likely that others will follow. If the history of private equity is anything to go by, this is a market that could grow rapidly. Already the value of units placed in the secondary market is more than three times the value of those redeemed in the primary market.[3]

Quarterly performance figures are available for the sector as a whole, but as yet are nowhere near as sophisticated as those in respect of, for example, private equity. At present they represent little more than a quarterly percentage yield, and the exact basis on which this is calculated is unclear (there can be considerable costs associated with redemption, for example, particularly of a large holding). It is also surprising that there are currently so few funds, or at least, so few funds covered by the available figures (only about 30) in what one would imagine to be an attractive sector both in and of itself and also for institutions looking to 'park' unutilised property allocation. Compare this to private equity, where there are a few hundred, or hedge funds where there are several thousand.

The figures do show, unsurprisingly, that there can be a large gap between the top and the bottom (the yield of the top performing fund can be double that of the worst) which is at first blush surprising in what would seem to be a fairly generic market, and this I think is a major drawback under the present approach since it means that, as with private equity and hedge funds, manager selection will make a dramatic difference to the returns achieved. I say 'under the present approach' because this would strongly suggest that unless one is making a sig-

---

[3] All numbers from the Association of Property Unit Trusts.

nificant allocation to this sector of, say, at least 10% of the total portfolio, then one is not going to be able to afford an in-house specialist with the expertise to select the right ones consistently.

A more attractive option would be to be able to invest in a property derivative, such as an index fund, and this option is being explored with increasing interest. While it is not currently possible to do exactly this, a number of derivative contracts were set up at the beginning of 2005 based on the IPD indices. By buying and selling contracts, investors should be able to duplicate the cash returns generated by the underlying index. This development is yet in its infancy, but is an interesting one and deserves to succeed. It is likely that increasingly sophisticated instruments will become available, and that their progress may be at the expense of vehicles such as PUTs, but time will tell.

However, in the light of these comments it is only fair to record that the PUT sector continues to grow rapidly in popularity. According to the Association of Property Unit Trusts, over £200 million was raised from new investors in the first three quarters of 2005 alone.

Private Institutional Funds (Limited Partnerships)

The third possible form that indirect property investment might take is a private institutional fund, usually a Limited Partnership, since this is a vehicle with which most investors are already familiar from other asset classes, and is tax transparent, thus being of particular benefit to investors who are tax exempt in their own country. There has been a growing trend of late to refer to this as Private Equity in Real Estate, or 'PERA', particularly in the United States. Personally I deplore this epithet since there is in fact no resemblance to private equity apart from the type of vehicle being employed, and the use of such a term can only serve to confuse the uninitiated.

However, to confuse matters still further, a number of property portfolios have been sold recently by German vendors to UK and US investors who either are private equity firms or are closely related to them; the first such transaction, the sale of over 100 000 railway-owned homes, took place as long ago as 2000. I do not intend to consider this development in detail, since it lies beyond the scope of this book (and in any event the area of overlap is as yet so small in terms of monetary value that we may safely regard it as being *de minimis*). However, coming as it does at the same time as talk of buy-out and hedge funds co-investing, it could point the way to a much closer interaction between our three 'alternative' asset classes, which could make it more difficult both to stick rigidly to preset allocations and also to achieve the level of correlation required.

Naturally these private institutional funds will have higher fee levels than a REIT-type vehicle and one might ask why any investor should want to incur this extra cost. The answer is once again that there is a price for liquidity and, although there is no firm evidence on this since real estate Limited Partnerships are a fairly recent innovation among institutional investors (at least, outside the USA), the hearsay that has come my way seems to suggest that investors are expecting a significantly higher return from such vehicles, even on a cost-adjusted basis.

One possible reason for this is that the managers of such funds are happy, where appropriate, to take on high levels of debt, even to buy-out-type levels of gearing. This is of course a relatively easy matter when one has property assets against which to secure such borrowing. By contrast, many institutional investors who invest directly in property do so on an entirely unleveraged basis (we will discuss this further below) and it is as yet unclear what levels of debt a REIT-type vehicle will be allowed in the UK. Thus, a private institutional fund offers the advantage of being able to leverage a property portfolio but on a non-recourse basis, since the debt will usually be ring-fenced within the fund by separate companies in just the same way as in a buy-out fund.

WHAT PERFORMANCE BENCHMARKS SHOULD WE USE?

Many property managers and investment houses produce their own data on property investment performance but, unlike hedge funds, for example, there is usually broad agreement. I have chosen to use the Investment Property Databank (IPD), which is widely used as an industry standard and has been kindly provided by IPD for the purposes of this book. There is a wide range of data available covering all sorts of different geographic markets, but for the reasons stated above I have decided to restrict myself to considering the UK market.

What Level of Correlation Exists with Quoted Equity Returns?

We must be very sure that we are comparing apples with apples. When measuring correlation of returns, including those for public markets, we have been taking the total return, i.e. both the index return and the dividend yield. We will do the same thing for property returns, adding the rental yield to the capital gain to arrive at a total return. The resulting figures can be seen in Table 9.1.

You will see that the correlation between the two series of data is only 14.8%. This is great news, as it means that UK property has passed the first test on the way to becoming one of our asset classes. In fact, as you will see from Table A1.3 in Appendix 1, UK property exhibits very little correlation with any of our potential asset classes, making it by far the most attractive from this point of view; for example, it is almost perfectly uncorrelated with the NASDAQ (only 1% correlation). It does show 40% against the DAX, although this difference may be partly a function of having to calculate the latter over a shorter time period because of the currently late development of DAX data in its present form (i.e. from 1991 rather than 1984).

What Levels of Return Risk and Capital Risk does UK Property Exhibit?

As we have done with our other classes, we need to convert our annual total return figures into vintage year returns.

Table 9.2 shows that property more than satisfies our possible return requirements. In fact, it looks as if it could be second only to private equity in terms of attractiveness. There is an 88% probability that it will return at least 9% compound return over time, and three chances in four that it will achieve at least 10%. You have to push the target return up above 11% before a return risk of 50% is encountered.

As for capital risk, it is the lowest of any of our asset classes; so low, in fact, that it is incapable of calculation. The normal distribution function indicates a probability of 100% that no capital loss can be expected.

Let us put this against the FTSE 100 return risk and capital risk figures by way of comparison (see Table 9.3). This looks like a massive difference; UK property has three chances in four of achieving at least 10% compound while the FTSE index has only one chance in four.

Let us move to the next stage and run the calculations again on a weighted vintage year basis (see Table 9.4). The weighted vintage calculations are of course the acid test, since this is what gives us our definitive figures for return risk. Just look at the difference between the two asset classes! Once you get up to around 12% target rate of return there is little difference, but below that number there is a dramatic gap. For example, there is a 93% probability that UK property will return

Table 9.1 Correlation of UK property total return and FTSE 100 total return

	1985	1986	1987	1988	1989	1990	1991	1992	1993	1994
Property income yield (%)	6.34	6.43	6.22	5.64	5.32	6.15	7.75	8.64	8.98	7.70
Property capital gain (%)	1.86	4.57	18.70	22.72	9.60	-13.78	-10.13	-9.53	10.36	3.90
Property total return (%)	8.19	11.00	24.92	28.35	14.92	-7.63	-2.38	-0.88	19.34	11.60
FTSE dividend yield (%)	4.45	4.17	4.57	5.03	4.2	5.46	4.88	4.21	3.56	4.21
FTSE index gain (%)	14.78	18.83	2.03	4.67	35.14	-11.51	16.28	14.20	20.06	-10.30
FTSE total return (%)	19.23	23.00	6.60	9.70	39.34	-6.05	21.16	18.41	23.62	-6.09
Correlation	14.8%									

	1995	1996	1997	1998	1999	2000	2001	2002	2003	2004
Property income yield (%)	7.76	7.95	7.60	7.04	6.81	6.68	6.72	6.87	6.75	6.28
Property capital gain (%)	-3.90	1.94	8.57	4.44	7.23	3.55	0.06	2.61	3.86	11.40
Property total return (%)	3.86	9.89	16.17	11.48	14.05	10.24	6.79	9.47	10.62	17.68
FTSE dividend yield (%)	3.9	3.88	3.16	2.37	2.04	2.18	2.59	3.55	3.2	3.16
FTSE index gain (%)	20.32	11.66	24.69	14.54	17.80	-10.20	-16.17	-24.48	13.63	7.53
FTSE total return (%)	24.22	15.54	27.85	16.91	19.84	-8.02	-13.58	-20.93	16.83	10.69
Correlation										

Table 9.2 Return risk of UK property total return vintage year performance

	1984	1985	1986	1987	1988	1989	1990	1991	1992	1993	1994
Vintage year (%)	10.47	10.56	10.69	10.67	9.88	8.82	8.43	9.68	10.66	11.68	11.01
Mean	11.26%										
Standard deviation	1.91%										
Return risk at	8%	9%	10%	11%	12%						
	0.3%	12.0%	25.5%	44.4%	65%						
Capital risk	Nil										

	1995	1996	1997	1998	1999	2000	2001	2002	2003	2004
Vintage year (%)	10.95	11.77	12.01	11.43	11.42	10.90	11.07	12.53	14.09	17.68
Mean										
Standard deviation										
Return risk at										
Capital risk										

Table 9.3   Return risk of UK property versus FTSE 100

Return risk at	8%	9%	10%	11%	12%
UK property	0.3%	12.0%	25.5%	44.4%	65.0%
FTSE 100	64.0%	71.2%	77.6%	83.2%	87.7%

Table 9.4   Return risk of UK property versus FTSE 100 on a weighted vintage year return basis

Return risk at	8%	9%	10%	11%	12%
UK property	1.1%	7.2%	27.1%	59.5%	86.0%
FTSE 100	55.5%	65.9%	75.1%	82.9%	88.9%

9% over a long period, but only a 34% probability that the FTSE can do likewise.

These results really are very dramatic. Apart from anything else, they show that once again the theoreticians have got it wrong and that rather than property being a riskier asset class than quoted equities, the contrary is true. When we run the calculations in our final chapter, we will see that pension funds would have been much better off investing in UK property than in UK quoted equities. Yet their consultants advised them to do exactly the opposite. Perhaps nowhere are the short-comings of the traditional risk model, and its adherents, more amply demonstrated.

HOW HAVE RETURNS VARIED BY SECTOR?

Table 9.5 shows the total annual return numbers broken out by sector. One point that struck me straight away about these figures is that they do not bear out the doom and gloom that is often transmitted by institutional investors about the UK property market. One hears of long periods of negative returns, with property values plummeting, but the reality appears to be different. In common with the other asset classes we are considering, there is no period of negative returns of more than three years. The worst such period occurs in the commercial sector between 1990 and 1992, but even then I calculate that only about 25% of the portfolio value would have been lost.

Table 9.5 UK property: total returns by sector

	All property (%)	Retail (%)	Commercial (%)	Industrial (%)
1984	8.8	13.8	6.9	6.0
1985	8.3	12.7	7.7	3.5
1986	11.3	11.7	12.1	9.2
1987	26.0	20.8	30.7	25.1
1988	29.5	24.8	31.1	39.3
1989	15.4	9.9	16.5	28.7
1990	−8.4	−8.2	−9.9	−3.5
1991	−3.1	3.4	−10.8	9.1
1992	−1.6	3.6	−7.2	1.4
1993	20.2	20.7	19.3	21.2
1994	11.9	12.9	10.7	11.8
1995	3.6	4.1	3.0	2.8
1996	10.0	11.8	7.5	10.3
1997	16.8	18.5	14.5	16.4
1998	11.8	11.6	11.6	13.2
1999	14.5	13.9	14.3	17.5
2000	10.5	6.7	15.4	13.6
2001	6.8	5.6	7.7	8.3
2002	9.6	14.0	3.3	10.7
2003	10.9	15.5	3.2	11.2
2004	18.3	20.5	15.2	16.9

Source: All figures supplied by and reproduced by kind permission of IPD.

By contrast, during the three years from 2000 to 2002 a portfolio wholly dependent upon the total return of the FTSE 100 (the most likely alternative use of funds for a sterling investor and allegedly a less 'risky' investment) would have lost 29% of its value. Five years later (i.e. after two more years) the compounded value generated by the FTSE total return stood at 91.6% of its pre-fall value; in other words, you would have lost 8.4% of value over five years before even considering the effects of inflation. Five years later the value generated by the total return of UK property had recovered to stand at 98.5% of the pre-fall amount.

Thus even if one looks at the most protracted period of negative returns, and the sector most badly affected (whereas in fairness we should probably be using the figures for 'all property'), UK property seems to exhibit less volatility of return than UK quoted equities. But isn't volatility of return supposed to be the same thing as risk as far as the traditionalists are concerned? If so, why are they recommending that one should invest most of one's portfolio in an asset class that is

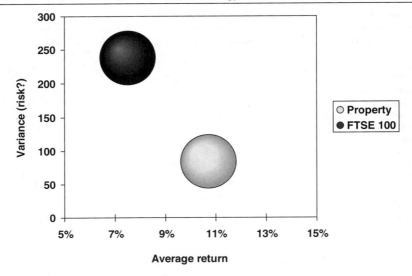

Figure 9.1   UK property and UK equities: variance versus return

higher risk, but generating lower returns? The variance of the property total return over a 20-year period is about 84. That of the FTSE 100 total return for the same period is about 238 – nearly three times as high. The weighted average vintage year return on property is 10.7%; the weighted average vintage year return for the FTSE 100 is 7.5%.

Can you spot the deliberate mistake in Figure 9.1?

Actually there isn't one. The only mistake has been made by those investors who have avoided property, and other so-called alternative asset classes, in favour of massive overexposure to quoted equities, and by those who have advised them to do so. This is yet another piece of glaring evidence that the traditional risk model may be fine in the artificial confines of the lecture room, but simply does not work in the real world. If one constructs a 'market portfolio' consisting of 50% property and 50% FTSE (total returns in each case), then property has a beta of 0.51 while the FTSE has a beta of 1.39.

Remember this formula for the Capital Asset Pricing Model?

$$\text{Expected } r_a = r_f + \beta(\text{Expected } r_m - r_f)$$

where r_f is the risk-free rate. Thus, if we assume a risk-free rate of, say, 5.5%, and calculate the average annual return of the market portfolio as 11.4%, the CAPM would calculate the expected returns of each asset class as follows:

$$r(\text{Property}) = 5.5\% + 0.51(11.4\% - 5.5\%)$$
$$= 8.5\%$$

$$r(\text{FTSE}) = 5.5\% + 1.39(11.4\% - 5.5\%$$
$$= 13.7\%$$

If we now look back to our risk return calculations, there is a 97% chance that property will achieve the predicted return compounded over a long period, which clearly means that it is much too low. There is, however, more than a 95% chance that the FTSE will *not* achieve the return predicted by the CAPM, which clearly means that it is much too high. Of course, we are using vintage year returns while the CAPM is using annual returns, but these very stark figures only serve to underline exactly why any investor should be concerned with the former rather than the latter.

However, even if we analyse the annual returns of each asset class, there is a 46% chance that the FTSE will hit its predicted number in any one year, but there is a 60% chance that property will. Why should this be if the beta of an asset class represents all its risk, and this can be precisely calculated? Surely one would expect both figures to be the same? The answer is quite simple. Beta is simply not a very good way of predicting likely returns in the real world, and, even if it were, it operates only on annual returns, which are largely irrelevant. Mean variance analysis, such as the phi calculations we have been using throughout the book, offer a much more reliable method since they look purely at the returns of the asset class itself. In addition, by applying this to compound rather than annual returns one can both increase dramatically the level of statistical comfort, and give the investors answers to the practical questions that actually concern them in the real world.

CAN PROPERTY RETURNS BE IMPROVED BY LEVERAGE?

One characteristic of the direct property portfolios of institutional investors is that they are unleveraged. This has always struck me as slightly strange since, given its legal characteristics, property is the asset class that lends itself most readily to the granting of security, and thus to the extension of debt facilities on favourable terms. Given that the individuals making the investment decisions within institutions, such as pension funds, will almost certainly be tolerating high levels of debt secured on their own home (presumably their most precious possession) then their reluctance to incur borrowing in their professional lives is perhaps difficult fully to understand.

Given that it is the UK property market that we have chosen to consider in detail, it would be wrong not to mention in this context the 'buy to let' market, which has become such a large part of the investment plans of many private individuals. The basic concept is simple. You buy a property (usually an apartment in a residential area), which you purchase partly with debt secured by a mortgage on the property. Typical loan to value figures are about 70%, since this is about the amount that most lenders are officially prepared to countenance for rental properties, although one hears anecdotal evidence of borrowers being geared as high as 95%. If such high ratios really exist, however, they could place one in severe difficulty, since the idea is to have the loan interest and repayments covered by the rental income, and it is currently difficult to obtain net rental yields (i.e. net of agent's fees, etc.) of much more than 5%.

It may seem slightly strange to mention this phenomenon in a book that is aimed exclusively at institutional investment, but it does point out an important principle which ought, at the very least, to be examined by every institutional investor, if only so that they can happily reject it knowing that they have given every possible alternative due consideration. The idea, simply put, is to give up the income yield on an asset in the hope and/or expectation of being rewarded at the end of the holding period with a much higher capital gain than would otherwise have been the case. Clearly, the whole reason why debt financing is known as either gearing or leverage in different parts of the world is this very quality: the ability to ratchet capital gains up to an exponential level (not forgetting the concomitant ability to ratchet losses up to an exponential level).

In fact, while this undoubtedly explains the basic concept behind 'buy to let' in terms of strict investment theory, it overlooks two important practical considerations. The first is that individual investors are taxpayers and that in most circumstances the rental income produced by a property can be offset against the interest payments (but not repayments of capital) due on the loan. Since most 'buy to let' investors will be paying higher rate income tax (currently 40% in the UK) then this makes a huge difference, since after paying tax on the rental yield it would be struggling even to keep pace with inflation. Most investment institutions, and particularly pension funds, are tax exempt and can therefore take the whole value of the rental yield. Therefore, for the leverage to make sense on a tax-adjusted basis is clearly not the same thing as the leverage making sense on a tax-free basis.

Secondly, the people who are going into this sort of investment have no option but to borrow since (in the overwhelming majority of cases) they do not have the necessary capital resources to be able to buy the investment property on a debt-free basis. Thus, the expectation of capital gain is really no more than making (or hoping for) virtue out of necessity. An institution is different. An institution has a choice between incurring borrowing or not. A rational institution will wish to deploy its capital in the most efficient manner possible. It is therefore required at the very least to conduct a feasibility study into whether its property portfolio should be geared and, if so, to what sort of level.

You will remember that we conducted a similar exercise when looking at quoted securities. Again, that thought was prompted by happenings in the retail investment sector since margin lending has always been available to private investors in publicly quoted securities in the USA (though not in the UK, which is another reason for the popularity of 'buy to let' – in the UK it offers probably the only realistic chance for private individuals to invest on a leveraged basis). However, I think that different considerations apply when we turn to look at property.

The sensitivities of lender and borrower alike will focus on loan to value ratios (sometimes called 'asset cover') and income to interest ratios (usually called either 'interest cover' or 'debt service'). However, differences arise from the nature of the assets involved.

Security over property assets can be legally registered (as a fixed charge or mortgage) against those specific assets and there are clear and well established procedures for its enforcement. Without going into excessive detail, this is not really the case with shares (or bonds for that matter). A fixed charge is not usually available (at least, not over the specific assets which comprise the share portfolio, although it might be granted over assets by way of collateral), and there is usually no equivalent of registering the interest of the lender over the legal title to the shares. In most jurisdictions the task of documenting title to securities lies with the issuing company, and while they are generally required to maintain a register of charges over their own assets, this does not extend to third-party interests over the assets of others (i.e. the shareholders). Security over any portfolio of shares (stocks) is therefore a matter of legal agreement between the parties, and usually the subject of lengthy and complex documentation.

The other main difference lies in what might be termed 'the covenant' in property management terms. By this I mean both the financial quality of future cashflows representing the anticipated income yield, and the volatility of the value of the underlying capital asset.

Both a share and a property can produce cashflows. A share will commonly (except in the case of high-growth companies which require all their available capital to finance that continued growth) produce a stream of dividend income while a property will produce a stream of rental income. Consider the nature of these income streams, however. A company may choose whether to pay a dividend or not. In extreme circumstances it may not be able to pay a dividend for some years. A tenant may not choose whether to pay rent; the tenant has no choice but to pay rent. Of course, a tenant may become financially incapable of honouring its rental commitments under the lease, but in practice a new tenant can usually be found within a reasonable time and the landlord will be holding security (usually in the form of a year's rent, or equivalent bank guarantee) to tide it over until that happens. Thus, in practical terms, there is very little chance of the rental stream being interrupted for very long (if at all).

The natures of the capital values involved are also very different. Yes, at the end of the day any asset, whether it be a company share or an office block, is only worth what someone is prepared to pay for it in the open market, so in that strict sense both assets' values are subject to the vagaries of the market. However, the office block has an intrinsic value of its own, whereas a company share really does not. At the end of the day the office block must at least be worth the land on which it stands, or the net present value of the rental stream it can be expected to produce. A company share has no intrinsic value. If the company fails, perhaps as a result of, or accompanied by, some previously unsuspected accounting scandal, then the share becomes worthless, apart from any possible residual liquidation value in the company's assets. If the company gets into difficulty it might decide upon a share split or a loan swap, in both of which cases the value of the share can be dramatically reduced overnight. There are other possibilities, but no doubt you get the idea.

What does all this mean? It is reasonable to assume that, both for the borrower and the lender, property is a much more attractive class to subject to leverage than are quoted equities. Property may suffer the vagaries of the market from time to time in terms of its perceived capital value, yet the rational expectation is that it will increase in value steadily over time (if only because of the effect of inflation) even if the precise level and timing of that rise cannot be accurately predicted. Why else would mortgage lenders be prepared to lend such high proportions of the value of people's homes – up to 100% in certain cases? Thus, a lender should be much more relaxed about a temporary fall in the property market than about a fall in the price of a share, or in the value of a share portfolio. We have seen that this is in fact borne out in practice. In our analysis above we found that property returns have been more robust, and that the total return from UK property has the ability to claw back losses more quickly than the equivalent total return of the FTSE 100 index.

This has important practical considerations. If both borrower and lender alike can have a reasonable expectation that property values will increase over time, then long-term loan commitments can be entered into (say over 10 or even 20 years) with neither party needing to get particularly excited if the loan to value ratio should rise from time to time, particularly if the loan interest is more or less fully covered by the rental yield. The same is not true of quoted shares. Here a short-term price fall is likely to be viewed with much more concern and the borrower might face a call for more cash (a margin call) or security to cover the debt. In the former example the lender can feel fully protected, provided that the loan is granted as a prudent loan to value ratio in the first place, and the borrower can plan his or her cashflows over a long period. In the latter case, the borrower cannot. That is not to say that leveraging an equity portfolio is not practically possible, or that it could never make sense in investment terms; it is simply less attractive a proposition from all points of view than leveraging a property portfolio.

Analysing the Possible Effect of Leverage on a Property Portfolio

The workings here are fairly straightforward and are set out in Table 9.6. I have taken the total return for the UK property market broken down into the capital gain and the rental yield for each respective year. We can now model the effect of a very prudent level of debt on this portfolio (30% of each year's starting value) assuming an interest rate

Table 9.6 Modelling the effect of 30% leverage on a UK property portfolio (ignoring the effect of taxation)

	1984	1985	1986	1987	1988	1989	1990	1991	1992	1993	1994
Capital gain (%)	2.53	1.86	4.57	18.70	22.72	9.60	-13.78	-10.13	-9.53	10.36	3.90
Rental yield (%)	6.16	6.34	6.43	6.22	5.64	5.32	6.15	7.75	8.64	8.98	7.70
Total return (%)	8.69	8.19	11.00	24.92	28.35	14.92	-7.63	-2.38	-0.88	19.34	11.60
Leveraged return (%)	5.84	5.15	8.17	25.43	30.37	13.60	-15.06	-7.51	-7.04	20.04	10.97

	1995	1996	1997	1998	1999	2000	2001	2002	2003	2004
Capital gain (%)	-3.90	1.94	8.57	4.44	7.23	3.55	0.06	2.61	3.86	11.40
Rental yield (%)	7.76	7.95	7.60	7.04	6.81	6.68	6.72	6.87	6.75	6.28
Total return (%)	3.86	9.89	16.17	11.48	14.05	10.24	6.79	9.47	10.62	17.68
Leveraged return (%)	-0.01	8.37	16.34	10.11	14.42	8.90	4.70	8.76	10.27	19.60

Source: All property return figures supplied by and reproduced by kind permission of IPD.

of LIBOR plus 1%. The resulting leveraged annual return is then contrasted with the unleveraged annual return (total return).

I was intending to go on to model the same figures on a vintage year basis but, as you can see, this will not be necessary. One of the most satisfying things I have encountered while preparing the analysis that lies behind this book is the sensation of having had a strong preconception completely disproved, and that is the case here. Contrary to all my initial instincts, a leveraged property portfolio would have produced lower returns than an unleveraged one; there are very few years in which the leveraged return outperforms.

Having said this, there are a number of strong caveats to bear in mind. Firstly, a statement that interest rates in the UK were at much higher rates during the 1980s than now seems justified by other factors such as the rate of inflation measured on an RPI basis. This was because monetarist economic policies were being pursued by the government of the day (the Thatcher administration), attempting to squeeze the amount of money in circulation by discouraging borrowing. However, even in recent years, in a low interest environment, the leveraged option continues to look unattractive.

Secondly, I must stress yet again that these calculations are on a tax-free basis. If one subjects the rental yield to 40% notional tax, then the situation changes. This is because the arithmetic of the process is quite straightforward. For the leverage to make sense, the capital gain has to exceed the rental yield by more than the amount of the interest being paid. In the event, the rental yield has been a very important part of the total return over the period under review; the arithmetic has worked in only six of the years under review, and in only two of those six cases has it made any appreciable difference. Strip out the notional tax, however, and there are 14 years that would be favourable. These figures are shown in Table 9.7.

The message, therefore, seems to be that for a tax-exempt investor leverage is probably not a good idea with regard to a UK property portfolio, but that for a taxpayer investor (which will include some institutions such as banks, insurance companies and family offices) the opposite is true. In 11 of the last 12 years (which may be viewed as a more normal interest rate environment compared to earlier years) a leveraged portfolio would have outperformed – and sometimes very significantly so.

That concludes our look at property as an asset class. I am sorry that it is not possible within the confines of this book to look further at what

Table 9.7 Modelling the effect of 30% leverage on a UK property portfolio (assuming notional taxation of rental yield at 40%)

	1984	1985	1986	1987	1988	1989	1990	1991	1992	1993	1994
Tax-free return (%)	8.69	8.19	11.00	24.92	28.35	14.92	−7.63	−2.38	−0.88	19.34	11.60
Leveraged return (%)	5.84	5.15	8.17	25.43	30.37	13.60	−15.06	−7.51	−7.04	20.04	10.97
Positive outcome?	N	N	N	Y	Y	N	N	N	N	Y	N
Tax-adjusted return (%)	6.22	5.66	8.43	22.43	26.10	12.79	−10.09	−5.48	−4.34	15.75	8.52
Leveraged return (%)	5.84	5.15	8.17	25.43	30.37	13.60	−15.06	−7.51	−7.04	20.04	10.97
Positive outcome?	N	N	N	Y	Y	Y	N	N	N	Y	Y

	1995	1996	1997	1998	1999	2000	2001	2002	2003	2004
Tax-free return (%)	3.86	9.89	16.17	11.48	14.05	10.24	6.79	9.47	10.62	17.68
Leveraged return (%)	−0.01	8.37	16.34	10.11	14.42	8.90	4.70	8.76	10.27	19.60
Positive outcome?	N	N	Y	N	Y	N	N	N	N	Y
Tax-adjusted return (%)	0.76	6.71	13.13	8.66	11.32	7.56	4.10	6.73	7.91	15.17
Leveraged return (%)	−0.01	8.37	16.34	10.11	14.42	8.90	4.70	8.76	10.27	19.60
Positive outcome?	N	Y	Y	Y	Y	Y	Y	Y	Y	Y

Source: All property return figures supplied by and reproduced by kind permission of IPD.

is a fascinating subject, but hopefully it will have whetted your appetite to research the subject.

SUMMARY

- Institutions around the world already have significant amounts of capital deployed in property (real estate). In the UK, for example, public pension funds have nearly seven times as much exposure to property than they do to hedge funds and private equity combined.
- Investment takes one of two forms: direct or indirect.
- Direct investment in property (chiefly office blocks) takes place through specialist managers. Development joint ventures can be a fertile source of quality assets for the portfolio.
- Indirect investment can take the form of investing in quoted property companies, but these are not a satisfactory proxy for holding land directly.
- In the USA, but not yet in the UK, Real Estate Investment Trusts offer a realistic and tax sympathetic alternative to holding property directly. Investors in both jurisdictions can take advantage of private institutional funds. This latter option is often referred to misleadingly as Private Equity in (or for) Real Estate, or PERA for short.
- Many institutions use Property Unit Trusts as their predominant form of indirect property investment, but efficient manager selection poses a significant obstacle to optimal performance.
- UK property returns show a very low level of correlation with UK quoted returns (only about 15%), thus making it ideal for inclusion within a model MAC portfolio for a sterling investor.
- When levels of risk return are analysed, UK property is found to be superior to UK quoted equity markets. Given that property returns exhibit much less volatility when measured by portfolio variance than do quoted returns, then the traditional risk model should see it as a much more attractive (lower risk, higher return) option than UK quoted equities. Why, then, does the typical UK pension portfolio have nearly 10 times as much exposure to quoted equities than to property?
- It is an easy matter in practice to arrange leverage of a property portfolio through debt, and investors should be relaxed about

short-term fluctuations in property values provided prudent levels of debt are arranged in the first place – we have used 30% for the purposes of our examples.

- Contrary to my initial instincts, leverage does **NOT** seem to make sense in the context of an institutional property portfolio. This is because rental yield has historically been a very important component of the total return.
- On closer examination, leverage **DOES** seem to make good sense for those investors who are not tax exempt. Using even 30% of leverage would have produced a favourable outcome over an unleveraged portfolio in 11 of the last 12 years.

10

LDI and Portable Alpha: Rival Strategies?

It seems difficult currently to discuss any aspect of asset allocation for institutional investors, particularly pension funds, without stumbling across two concepts that are being marketed energetically by various consultants and investment managers: Liability Driven Investment (LDI) and Portable Alpha. The two are often linked (for example, at conferences) but in reality are quite separate. In fact all they seem to have in common is that they are both being promoted as the answer to all the problems of pension funds in deficit. Let us examine each in turn.

Before we begin, a quick word of apology and explanation. There is an element of repetition about some of what follows since I was obliged to introduce it in a different context when discussing investment strategy. I have tried to keep this to a minimum but in the end there is no alternative but to restate certain matters. I believe this should be preferable for a reader than darting around between chapters and I hope you will grant me your indulgence, particularly since we will be looking at things from a different viewpoint.

LIABILITY DRIVEN INVESTMENT

WHAT IS 'LIABILITY DRIVEN INVESTMENT'?

When I began to sketch out my ideas for this book, the need for a separate chapter featuring Liability Driven Investment (LDI) was not part of my plans. However, over the last year or so this has become a very topical subject, and I have been asked to speak on it several times, chair a two-day conference devoted entirely to the topic, and participate in various investor meetings and roundtable discussion groups. I am aware that this is a topic of particular relevance to the UK, where huge pension deficits exist, but I know that pension funds in other countries (the Netherlands, Sweden, etc.) are also discussing it, and so it will I trust be of general interest to all who are concerned with setting investment strategy.

It has become apparent that, sadly, a fundamental misunderstanding has arisen as to what LDI is and is not. This is particularly important in the context of this book, since it is assumed that a Total Funding approach will be used to calculate the target rate of investment return which is needed in setting a coherent investment strategy, and Total Funding is itself an LDI strategy (and indeed may be said to be quintessentially the only true LDI strategy, properly so called).

Total Funding is liability driven in that it takes the pension plan's potential future liabilities and uses these as the basis for calculating the required investment return, which is in turn used as the basis for asset allocation. The difference between this and the mistaken sense of LDI is deep and dramatic.

Treasury departments the world over routinely seek to meet anticipated outflows in the most effective manner. Frequently this takes the form of **matching** an outflow which is due in, say, nine months time with a bond held for its duration.[1] This is a perfectly proper exercise of the treasury function. They are seeking to take every last little advantage that can be squeezed out of the coupon payable on the bond, and thus keep to the absolute minimum the impact of the outflow on their overall cash position. But they are exercising a treasury function, not making an investment. As we saw in the first chapter, bonds are not a valid investment asset class for a pension fund. They are, however, a valid and appropriate cash substitute when planning how best to cover anticipated short-term liquidity needs. This is not a type of investment, still less is it 'Liability Driven Investment'. It is the exercise of a routine treasury function.

How we very rapidly get into treacherous waters is by confusing this routine treasury (i.e. cash and short-term liquidity management) function with the investment of pension plan assets. They are different in just about every respect. One is essentially short term while the other is necessarily long term in outlook. One is tactical, the other is strategic. One is not an act of investment, whereas the other is. One is concerned with how best to manage immediately foreseeable cash outflows, while the other is concerned with how best to deploy the

---

[1] NB: As will be explained in a subsequent footnote, except in the case of a zero coupon instrument, this is not the same thing as holding a bond to maturity, e.g. its termination date.

plan's assets to achieve the target rate of investment return over a period of many years.

Yet this is a misunderstanding which is so prevalent and has existed for so long that it strikes at the very heart of pension fund investment strategy, and is shared by consultants and trustees alike. It is as if they were wearing blinkers, keeping them focussed on what is immediately in front of them, but blinding them to the wider reality which is all around them. It is impossible for a pension fund in deficit (which in the UK, for example, is sadly typical) to match its liabilities since those liabilities are already effectively out of control, at least under the present approach. In British pension plans today, they will often already represent at least twice the present value of the fund, so how can any arrangement of the fund's assets 'match' them? And, if their investment strategy involves a large allocation to underperforming assets such as bonds, then those liabilities are getting further beyond reach with every year that passes. Thus, surely it should be obvious that any attempt to 'match' liabilities, for example by investing in bonds, can only result in those liabilities actually increasing!

A pension fund exists solely for the purpose of meeting certain future liabilities. Thus the only proper approach for a pension fund's investment strategy is to seek to be able to meet those liabilities in full as they fall due. So far as pension funds are concerned this can logically be the only possible meaning of 'Liability Driven Investment'. The Total Funding Model rests on these principles.

Unfortunately a more pernicious philosophy has been peddled by various pension consultants, and has been allowed to gain credence by precisely those people who could, and should, know better. In order to understand how this has happened, we need to think back to how the present funding situation as a whole has arisen. Let us discuss in more detail the background to this mistaken application of so-called LDI.

THE DIFFERING POSITIONS OF THE PENSION PLAN AND THE EMPLOYER

There are two important strands that run through the fabric of the new pensions world. The first is the need for sponsoring employers (particularly companies) to find a way of properly reflecting in their accounts their obligations towards their pension fund. The second is the need for trustees to find a way of being able to meet their pension obligations in the future, given that they may be able to plan on having only about half the money they require to do so. While the strands are clearly inter-related, it is very important to keep them separate. The failure to do so contains the seeds of the spread of what one might call 'false LDI'.

The first is clearly driven by the financial community within which the company operates, and the need for this is readily understandable. Financial analysts need to be able to fix with as much certainty as possible the financial health of the company. Investors need to be able to value its shares. Shareholders need to be able to predict the type of dividend yield and capital growth they are likely to experience. Suppliers and banks need to be able to assess the type of credit risk they are assuming when dealing with the company. In the new world, the pension fund will typically be the company's largest unsecured creditor, and so, for accounting purposes, it is vital that some way be found of treating this that is both consistent and gives a fair view (the two key requirements of financial accounting measures).

A number of accounting measures have been adopted in different countries to meet this situation, and further draft European standards are currently under discussion. The latest attempt at a solution to this problem in the UK is FRS 17 and perhaps I might take this as an example, although what I have to say is of universal relevance, regardless of whatever the appropriate accounting treatment is referred to in your own country. Let us simply note at this point that, like all accounting treatments of pension liabilities, FRS 17 states what many might believe to be an artificially low figure, since it works by discounting liabilities. There are also questions as to whether it properly takes into account either the rights of future members of a scheme or the future rights of current members.

There is nothing wrong with discounting, and indeed from an accounting point of view discounting pension liabilities is probably the only way to arrive at a true picture. After all, those liabilities do not have to be paid today but at various dates in the future, and in the meantime both inflation and (hopefully) the investment performance of the pension fund will have had an impact on the asset versus liabilities situation. I therefore take no issue with FRS 17 *as an accounting measure*.

In those last four words, however, lies the crux of a huge problem. FRS 17 is just that: an accounting measure. Strictly speaking, it is not even an accounting measure that applies to pension funds, but rather to the companies who sponsor them. It is not a measure of pension liabilities for the purposes of investment strategy within the pension fund. Not only is this not properly understood in practice, but the very fact that FRS 17 uses the bond rate as a discount rate has somehow filtered through into the consciousness of some pension trustees as a belief that if they could only invest their whole portfolio at the bond rate then they would be matching their liabilities!

Trustees who fail to see this, and who feel that they are somehow bound by the view that FRS 17 apparently imposes when analysing their situation and planning their strategy, make a grave mistake. What is required for their purposes is a tool that looks at the true extent of their liabilities and applies this in analysing their financial situation. That tool is the Total Funding Model, not a set of accounting rules.

The need to keep separate these two strands to the present problem point up a fundamental question, which may be crudely expressed as: 'who pays?' The reality of a pension fund deficit is that it is a liability of the sponsoring employer, and, although one may quibble with exactly how it does so, FRS 17 accurately recognises and represents this. However, at this point the questions arise and multiply. Is it really a 'liability' that the company's shareholders recognise as a debt that will eventually have to be paid by the company rather than simply a technical entry that must be carried in the company's accounts? Is it in the shareholders' interests to attempt to reduce that liability as much as possible? If so, how can this be reconciled with the risk of it becoming greater instead? How can this be reconciled with the needs of the finance department and the auditors for certainty? Is there not in fact a fundamental conflict at work that needs to be addressed?

HOW DOES LIABILITY MATCHING HELP?

Liability matching solutions (I will not continue the pretence of such solutions even being able to refer to themselves as liability driven) are aimed at the company's finance director (CFO) and are designed to appeal to a desire for certainty. In many cases, companies have seen their pension fund deficits soaring from year to year, and the CFO will be under great pressure from fellow directors to find a way to stop this happening. One has to sympathise with the CFO in this situation. The fellow directors will probably see the funding deficit as an accounting matter rather than an investment issue. Rather than discussing how the deficit arose in the first place, their concerns will quite properly be directed at running the business, and deciding what can be done about the deficit. Indeed, the pension fund in its totality may be seen as little more than an irrelevance or distraction to their everyday responsibilities. It would be very natural in this situation for the CFO, who has many day-to-day responsibilities other than the pension fund, to turn to the pension consultant and ask for advice on a way to stop the liabilities growing any further. Let us look at how these liability matching 'solutions' operate, and note in passing why they do not even do what they claim.

If you imagine the liabilities of a pension fund as a stream of cash-flows you will see that they represent a huge curve stretching out into the future, whether you represent them as monetary values or, as the Total Funding Model recommends, as a percentage of the starting value of the fund. Typically the liabilities of most reasonably mature funds will peak about 30 to 35 years into the future.

It is important to enter a caveat at this stage as this process will only embrace the three classes of current pension fund member (active, deferred and pensioner). In other words, future members are not considered at all, so unless the scheme in question is closed to new members, this process is inherently artificial. Even if the scheme *is* closed to new members, the process will frequently not take into account the future rights of active members, i.e. their potential entitlement to higher levels of benefit conditional on longer service with the employer.

It is possible to measure the **duration** of these liabilities. Since I would like to keep things as simple as possible for the purposes of this illustration, let us assume that the duration of the liabilities is simply the weighted average time to payment. Typically, the duration of the liabilities of most pension funds will be somewhere between 15 and 20 years.

As we have already seen, the theory of liability matching is nothing more than the matching of the duration of a guaranteed incoming cash-flow (usually represented by a bond) with the timing of an anticipated outgoing cashflow (in this case, the payment of retirement benefits). In its most simple form, the theory would suggest holding a portfolio of bonds, the overall duration of which was exactly the same as the duration of the liabilities.[2]

Obviously a more satisfactory approach would be to match separately each individual liability, or at least those that would occur in the

---

[2] The duration of a zero coupon bond will be the time to its maturity. The duration of an interest-bearing bond is a rather complex matter and there are various measures in existence, of which the best known is Macaulay Duration, which serves as the basis for the calculation of some others.

same time period. However, without going into unnecessary levels of detail, there are technical reasons why neither of these approaches actually works.[3] There are more complex solutions available (such as convexity matching and the use of interest rate swaps) that can go a long way towards addressing these shortcomings, but presumably at significant extra cost. However, it is not necessary to go into this (rather complicated) aspect of things, since there are sound practical reasons why this liability matching approach is simply not appropriate.

In a situation of pension fund surplus, or at any rate full funding, the objective of any CFO in entering into such an essentially artificial investment strategy would be to give the best possible chance of the fund being able to meet its future liabilities over a defined period in full, and to use future contributions to begin accumulating assets for use in paying retirement benefits after that period expires. In other words, the CFO would be attempting to lock in the scheme's funding position.

In a situation of pension fund deficit, as we have seen, the CFO's objective is different. It is to stop the accounting entry in respect of the deficit from increasing any further. In other words, the CFO is attempting to lock in the company's liability position (which is what has given rise to the misnomer of Liability Driven Investment when applied to such schemes). Yet, quite apart from any other consideration, will this actually work? The answer is: No, it won't.

Why Liability Matching does Not Work

It is not possible to guarantee that the liability will not increase. On the contrary, it is almost certain that it *will* increase, even with such a liability matching scheme in existence. Mortality assumptions are certain to change over the intervening 18 years or so, and possibly quite dramatically. These will have the effect of increasing the liabilities, and it is very difficult to conceive of any way in which one could hedge against something so inherently uncertain. Similarly, even the pension consultants will probably concede that it is not possible to hedge against salary inflation – surely a vital factor when considering the liabilities of final salary (DB) pension plans. It is precisely this sort of uncertainty

---

[3] Neither gives protection against either a non-parallel shift in the yield curve, or a large parallel shift.

that the Total Funding Model tries to take into account but the liability matching approach simply ignores.

Worse, by accepting that liabilities may increase, while at the same time taking away (by locking all your assets into a fixed income portfolio) any ability to earn superior returns, one can only be tacitly accepting that the impact of these extra liabilities could be exponential, since they will be wholly unprovided for in an investment strategy.

Common sense is frequently the enemy of financial theory, and particularly so in this case. However, consultants rarely allow the facts to get in the way of a good theory. For example, there simply are not enough high-quality bonds available of sufficient duration for pension plans to pursue such an approach. In the UK, there is already an acute shortage of long bonds (brought about by pension fund appetite), such that the yield curve has reversed itself: long bonds now offer lower yields than short bonds. And even if it was possible to come up with some incredibly complex and flexible instrument that would completely address all the above issues, what happens to the deficit? Liability matching approaches seem simply to shunt this question off into a siding and leave it to be dealt with at some indeterminate date in the future.

The problem with such a view is that it raises a whole host of new issues, the probable adverse impact of which are not generally taken into account, and which could completely outweigh the 'beneficial' (if indeed this is the case) outcome for a CFO of believing (wrongly) that the company's pension fund liability has been crystallised.

THE PENSION PLAN AS CREDITOR

As noted above, where a pension fund is in deficit, then that deficit will be treated as a liability of the company – a debt owed by the company to the pension fund. However, this is clearly capable of different nuances of meaning, and thus of approach, according to whether one sees it (at one end of the scale) as an accounting technicality that must appear on the balance sheet but as an irritant with little real significance, or (at the other end of the scale) as a very real debt that the company can be certain of having to discharge at various dates in the future.

If the pension fund trustees are making strenuous efforts to make good the deficit, and this is indeed the objective of their investment strategy, then, depending upon how realistic that objective is, everybody would be entitled to feel quite relaxed about holding the former view. If, on the other hand, a liability matching 'solution' has been adopted by the sponsor and imposed upon the pension plan, then nobody can be under any illusions. The liability is a very real debt, which will have to be discharged by the company in the future, and not only will it definitely survive into the future but it will probably grow.

We have spent some time discussing the position of the CFO. Let us now turn to the position of the pension trustees and consider the logical model (sadly a fantasy situation in the real world) where they are disinterested individuals, not connected in any way with the employer.

As we have noted above, the position of the pension plan in a new world deficit environment is that of an unsecured creditor of the sponsoring employer – usually indeed the largest unsecured creditor. It is therefore incumbent upon the trustees, in order to discharge their duty to their members, to act as any reasonably prudent and competent unsecured creditor would do. It is here that the conflict of interest between pension plan and employer (let us assume that this is a company for present purposes) becomes most evident, and the unacceptability of individuals and consultants attempting to serve both parties simultaneously must surely be clear to anyone of even average intelligence (which sadly excludes many politicians and regulators, the only people actually in a position to be able to do anything about it).

If you were an unsecured creditor of a company to the tune of many millions, would you happily sit back for year after year, accepting the company's assurances that the debt will be paid one day? I think not. Pension trustees in such a position bear a heavy responsibility. They are obliged to think themselves into the shoes of a commercial creditor, and the issues they must resolve are clear.

Firstly, they need to seek to turn themselves into secured creditors, at least in part and preferably in total. The most obvious way they could do this would be to require the company to grant the pension plan a fixed charge over specific assets (such as buildings) and/or a floating charge over all the company's assets. The latter would need to include the right to appoint a receiver should the company ever default.

Secondly, there needs to be a requirement for interest to be paid on the debt. After all, if the pension plan had the use of the money today, it could be earning a return, so why should they give away the use of the money to the company without compensation? The interest rate would be a matter for negotiation, and the greater the degree of security that could be given, then probably the lower the rate of interest that would be appropriate.

Thirdly, there needs to be some sort of definite payment plan, showing how the deficit is to be paid off over a fixed period, presumably by way of increased contributions. Indeed, the need for pension plan and sponsor to agree such a rescue plan is a requirement of yet another new pension regime currently being introduced in the UK.

THE STRATEGIC DILEMMA

So let us come full circle and consider again the situation of the CFO, which I hope you will now appreciate is nowhere near as straightforward as was first assumed. In the imperative from the CFO's colleagues to crystallise as far as possible the amount of the deficit in the company's accounts, lie the seeds of a potentially far worse situation in which the company may find itself.

Any attempt to crystallise the deficit as a liability will involve one or other of the imaginative liability matching solutions currently being touted by consultants and investment managers. However, as we have seen, any such approach necessarily involves both sides of this particular coin. Yes, one can attempt to minimise any further increase in the deficit, but only at the expense of any attempt to reduce it through investment strategy. Thus, the adoption of such an approach must be accompanied by acceptance of the fact that the deficit is indeed a liability that will actually have to be paid by the company.

This in turn brings into play all the potential problems of the pension plan as creditor that are outlined above. As long as the pension plan is being allowed, or even encouraged, to plan for the reduction or elimination of the deficit through investment strategy, then the view that the deficit is simply something that must be carried on the balance sheet as an accounting requirement is tenable. Once that ability is taken away from the trustees, then the spectre of them beginning to act as commercial creditors becomes reality.

For the company, of course, it is a choice between unpalatable alternatives. Would the company rather carry the contingent liability of paying off a deficit that might theoretically one day be higher than it is today, or would it rather be shackled by payment plans, interest payments, charges over its assets and the possibility of receivership?

Clearly there is no good outcome from the company's point of view but it is important that it should be able to take an informed decision with a full understanding of all the relevant issues, rather than resort to knee-jerk reactions.

It is interesting to consider what the company's shareholders would make of this. Sadly there is no real mechanism (other than the company's annual meeting, which is usually heavily stage-managed) for allowing them to express their opinions, although in practice any company will stay in close touch with its largest shareholders and will canvass their views. However, these large shareholders tend to be financial institutions who do not always take a long-term view, and indeed will probably prefer the 'jam today' of maintained dividend levels to planning to improve the company's position in the long term.

The view of those consultants who champion such schemes is to dismiss the alternative (trying to reduce the deficit through investment performance) as 'the double or quits option'. Yet this glib response is not only unthinking but also downright hypocritical. For any intelligent approach to investment strategy will involve the MAC approach of spreading one's assets over a range of asset classes with as little correlation as possible, and involving very little capital risk. Yet it is precisely this approach that almost all consultants (certainly outside the USA) have advised their clients to avoid! Thus to characterise the alternative as a 'double or quits option' is to damn the very investment strategy (putting all your eggs in one basket) that they have advised their clients to employ for the last 20 years or more.

There is one final point that I hesitate to make because I am aware that it may be hugely controversial, but it arises as an inexorable logical progression from what we have just been discussing. Where a pension fund is in deficit, it is surely hugely undesirable for the same people to sit both as directors of the sponsoring company (or as officials of the sponsoring public body) and as trustees of the pension fund. The conflicts of interest are so massive that it seems grossly unfair to expect any individual to reconcile them. This situation can only be exacerbated further by any attempt to adopt a so-called LDI scheme. How can you, as a trustee of the pension fund, seek to protect its position as a creditor, when you also act as a director of the debtor company? It is curious, to say the least, that the recent UK Pensions Act should have chosen to institutionalise and perpetuate this conflict rather than remove it, but such a discussion lies beyond the scope of this book.

SUMMARY OF LDI

- Liability Driven Investment and Liability Matching are different concepts and should not be confused.
- All of the so-called 'Liability Driven' solutions that are currently being suggested are in fact Liability Matching, not Liability Driven.
- Liability Matching approaches are driven by the company's desire to crystallise the size of the pension deficit for accounting purposes.
- In fact, no Liability Matching solution can guarantee that the size of the pension deficit will not increase. On the contrary, it is almost certain that it will increase.
- Many Liability Matching approaches cannot protect a liability-matched portfolio from non-parallel shifts in the yield curve, or even from large parallel shifts. Such protection is theoretically possible with some schemes, but will carry a higher price.
- Any Liability Matching approach takes away any chance to reduce the size of the deficit through investment strategy. This makes it certain that the deficit is not merely an accounting entry, but a real debt that will one day have to be paid by the company.
- This in turn requires the pension trustees to act as if they were commercial creditors. They should request from the company: (1) security, (2) interest and (3) a definite plan of scheduled payments.
- In the circumstances, it is clearly highly undesirable that the same individuals should act at the same time as directors or employees of the company and as pension trustees. Sadly this was altogether too sensible an approach for the UK Government to adopt.

PORTABLE ALPHA

I must begin this section with an apology since I fear I am about to confuse you horribly. In mitigation I can say only that the confusion is not of my making, but arises from a usage of the word 'beta' which is completely inconsistent with that which we examined earlier in the chapters on risk. You will remember that 'beta' is commonly used as a measure of the specific risk of investing in any individual asset that forms part of the market portfolio, as opposed to the risk of that market portfolio itself, which we referred to as the systemic risk.

Unfortunately, when it comes to a discussion of portable alpha, we need to switch these concepts around, and beta, rather than representing the specific risk of an individual asset, now becomes the systemic risk of the market portfolio. Personally I deplore the introduction of yet another unnecessarily confusing element into the world of the institutional investors, but I am afraid we are stuck with it and will just have to make the best of it.

In fact, it is not quite as crazy as it sounds. Remember that we looked at beta as representing the specific risk of a particular asset and as a mathematical operator calculating the risk premium over the risk-free rate? Remember also that we talked about being able to diversify away specific risk by investing in a relatively small number of individual assets? Well, all such specific risk is now in fact assumed to have been diversified away or, if you prefer, when we use the word 'beta' in this context we are simply talking about a beta with a value of 1.

There is also some confusion about the use of the word 'alpha' and this is more pernicious, since, as we will see, there is the danger of it being used deliberately to confuse an investor.

The traditional use of the word 'alpha' was to describe all returns that could not be explained by beta. In other words, if a portfolio based on the FTSE 100 still had a beta of 1 but, presumably through some subtle and skilful stock-picking, enjoyed a higher return than the index itself, then that extra return was referred to as 'alpha'. Since it was a manager who made the stock-picking decisions, this became known in turn as 'manager risk'.

Does any of this sound familiar? It should. We discussed exactly this concept when we examined the debate between the active dollar and the passive dollar. So 'alpha' in that context would represent the risk (and the potentially associated extra return) associated with using an active manager rather than a passively managed portfolio.

A subtle transition has taken place, however, and 'alpha' now apparently means any attempt to add value by accepting risk higher than the market risk. I am sure you appreciate the distinction: whereas previously alpha was gained by selecting from assets already contained in the beta portfolio, it now apparently refers to investing in assets that are different from the beta portfolio, the most common of which are hedge funds.

THE CONCEPT

In its purest form, the idea of portable alpha relies upon an investor being able to lock in her beta return by using less than the full amount of her capital. This can be achieved by the use of derivative instruments, which are of course leveraged, requiring only relatively small payments up front. Put another way, what the investors are being urged to do is effectively to eliminate their exposure to beta risk in respect of some part of their overall asset base, thus theoretically leaving so-called 'pure alpha'. It is this apparent ability to separate beta from alpha that leads to the idea being called 'portable alpha'.

For example, an investor might choose to put 30% of her assets into the domestic quoted index, but instead of investing the whole 30% into the index fund she might put 15% into the fund and 15% into the corresponding futures contract, thus freeing up capital (the 15% allocation to the futures contract less the purchase price of the contract) to give to a pure alpha manager to achieve returns superior to the beta return.

Problem 1: The Traditional Risk Model

The most obvious problem from our point of view is the fact that this theory is based upon annual returns and the traditional risk model, neither of which is appropriate for modern investment strategy. I do not think there is any need to repeat here what we said about all this earlier. By using the traditional risk model to promote a particular approach, one is simply encouraging an investor to adopt a profoundly mistaken view of how performance should be assessed, and asset allocation undertaken.

This is rather like Nietzsche's objection to much of traditional philosophy. If you are going to base a belief system on the existence of God, what do you do when you encounter someone who does not believe in God, and you discover that you cannot prove that God actually exists at all? Just as an atheist can say 'I don't believe in God', why cannot an investor say 'I don't believe in beta (however you happen to be defining it today)'?

This is the fundamental difficulty that lies at the heart of portable alpha; it makes the usual assumption that extra risk and extra return are directly and unshakeably linked. Further, it assumes that risk is absolute and can be measured, and that this computed value can then be used to calculate 'risk-adjusted' returns and target returns. Reality, of course, is different. Risk is relative, not absolute. Risk cannot validly be measured in the way suggested (as a simple matter of variance and covariance of historical returns), and, even if it could, it almost certainly never captures all of the different types of risk inherent in a particular investment. Finally and most damningly, there is no direct link between extra

Table 10.1 Correlation of market-neutral hedge funds with quoted returns (CSFB/Tremont market-neutral index return versus S&P 100 total return)

	1994	1995	1996	1997	1998	1999	2000	2001	2002	2003	2004
Market-neutral annual return (%)	−2	11.04	16.6	14.83	13.31	15.33	14.99	9.31	7.42	7.07	6.48
S&P 100 total return (%)	2.61	38.97	24.66	29.23	32.49	32.31	−12.32	−13.49	−21.91	25.59	6.32
Correlation coefficient	0.37										

risk and extra return; on the contrary, we have demonstrated consistently in earlier chapters that high returns can be earned from low-risk assets, provided that risk is assessed in a way that is consistent with the real life concerns of real world investors.

Problem 2: Pure Alpha

Even the protagonists of portable alpha accept that for the concept to be valid there must be a source of pure alpha available, but where is that source to be found? Contaminate the alpha return with even a small proportion of beta and the idea no longer works.

Most professionals whom I have heard advocating this approach have been touting the use of market-neutral hedge funds, but on the evidence of the figures I have available to me, I must submit that this simply does not qualify. Table 10.1 sets out the annual returns for the market-neutral CSFB/Tremont hedge fund strategy index against the total return on the S&P 100 for the same period and shows the correlation between them; as you will see from Table A1.3 in Appendix 1, there is positive correlation of 37% with the S&P 100 and even more with the FTSE and DAX indices (about 44%). Not huge, perhaps, but hardly 'pure alpha'!

I have tried very hard to find another possible asset class that exhibits zero correlation with the S&P 100, but without much success. UK property is the closest (only 8% with the S&P 100 and down to 1% with the NASDAQ) but would property be a sufficiently liquid asset for these purposes? (Money has to be available at short notice to be moved back against the futures contract and/or to meet margin calls, depending on which approach has been adopted. If not, this can only be covered by a loan facility, which imposes yet more cost.) There are one or two asset classes that exhibit negative correlation, but for reasons we have already discussed, negative correlation should be avoided. However, I have a completely open mind on this point and would welcome someone coming forward to identify any such source of pure alpha that may actually exist.

Problem 3: Exactly What is Being Suggested?

It is very easy, when confronted with self-confident investment professionals glibly talking about concepts such as portable alpha, simply to assume that what they are saying makes sense. This is in fact by no means a foregone conclusion, particularly where the same words ('beta' and 'alpha') are used in different senses in different situations. If you want to know why this is, then a cynic might suggest that it is for the same reason that consultants are usually either unable or unwilling to explain their concept of 'risk' in laymen's terms. In any profession (lawyers, engineers, IT specialists, etc.) there is always a group who do not actually care if the client does not understand what is being said, and investment is no exception. However if, as here, the process is aimed at persuading a potential client to buy one's product or services, then I feel it is particularly objectionable.

Let us be clear. Portable alpha has nothing to do with the passive versus active management debate, because there we are talking about the active manager selecting from the same (broadly, at least) population of investment opportunities as is represented by the passive portfolio. Here we are talking about giving money to a manager to use with reference to a completely different set of investment opportunities. But . . . isn't this just advocating MAC investing? And, if it is, why not just say so?

Portable alpha enthusiasts are simply advising investors effectively to leverage some part of their existing portfolio in order to release money for deployment in other asset classes. As will have appeared elsewhere in this book, I have no problem at all with using leverage where it may be appropriate (see, for example, the chapters on quoted equities and property) although for the purposes of this book I have stuck to the more simple example of debt, since an examination of the use of derivatives probably merits a book all to itself. However, as with all these things, we should not lose sight of the essential question: 'Why?'

Why should an investor leverage a particular asset class? Surely because she believes that by doing so she can increase the returns of that asset class – property would be an obvious example – without incurring any significant extra risk. Or, to put it in terms of the risk premium, that the extra return she is likely to gain from the asset class outweighs any amount of extra risk she incurs by way of the leverage employed. To suggest that she should incur extra risk in one asset class just to receive, possibly, a higher return in another asset class is surely stretching a point. In fact, it is doing more than stretching a point; it is downright misleading. In fact, the extra return represented by the allocation to the other asset class could be gained quite simply without any leverage at all.

In other words, all portable alpha offers is an opportunity to access the returns of a different asset class at significant extra cost than might otherwise be the case. (This 'extra cost' is not just the literal cost of the portable alpha manager's fees – not to mention all the various consultants who will cluster round to offer opinions and prepare strategic studies – but also the theoretical costs of the extra risk represented by the leverage.)

Portable alpha is the coward's version of MAC investing. The intellectual coward knows that the real message is 'you cannot generate enough return or diversification from your existing portfolio and therefore you should be looking to invest in multiple asset classes', but he knows that this message may not be well received as it runs counter to the advice that investors have been receiving for many years. The message is therefore modified to 'we're sure you are doing the right thing, but have you ever considered how you could increase your returns without actually changing very much at all?'.

The investor is being told to invest in a different asset class, but without actually making it explicit that this is what she is doing; perhaps she may be happy to play along with this, feeling that it might be easier to get past her board of trustees or investment committee than an outright suggestion of allocating, say, 15% to market-neutral hedge funds. However, all of these approaches overlook one issue of staggering simplicity. The investor could simply adopt a MAC investment model and gain the extra return from other asset classes, without having to take on unnecessary leverage, and without the expense and deliberate complexities of a portable alpha scheme.

MAC investing makes sense. Portable alpha does not.

Problem 4: Alpha Returns

Look again at Table 10.1. In three of the years under consideration the alpha return was positive while the beta return was negative. Probably therefore (I say 'probably' because without knowing exactly what derivatives were being used, and on what terms, it is not possible to say for sure) in those years the alpha return would have slightly reduced the negative beta return. One year is too close to call. Yet in all the others, including six consecutive years from 1994 to 1999, the beta return was dramatically higher than the alpha return.

I must enter the usual caveats at this point. We are dealing with only one of several possible measures of hedge fund returns. We are dealing with a relatively short data series. Past returns are not necessarily a good guide to future performance. Yet the fact remains: portable alpha theories are built around the concept that the alpha manager will outperform the beta, thus generating a source of extra return, when much of the evidence suggests the opposite. If the alpha manager in fact underperforms (and using a market-neutral hedge fund strategy seems to point in this direction) then the investor will not make money but lose money, to which loss must be added all the extra costs that she has incurred in order to pursue the portable alpha strategy.

SUMMARY OF PORTABLE ALPHA

- Portable alpha is an investment approach which leverages some part of an existing portfolio, usually by use of derivative instruments, to release cash for investment in a different asset class, often market-neutral hedge funds.
- The word 'beta' is used here not in the context we have discussed earlier, but in the sense of the return that investors are likely to earn on their existing portfolios.
- The word 'alpha' is used here not to represent manager risk per se (although that is necessarily part of what is implied, since different managers are used) but the return that may be earned in excess of the beta return.
- The phrase 'portable alpha' is based on the supposition that the return earned by the alpha manager (i.e. the manager who would not have been used but for the leverage) is pure alpha, i.e. untainted by any beta return, and that this extra return is essentially something discrete that may be identified and notionally moved around.
- Portable alpha is based on annual returns and the concept of the traditional risk model, both of which we have already rejected. It therefore encourages investors to persist with the traditional, mistaken approach rather than to embrace the new.
- The assumption that sources of pure alpha are available does not seem to be supported by the facts. In particular, market-neutral hedge funds appear to exhibit some significant degree of correlation with quoted indices and do not therefore qualify as a source of 'pure alpha'.
- All that is being suggested here is the basic principle of widening the scope of a portfolio to invest in other asset classes. This can be achieved better and more cheaply by MAC investing. The portable alpha investor is being forced to pay extra costs, in the form of fees and leverage, for something that could be obtained without extra cost.

- The assumption that the alpha return will always exceed the beta return (and presumably by more than the extra costs involved) also appears to be unsupported by the facts. The figures made available for the preparation of this book suggest, on the contrary, that returns may be more likely to be lower rather than higher.

RIVAL STRATEGIES?

I hope you noticed, dear reader, the question mark that I cunningly placed at the end of the title to this chapter. Do either LDI or portable alpha really represent the rival strategies to MAC investing, which they are commonly believed to be? I think not, and certainly not for a pension plan in deficit.

LDI reminds me of a question from a history exam: 'The Glorious Revolution[4] was neither glorious nor a revolution – discuss.' As we have seen, it is neither 'liability driven' nor is it 'investment'. It is liability matching, and therefore completely inappropriate to a pension fund in deficit, whose liabilities are already, by definition, wildly out of control, and it is at best a glorified treasury function, not an investment process.

It remains an open question whether it is appropriate to a pension scheme in surplus. Theoretically, it may well be, but it would be unwise to rely upon it completely. Firstly, in addition to guarding against inflation, the return would also have to take care of the rest of the escalator function, and one would need to quantify what this might turn out to be. It is therefore quite possible that a bond return might not after all prove sufficient. Secondly, the nature and timing of the liabilities might change for non-demographic reasons. Suppose, for example, that the business of the sponsor goes through a period of enforced restructuring, and as a result of this the sponsor decides to offer voluntary redundancy to many of its workers, including early retirement benefits.

For this reason, I would suggest that even in the benign environment of a pension surplus it should be applied only to part of the fund's present value, leaving the remainder to be deployed in a MAC portfolio.

It may seem to be engaging in sophistry to say that because LDI is not an investment strategy it cannot be a rival investment strategy to

---

[4] The overthrow of James II of England in 1688 in favour of William of Orange.

MAC investing. Yet the implications go well beyond this. LDI is a decision not to have an investment strategy. It is a blank refusal to engage in the investment process in any way. It is a decision to crystallise the losses already suffered by the pension plan and never attempt to recover them, even in part. The message to its members and sponsor is 'the bond return is all you are going to get, so make the best of it'.

Finally, not only is it profoundly unattractive from an investment point of view, but, as we have seen, it triggers some very serious related issues; issues with which even now pension trustees (certainly those of whom I am aware in the UK) have not begun properly to grapple.

Portable alpha is an investment strategy, albeit a rather strange one. It forces investors to pay for what they could have at no extra cost, and it does not even guarantee an extra cost-adjusted return. On the contrary, on the figures available to me (see Table 10.1) there is a good chance that their overall returns might actually be depressed rather than enhanced.

Portable alpha seems to be for those who know that MAC investing will not be welcome at the front door, and therefore try surreptitiously to sneak a bastardised version of it in at the back door, hoping they can persuade their parents (trustees, directors, etc.) that this really is the acceptable face of something they instinctively dislike. And the parents sigh and accept it as the lesser of two evils, and start concocting an explanation for the neighbours.

Investing in different asset classes is good. Investing in a very narrow selection of assets is bad. Both the portable alpha and MAC investing schools would agree with that proposition. The difference is that the MAC enthusiasts are prepared to take a full frontal approach, while the portable alpha group feel the need for a fig leaf, but still spend most of their time hiding behind the trees. If MAC investing is the way ahead then why not say so? If investors do not agree, then try to persuade them through logical argument. At the end of the day bamboozling pension trustees to sample a very small part of MAC investing in adverse circumstances is surely not the answer.

11
Liquidity

The bad news is that many stumbling blocks have been placed in the path of the MAC investor. The good news is that these are mostly shibboleths from the past and can be circumvented by logical argument – assuming of course that the investors in question are willing to listen to logical argument rather than simply repeat the mantras they have been taught to intone when danger threatens. One such mantra is 'ah yes, but we must have liquidity, you see'. The obvious question, asked so often in this book, is 'why?'. As with many such questions, all too often the answer is 'because that's what our consultants have told us'.

As long ago as 1935[1] Keynes identified what he called 'the fetish of liquidity'.

> Of the maxims of orthodox finance, none, surely, is more antisocial than the fetish of liquidity, the doctrine that it is a positive virtue on the part of investment institutions to concentrate their resources upon the holding of 'liquid' securities.

Keynes was writing 70 years ago but little seems to have changed in the thinking of some of the world's largest investment institutions in the meantime. Many still have virtually all their assets in quoted equities and bonds.

We have already heard what Swensen thinks of this, but it bears repeating:

> Managers willing to accept illiquidity achieve a significant edge in seeking high risk-adjusted returns. Because market players routinely overpay for liquidity, serious investors benefit by avoiding overpriced liquid securities and locating bargains in less widely followed, less liquid market segments.[2]

This seems so obvious as to need no further justification, but in reality many investors, particularly pension funds, cling to their

---

[1] There is some disagreement here. Some sources say 1934. John Maynard Keynes, *The General Theory of Employment, Interest and Money*, currently published by Prometheus Books, London 1997.

[2] *Pioneering Portfolio Management*, already referenced.

claimed need for liquidity to justify their asset allocation. This generally occurs when they have run out of all other excuses, such as 'there are no available benchmark returns' or 'returns of that asset class have been highly volatile' or 'that's much too high risk for us', but let that go. Let us focus on liquidity.

The fetish of liquidity stands in our path and must be circumvented if we are to proceed. There are three possible paths we can adopt. Firstly, we can try to satisfy the craving by actually producing exactly the liquidity that the investors demand. Secondly, we can question whether they actually need the liquidity they say they do. Thirdly, we can show that their views on the nature of liquidity are outdated and mistaken.

CREATING ARTIFICIAL LIQUIDITY

I am aware that the first approach is actually being taken by a number of people, since my views on it have been sought by various investment managers and pension funds. I have heard several imaginative suggestions of nominal listings, unit trust type redemptions, and even insurance and annuity-based solutions. For me, they all fall foul of two fundamental issues.

Firstly, certain asset classes (and private equity is the most obvious) simply are not liquid in the legal sense of the word, and any attempt to shoe-horn them into an artificial structure which creates that liquidity, while legally possible (given great ingenuity), is fraught with difficulty in practical terms since the underlying cashflows involved are highly unpredictable. Many of the ideas that I have seen and discussed are ingenious, but can only be made workable by conditions and associated extra costs that I fear investors will quite understandably reject out of hand.

Secondly, a private equity programme takes many years to become fully mature and comparatively little money is drawn down in the early years (in normal circumstances). Thus, any vehicle which claims to provide liquidity does not fit the pattern of operating cashflows that will be generated and simply passes the problem of what to do with all the remaining money in the interim onto the manager of the vehicle. We have already seen, in Chapter 8, that the solutions generally adopted by investors in this regard are suboptimal, to say the least, and there is no guarantee that things would be so very different in this case.

For example, one particular version of this approach is to invest in one of the existing quoted private equity vehicles. However, while providing nominal liquidity, this does not solve the cashflow problem since many of these vehicles are themselves cash rich – a problem exacerbated historically by some managers running a private institutional fund with a very different remuneration structure alongside the public vehicle, and both of them competing for the same dealflow. Even if allocated scrupulously pro rata, the outcomes were rarely satisfactory. Interesting developments are still taking place in this area, including the securitisation of specific secondary portfolios, and I think progress will continue to be made in this direction, but the basic problem with this approach is that you are straining to provide the investors with something they think they must have (often at considerable extra cost and/or at the expense of lower returns) when a more straightforward approach would be to show that they really do not need it at all, and that, consequently, there are easier and potentially more attractive ways to achieve their objectives.

'Market players routinely overpay for liquidity' says Swensen, and the world's sophisticated investors agree, choosing, for example, to invest in private equity through institutional limited partnerships (even though these have higher up-front fees) than through quoted vehicles for the simple reason that they expect the former significantly to outperform the latter on a cost-adjusted basis.

WHY DO INSTITUTIONAL INVESTORS NEED LIQUIDITY, AND HOW MUCH LIQUIDITY DO THEY NEED?

Since we know that we must pay an extra price for liquidity, then clearly we want to have as little liquidity in our portfolio as possible. The *reductio ad absurdum* of this proposition would be to have no liquid assets at all, and so perhaps a useful starting point would be to ask what the function of liquidity should be within a portfolio, and thus understand why it is required, at least in some measure.

Pension plans, endowments, foundations and various other types of institutional investors have specific outgoings which they know they are going to need to pay. In the case of those which are likely to occur in the near future, the precise date of these outgoings can be fixed with confidence. The further into the future they are likely to occur, the more difficult such precision becomes, but the general amount and periodic impact should at least be capable of estimation.

These are generally liabilities that the institution *must* make. The payment of retirement benefits by a pension plan is not optional, but obligatory. Not having the necessary cash available to honour such an obligation is simply not an option. Therefore any such institution will clearly need to maintain both a cash 'float' for the day-to-day expenses of the management budget and some sort of reserve of liquid assets to fund these projected liabilities. I think the need for liquidity is clear; if an institution is going to have to make payments in the short term, then there is no point in having all its money tied up in assets that cannot be readily realised (turned into cash with which to make the payments). So far, so good, but just how much liquidity does an institution really need?

Obviously this will in most cases be a subjective decision, based on the preferences of the individual investor. However, there are two important points that need to be made.

The first point is that most such decisions will simply not be valid on logical grounds since the people making the decision have not grasped the principle of 'paying for liquidity' and thus do not properly understand the adverse impact they are visiting upon their fund's performance. In my experience, including the specific research that I conducted in preparing this book, most pension funds grossly overestimate their need for liquidity, and I am convinced that if they properly understood the cost/benefit implications of their decision they would not be so unnecessarily profligate with their fund's assets.

The second point leads on from the first, in a way. Would it not be much more desirable if some objective test could be suggested? Firstly, an objective test, if properly thought out and structured, should always be preferable to a subjective approach since it is likely to lead to more optimal outcomes. Secondly, we know that, in practice, the subjective approach is in fact leading to bad decisions being taken on a consistent basis.

So, what form might such a test take? I would suggest one that most closely matches the circumstances of such an institution (a pension fund, for example). They are concerned with the relationship between time and money (since certain outgoings can be predicted to occur at certain times) and with the time value of money (since we have already established that it is only with returns compounded from year to year that a pension fund should be concerned). Earlier we talked about thinking of net annual outflows as percentages of a fund's present value. Let us assume, for example, that the net outflow of a pension fund for each of the next few years is likely to be about 2.5% of present value (not an unrealistic figure). This gives us something to work with.

How many such outflows do we need to plan to cover? Let us think about this in practical terms. Assuming that one could liquidate enough assets to cover 2.5% of present value (a reasonable assumption), why would one not wish to? The only reason I can think of is that financial markets might be falling and that one might not wish to sell assets into a buyer's market.

Actually, this is illogical. The whole point of holding liquid assets, according to those who advocate such things, is precisely because they have a market value that is continually quoted and can be turned into cash in the space of a phone call lasting a few seconds. That value is the price the buyer is prepared to pay for them, and is thus a function of the market. If you view liquidity as a substitute for holding cash, or at least as a means of readily realising cash when required, then surely this is exactly what you bargain for when you buy the assets in the first place? Thus, if you expect quoted equities to outperform bonds, for example, there is no logical reason to hold any bonds in your portfolio since the shares can be turned into cash just as easily and you expect them to be more beneficial for your portfolio while they are in it.

Let us leave this to one side for the moment. Let us accept for practical purposes that we operate in an illogical world and that investors are not prepared to see quoted equities as a substitute for ready cash. (In fact, it is doubly illogical, because if not, then why hold quoted equities at all when you could deploy that money in asset classes with higher anticipated returns?) How much liquidity does such an investor actually need? Well, we have hypothesised that the most likely reason for reluctance to sell quoted securities would be the irrational fear of selling into a falling market. How long would such a state of affairs be likely to persist?

Looking at the data on quoted markets that I have been using for the purposes of this book (which broadly covers the period from 1984 onwards) the longest spell of continuous negative returns on any of the indices (S&P 100, FTSE 100, DAX, Nikkei, NASDAQ) has been three years. It is true that negative returns have occasionally been savage in a particular year, and in many cases indices have struggled to recapture lost value, but the longest period over which a market has fallen continually has been three years. This seems to suggest that a period of three years' net outflows would represent a prudent liquidity reserve for a pension fund to maintain. Assuming that our assumption of 2.5%

is valid, then this would mean a liquidity reserve of somewhere around 7.5%; let us err on the side of caution and say 8%. Of course, there may be pension funds that are much more mature than the typical example I am considering, in which case the actual figure should of course be substituted for 2.5%.[3] I am using the figure for illustrative purposes only.

So, we will adopt a figure of roughly three years' net outflows, which we will estimate at about 8% of present value, and place this in a portfolio of bonds, with the duration of the bonds matched as far as possible to the timing of the individual outflows. This will, of course, not be allowed to decay, but will be reviewed annually (perhaps even quarterly, if desired) so that the investor will *always* have her next three years' liabilities covered and matched. In this way we can also allow for changing maturity profiles.

Thus, if we are assuming that no major quoted index is likely to show negative returns for more than three consecutive years, and if we have our next three years' liabilities covered in advance at all times, where is our liquidity risk? Why do we need to have almost all of our money in expensive liquid assets (as many pension funds do, at least outside the USA) when a mere 8% or so will suffice, and arguably even that is unnecessary?

ARE SO-CALLED ALTERNATIVE ASSETS REALLY ILLIQUID? AND, IF SO, JUST HOW ILLIQUID?

Illiquidity is the most common excuse I hear from pension trustees for not investing in so-called alternative assets such as hedge funds, private equity and property. We have just demonstrated that their thinking as to their need for liquidity is profoundly mistaken. We will now turn our attention to their perception of the liquidity of certain asset classes and see that this, too, is misconceived.

Firstly, let us look at quoted equities, which are likely to make up about 37% of our portfolio if we go for an equal distribution approach. Would anyone deny that quoted securities are liquid, at least if held through the medium of a major index such as the S&P 100? Of course not. On the contrary, they are the classic example of a liquid investment capable of being turned into cash instantly, subject only to the time it may take the broker to clear funds into the investor's account.

---

[3] For a brief discussion of the position of mature pension funds, please see Appendix 2.

As pointed out above, it is strange that investors should apparently find this hard to accept, since the need for liquidity is usually advanced as the justification for holding them rather than other asset classes that seem to promise higher returns.

This means that our model MAC portfolio is going to have about 45% of its present value allocated to asset classes that are indisputably liquid, capable of being turned into cash at a moment's notice. Thus, we have at least our next 15 years' liabilities covered by liquid securities, even if the return on our quoted equities was to be zero for the whole of that 15-year period (an unrealistic assumption, I am sure you will agree). If the quoted equities were to make even a modest return, even on a declining balance as they are progressively sold, then in reality we may well have at least our next 20 years' liabilities covered. What cataclysmic event can anyone consider that would prevent us being able to fund our next 20 years' net outgoings? Particularly bearing in mind that during the intervening period it would be possible to take all sorts of palliative action, including increasing employer contribution levels, if necessary. It must therefore follow that on any view our model MAC portfolio offers significantly more liquid liability cover than even the most prudent investor could wish for.

Strictly speaking, therefore, a discussion on the liquidity of the remainder of our portfolio becomes irrelevant, but let us have it nevertheless. What about hedge funds, private equity and property?

Hedge Funds: Liquidity Considerations

Hedge funds would satisfy many of the legal tests of liquidity since they usually enjoy some sort of quote or listing and are structured to allow redemptions. However, nowhere is the dictum that liquidity comes at a significant price better demonstrated. Let us look at this aspect of hedge funds in a little more detail.

Hedge funds frequently have long lock-up periods. With many US funds this is for one year, and the most usually advanced reason for the need for this was that performance fees were assessed annually, and one year was the fairest minimum time for which money should be made available. When offshore funds were set up, hedge fund managers came under pressure from other sorts of investors (notably the Swiss banks) to provide shorter lock-up periods and so these were frequently reduced to one quarter, but with the performance fee being assessed and paid quarterly as a quid pro quo.

Currently, attempts are being made to extend the lock-up period on some US funds to two years. Can you remember that in the hedge fund chapter we discussed the reluctance of many US hedge fund managers to register and be regulated? Well, one of the possible exemptions seems to be in respect of funds that have at least a two-year lock-up period. Thus, a reluctance to register with the SEC, which many would see as an investor-unfriendly issue, is being used to justify the imposition of another investor-unfriendly issue. One hopes that the obvious injustice of this will ensure that such attempts will fail, but as it is frequently difficult to discern any logic in the actions either of investors or of regulators, you can never predict such things with confidence.

Be that as it may, the lock-up period is not the end of the story, since, as Swensen points out, liquidity always comes with a price tag attached. Most hedge fund documentation provides for 'exit windows' through which a departing investor may slip away, but the key that unlocks the window is a penalty payment, and these can be substantial. However, all this is a question of degree and there will frequently be no black and white answer.

For example, if a hedge fund has a 'tilt' that requires long investment periods, such as many event-driven strategies do, then is a one-year lock-up really so unreasonable? Having to unravel a position unexpectedly and in haste in such circumstances could entail significant losses. One could argue that the investor knew exactly what she was getting into when she selected a manager with this specialty and should not be allowed to change the rules of the game halfway through. The *non plus ultra* of this approach would apply equally to private equity funds (in theory, at least). Yet if another hedge fund manager were operating in an environment where he could offer weekly (or even daily) valuations, and where the underlying hedge fund portfolio was largely liquid, would it be unreasonable to expect investors to be able to withdraw funds at, say, seven days' notice?

Similarly with exit fees. Is it really reasonable to expect the continuing investors to bear the brokerage fees for liquidating the position of a departing investor? Clearly not, so an exit fee of, say, 1% would hardly be objectionable. Yet what about a 5% fee, particularly where the fund is currently cash rich and may therefore not actually incur any significant extra costs at all? Yet one cannot judge every situation on its merits, because all of this will need to be agreed and documented when the fund is first formed, and those decisions will often have to be taken in situations where bargaining positions may be unequal, lawyers rather than investors are in charge of the process, and in any event nobody can foresee what may happen in the future.

So, how can we summarise the liquidity of hedge funds? Like other concepts we have encountered in this book, I would suggest that the answer may be at least partly relative, depending upon one's own personal circumstances. In our model MAC portfolio we already have something like the next 20 years' liabilities covered. Are we therefore ever going to be in a situation where we need to liquidate our hedge fund portfolio at a moment's notice, or even in less than the prescribed lock-up period? No.

However, if we were an investor who is largely illiquid, and faced with an unexpected demand for cash, how long would it take to liquidate our hedge fund holdings? This would obviously depend on the terms of the individual hedge funds themselves, but if the investor knew that liquidity could become an issue then she would be more likely to have selected funds with short lock-up periods, possibly a majority of which would be offshore. Given this, it seems reasonable to assume that at least a large part of the holding could be liquidated in little more than three months, with little significant cost (particularly if one bears in mind that there is always going to be *some* cost associated with the alternative of liquidating a quoted portfolio). In other words, liquidity is never likely to be an issue, provided the liquidation can be planned and executed in an orderly manner.

Private Equity: Liquidity Issues

Private equity is usually cited as the *bête noire* of the liquidity fetishists. On the face of it, they are right to be concerned, but in practice, as opposed to strict legal theory, this is in fact a surprisingly liquid asset class.

Viewed by a lawyer, little could appear less liquid than a private equity fund, tying the investor up as it does for anything up to about 12 years, although most limited partnerships (and the overwhelming majority of private equity funds take this form) now contain what have become known as 'no fault divorce' clauses which allow a certain majority of the limited partners to force the dismissal of the manager (usually the general partner or a related party) or even, in certain circumstances, to force the winding-up of the fund.

In passing, the same justification for long lock-up periods advanced above in support of certain hedge fund strategies holds true in spades for private equity funds. An early stage venture fund, for example, might quite genuinely have a fund investment/divestment cycle of anything up to about 12 years, with totally unpredictable cashflows (both in and out of the fund) and one or two equally unpredictable big winners ('home runs') generating the bulk of the fund's return. Allowing limited partner capital to be withdrawn early might leave the fund in a situation where it is unable to honour contractual commitments already entered into, and would almost certainly significantly (and unfairly) impact upon the manager's carried interest (performance fee).

Fortunately for all concerned, however, the strictly legalistic analysis takes no account of practical reality. Remember that in the private equity chapter we touched upon the concept of secondary funds? This is where they come into their own.

Secondary funds are a thriving section of the private equity community that might be thought of as essentially cannibalistic in that they feed upon interests in other private equity funds. Thus while it is not possible to withdraw your capital from a private equity fund it is possible to transfer your interest, together with the capital already subscribed, to a third party, who will take on the interest and thus also the liability to pay the remainder of the capital amount as it is called down by the manager. That interest has a value, and the secondary player's expertise lies in being able to assess it and structure a deal that will still provide them with a reasonable return while hopefully giving the initial investor (i.e. the seller of the interest) a satisfactory outcome.

Obviously there is a cost involved here, as one might expect. The price paid may look reasonable at first sight when compared to the stated NAV of the fund, but many private equity managers, particularly in Europe, are loath to write their investments up and thus the potential gain that might be realised when one of these investments is sold may bear little relationship to the stated value (without going into unnecessary detail, European valuation guidelines impose mandatory downgrading requirements when a company misses its targets, but make it relatively difficult to increase a company's valuation significantly, so European private equity valuations are frequently conservative). The secondary player, since this is their specialist area, is more likely to be able to assess the potential value of the underlying investments than you are, but frankly most investors do not care too much about this. They just want a price for their interest.

Given the effects of the J-curve, exiting a private equity fund in the early years of its life is likely to be a relatively expensive business, but one would never need to do this within a properly planned MAC portfolio. Firstly, other asset classes (the bond-based liquidity reserve, quoted equities, hedge funds, etc.) would be exited first and it seems inconceivable that one would ever need to get down as far as private equity in the liquidation pecking order. Secondly, if one had anything like a mature private equity portfolio then one would exit the older funds (where the effect of the J-curve has been absorbed) before the younger ones (where it has not), and the buy-out funds (where it is easier to guess at eventual value) before the venture funds (where life becomes much more uncertain). Also, bear in mind that in many cases quite small amounts of money might have been drawn down. It is not impossible that if one commits $20 million to a venture fund, perhaps only about $1 million has been drawn down after two years, and perhaps $3 million after three. So the cost, though high in terms of what has been paid into the fund, may actually be very low in relation to the amount committed (which is what matters in terms of the investor's overall portfolio).

In terms of time, it should be possible to sell any portfolio of secondary interests in less than six months, perhaps even less than three if full documentation and reporting are promptly available. (I once closed such a transaction in less than a month from start to finish.) So, if anything, liquidating a private equity portfolio might actually take less time than for a hedge fund portfolio, which is ironic given that most investors seem instinctively to assume that hedge fund investments are liquid, while private equity investments are not.

Property: Liquidity Issues

The liquidity of this asset class will obviously depend upon the route that has been taken when choosing between direct and indirect investment. It may well be, of course, that some combination of options has been chosen.

Liquidity of directly held property assets will obviously depend upon market conditions at the time of liquidation, but my instinct is that in most of the world's major property markets there will always be a buyer available somewhere. Even in a weak market a property asset will sell if you price it low enough (this is really the flip side of the maxim about never being a forced seller of any asset class – liquidation carries the implication that you *are* a forced seller) and thus, as with other asset classes, liquidity is available, but comes at a price.

If the leverage has been obtained partly through fixed term loans, then there may also be some penalty fees payable under the loan agreements for paying off loans early, but this is a small point, and while I have included it for the sake of completeness, I think it can safely be ignored.

A commonsense view would be that any property assets could probably be sold in an orderly manner in about six months, so, again, there is very little issue as to timing. Indeed, unless the portfolio is very large it may well be possible to structure the sale of the portfolio as one large job lot.

A slightly more exotic option, should property market conditions be very unsatisfactory, would be to consider using an investment bank to securitise the portfolio. In this way a better value might be realised, although it may not be advisable to sell all the shares at once.

If any part of the property allocation is currently being held in REITs or other quoted vehicles, then these are of course liquid in just the same way as any other publicly quoted security.

It is the property funds that are likely to do worst when viewed from the viewpoint of potential liquidity. I am not aware of any large secondary PERA market operating in the same way as for private equity, but logically there is no reason why a secondary transaction should not be entered into in exactly the same way – after all, the same legal structures and considerations are involved.

Liquidity of So-called Alternative Assets

As we have demonstrated, fears as to the purported illiquidity of some asset classes, most notably private equity, but also others, are largely misconceived. Hedge funds may be exited (effectively by redemption). A thriving secondary market exists for interests in private equity funds. Property may be sold in the open market. Therefore both strands of our argument hold true – (1) that pension funds do not actually require anything like the levels of liquidity to which they cling, and (2) that a MAC portfolio offers all the liquidity and more that any pension fund may need.

The situation might be summarised as shown in Table 11.1.

In fact, the situation is even more favourable than that shown in the table since this takes no account of any investment performance in the interim, i.e. it assumes that all assets would be liquidated and held in cash, which would not of course be the case. Thus increasing amounts could be added to each figure in respect of cumulative years' exposure. It is quite possible, for example, that assuming an investment per-

Table 11.1   Liquidity of the model MAC portfolio

	% of portfolio	Cumulative annual outflows[a]
Liquidity <24 hours		
Bonds	8.0	3
Domestic equities	18.4	9
Foreign equities	18.4	15
Liquidity <6 months		
Hedge funds	18.4	21
Private equity	18.4	27
Liquidity <12 months		
Property	18.4	33

[a] Based on the assumption that each annual outflow will be approx 3% of NPV.

formance of 5%, the amount held in instantly liquid securities could actually exceed 20 years' anticipated outflows.

Which prompts the question: has any liquidity event ever occurred that has required a pension plan suddenly to have to payout the equivalent of 15 or more times the outflow of any normal year in the space of just one? I cannot think of one, and indeed it seems inconceivable that this could ever happen. Even a mass redundancy programme could hardly generate a need for that much cash up front, since this would normally just involve people being allowed to take their retirement benefits from an earlier age.

IRRATIONALITY OF LIQUIDITY CONCERNS

Having examined the liquidity of the various parts of the MAC investment model in turn, the only possible conclusion is that the liquidity needs of any pension plan are grossly overestimated. Yet it remains the case that 'liquidity' is the most often proffered excuse that I encounter for a failure to implement the MAC model (apart from 'we need to match our liabilities', of course!) and it would be intriguing to know why this is. Is it just a genuine misunderstanding of the position? Does it, for example, confuse 'liquidity' with 'solvency'?

I confess I am at a loss. I can think of no single reason why a pension plan should want more than 45% of its assets in instantly liquid securities, nor why it might want more than 85% in assets that can be liquidated within six months. I said at the beginning of the book that the strategic planning process required the rigorous application of logic, and I am afraid that what we encounter here is one of those pockets of irrational, emotional sentiment which, though mistaken, are blindly and stubbornly mistaken.

That said, this is clearly an area where trustee education is urgently required and where consultants, if they choose to, can play a major role. Nor would it be right to look at the area in isolation, for bound up in this prejudice are concerns over the validity and comparability of alternative asset class returns, and mistrust of anything that cannot be slotted conveniently into the traditional risk model.

Let us do all that we can, which is simply to say as loudly and as often as possible that there is simply not the liquidity requirement that pension funds seem to believe exists, and that by clinging obstinately to false beliefs, they are costing their members a great deal of money in terms of the extra cost that Swensen refers to as being payable for liquidity.

SUMMARY

- The Yale Model and MAC investing turn the accepted notion of liquidity on its head. Liquidity is bad, not good. There is a heavy price to pay for liquidity in the shape of underperformance against less liquid asset classes, and liquidity should accordingly be kept to the absolute minimum within any portfolio.
- Institutional investors, particularly pension funds, routinely grossly overestimate the amount of liquidity they require. If one has a properly diversified portfolio then holding three years' net outflows in a liquidity reserve at any one time will normally be ample. In reality, the model MAC portfolio will usually see anything up to 20 years' net outflows held in instantly liquid assets.
- Institutional investors and their advisers routinely misunderstand the liquidity of so-called 'alternative' assets by applying an overly legalistic approach to the term. In the real world even private equity fund holdings (often regarded as totally illiquid) can be realised in the open market within a timeframe of a few months.
- Liquidity concerns are the most frequent excuse proffered for poor asset allocation. MAC investing exposes this excuse for what it really is: not prudence but intellectual laziness. There is no logical objection to MAC investing on liquidity grounds, even for a fully mature pension fund (though obviously the asset mix may vary to match different anticipated cashflow profiles).

12

Portfolio Performance

Finally, it is time to put all we have been talking about into perspective. The theory is very interesting, but we need to see how a MAC portfolio might actually perform in the real world. We know that in theory it should outperform a non-MAC portfolio, but we need to demonstrate how this might work in practice. As usual when looking at investment returns, we have little option but to examine what has happened in the past, but bearing in mind any environmental factors that might suggest that historic figures may not be a good guide to future performance.

We also need to bear in mind everything we have been saying throughout the book about long-term compound returns. This is the environment in which institutional investors operate, and so not only is it the way in which they need to approach their planning process but also it is the way in which we need to assess portfolio performance. We will therefore be concerned only with returns that are compounded over a period – in this case the decade or so since 1994. This is an instructive exercise since, if you look again at the annual return performance figures, you will see that they can fluctuate quite dramatically from one year to another. With compound returns, however, this volatility is smoothed out and we get the true picture of what an asset class can actually achieve over time.

Now for the acid test; it is time to see how our model MAC portfolio would have performed over, say, the last 10 years or so. First let us set our parameters, then let us remind ourselves of exactly what that portfolio would be, and why. By the way, all the relevant figures have been gathered together in Appendix 1, although many of them have already been used in preceding chapters.

Since we chose to examine the UK property market, it seems sensible to approach our analysis from the viewpoint of a sterling investor, although if you have read this book you will be equally able to perform exactly the same exercise for a dollar or euro investor. The only additional information you will require is that of the relevant domestic property market.

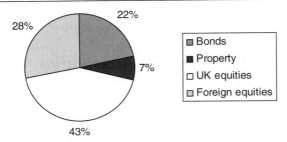

Figure 12.1   2005 typical UK public portfolio

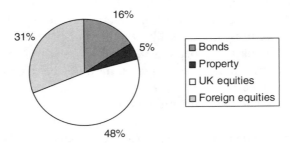

Figure 12.2   1994 typical UK public portfolio

Figure 12.1 shows the asset allocation model of the typical UK public pension fund today, while Figure 12.2 shows how it was in 1994[1] (which we will be using as the starting point of our analysis). See how exposure to bonds has actually risen during the intervening period.

Note also the huge overexposure to quoted equities, particularly domestic equities. As David Swensen says dryly, with masterly understatement, overcommitting to any asset class, but particularly to domestic stocks, 'exposes investors to unnecessary risk'.

Now, what is the model MAC portfolio for a sterling investor? Well, first of all remember that we are setting aside 8% in bonds to cover our liquidity needs for the next three years. This should ensure that we should never need to be a forced seller of any asset class and this, in turn, will minimise the chance of our ever suffering a capital loss within any particular asset class.

We next need to consider whether quoted equities can properly constitute two separate asset classes, or just one. We looked at this issue

---

[1] All figures from the WM Annual Report, 2004.

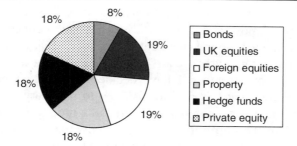

Figure 12.3   The model MAC sterling portfolio

in an earlier chapter and found out that it all depends on the foreign index you have in mind to set against the FTSE 100; if you choose the S&P 100, then the answer is 'no' because they are too highly correlated with each other. If you choose the NASDAQ, however, then the answer is 'yes'. So, we will assume that we will use the FTSE 100 and the NASDAQ as separate asset classes. That means that with the addition of hedge funds, private equity and property, we will have five asset classes in all (Figure 12.3), and we will assume that each is given an equal weighting of 18.4%.

Given our conclusions from the earlier chapter about quoted equities we will be taking a passive approach to the first two asset classes, looking simply to duplicate the index rather than 'stock-pick'. I started my research for this book with a completely open mind on this subject, but in the end I was swayed mainly by one thing: it would be the easiest and most natural thing in the world for any active manager who could conclusively prove that he had consistently outperformed the relevant quoted index over a long period to come forward and show exactly that – so why has no one done so? It seems that successful active management of quoted equities on a cost-adjusted basis is rather like the Loch Ness monster; everybody would like to believe in it, if only because of our romantic notions, but we cannot find anybody who has actually seen it. This also has important implications for the costs of managing the portfolio.

COST-ADJUSTED PERFORMANCE

It is important that we look at relative performance on a cost-adjusted basis if it is to be valid and relevant. However, there are problems here in that we are going to be forced into making some assumptions. Before we look at these, however, there are also what one might call the over-riding costs of portfolio management to consider – that is, the ongoing costs of running the central team which manages the pension fund, or endowment or whatever. I have decided simply to ignore these, although I accept that this position is open to some argument. While the costs of the organisation can be said to be the same whatever the performance of the portfolio – in other words, they are a function of the decisions made by the organisation about staffing and remuneration levels – that is only partly true. It seems difficult to believe, for example, that an investor with no previous exposure to the asset class would embark on a programme of allocating nearly 20% of the port-folio to, say, hedge funds or private equity without taking on at least one individual who was already experienced in the relevant area. My difficulty here is that the extra cost is essentially unquantifiable; it would make a great difference to the level of internal skill required, for example, if the investor decided to pursue a fund of funds approach in either area rather than selecting its own managers. So, I state and acknowledge the issue but will ignore it for the purposes of the remain-der of this chapter, taking account only of the presumed costs of exter-nal managers. Investors will, of course, be able to conduct their own budgeting exercises where necessary.

The difference to the cost level of running a quoted equity fund on a passive versus an active basis can of course be substantial: 50 basis points (or even less in the case of a large and influential investor) com-pared to perhaps three times that amount or more. So, 50 basis points seems a reasonable assumption to make here. However, please be aware that this will result in performance figures that will flatter the average investor. Very few pension funds, for example, adopt a purely passive approach to quoted equities; the 2004 WM report on public pension funds in the UK shows that less than 20% of equity exposure by value was indexed. Most corporate pension funds use active managers – there was a high profile law case in London recently featuring the Unilever pension fund on exactly this point. The Abu Dhabi Investment Author-ity, one of the biggest investors in the world, uses active management almost exclusively, both externally and internally. Yale, as we have seen, also adopt an active management approach. Therefore my figure of 50 basis points is obviously much too low on an average basis. However, I am in a difficult position. This book will undoubtedly be seen by many as an attempt to boost so-called 'alternative' asset classes at the expense of bonds and equities (which it is not – it is simply an attempt to have them all viewed on their own merits and used properly together) and so I am loath to use any cost assumptions in respect of quoted equities that may be attacked as being too high. So, I will adopt 50 basis points but subject to the reservation that, in practice, this is almost certainly a very generous assumption to be making.

Both the hedge fund and the private equity returns I am using (CSFB/Tremont and Venture Xpert respectively) state returns net of all fees, the former by extracting them before stating the figures and the latter automatically, since they measure only net cashflows to investors. Thus, it could be said that all the external costs of investing in each asset class have already been accounted for. Strictly speaking that is true, but in reality most investors are likely to travel by way of the fund of funds route and this would necessarily entail an extra layer of fees. In the case of hedge funds this seems to be pretty much cast in stone at 1%. In the case of private equity this is also broadly true, but for large amounts can be much lower; I am aware of one high-quality fund of funds whose fees are as low as 50 basis points. There can however be performance fees, or carried interest on top of this.

We should also bear in mind that there would be an element of double counting here since, unless the amounts involved were very large, then the fund of funds fees might well be less than the extra cost to the organisation of having to put their own skilled specialists in place; at the very least, they would offset some part, probably a large part, of this extra cost. However, we have already decided to ignore this factor, so I think the fairest thing to do is to charge a hedge fund cost of 150 basis points and a private equity cost of 100 basis points.

In the realm of property investment the picture becomes even more muddied, since much will depend on the selected mix of direct and indirect investment and exactly how any such programme is carried out. For example, private institutional funds will carry private equity or hedge fund type fees but, unlike these two asset classes, my figures for property investment returns are total returns before taking fees into account. So, if we want to consider performance figures that will be broadly compatible with those for other asset classes on a cost-adjusted basis, then we are forced into making an assumption. After much thought, I have decided to adopt the same figure as for hedge funds (150 basis points) which will hopefully be generally representative of the costs involved despite the mix of direct and indirect decided upon in any particular case.

WHAT RETURNS WILL WE USE?

I have not given any figures for bond performance because we have not been treating it as an asset class for investment purposes, but rather as a cash substitute for liquidity reserve purposes. Incidentally, even this is a questionable assumption since a Barclays Capital report that has been widely quoted in the press states the 50-year real return on bonds in the UK as 1.7% and the same return on cash as 1.9%. As far as the future is concerned, the most recent consensus forecast returns for bonds among UK public pension funds was 4.5%, as against 7.2% for equities. In other words, if one assumes UK inflation will run somewhere around the 3% mark, then UK investors are expecting the historic rate of real return to continue.

However, what of the past? We have no option but to consider this when looking at portfolio performance, since bonds have formed a large part (typically 30% or so) of many traditional pension fund portfolios. We therefore need to be able to plug some historic bond performance figures into our calculations.

It is surprisingly difficult to find such figures which actually seem consistent with each other. I think there may be a number of reasons for this. Some samples may include government bonds but not corporate bonds. Others may include corporate bonds, but only of a certain minimum rating (perhaps triple A). I also suspect that some returns stated as 'annualised' may in fact be average annual returns rather than proper vintage year returns calculated on a compound basis from year to year. However, the FTABG index gives a 10-year Gilt return of 7.7% assuming reinvestment of dividends, and this is the figure that I propose to adopt. Since it will be used consistently across all our simulations I do not think it matters that it may be slightly different from figures advanced by other sources. We will assume management costs of 50 basis points, the same as for passive equity investing.

Incidentally, since we have ignored them thus far it might be interesting to note one or two features of recent bond returns. Firstly, if the numbers are to be believed, they have been very volatile over the course of the last decade. For example, UK public pension plans claim that they made an annual return of 19.4% from bonds in the calendar year 1998 compared with 0.6% in 2000 and 3.6% in 2004.[2] Without wishing in any way to cast doubt on these figures, I would say that such fluc-

---

[2] WM Annual Report, 2004.

tuations seem very hard to understand in the context of what is essentially a fixed rate investment, at least in the absence of any sudden and unexpected changes in interest or inflation rates.

Secondly, the three-year bond return is significantly lower than the 10-year bond return. This too is strange to understand since 10 years ago in the UK we already enjoyed low interest and inflation rates. I believe this could be a function of supply and demand; we have already seen, for example, when discussing so-called Liability Driven Investment, that overdemand for long-term bonds in the UK has led to an inverted yield curve and perhaps this is a manifestation of something similar. Interestingly, the proportion of asset value that UK public pension plans had invested in bonds rose by 36% between 1997 and 1999, which might explain the high return figure for 1998 if excessive demand pushed prices up (and yields down). If so, this is yet another example of investors harming themselves by blindly playing 'follow the crowd' instead of thinking for themselves.

Whatever the case, even the pension industry seem to recognise that historic returns are not a good guide to future performance, as the consensus forecast demonstrates. A return of 4.5% is most unlikely even to match the escalator factor, and thus investing in bonds can only operate as a drag on fund performance, making the job of the remaining asset classes even harder.

In respect of all other asset classes that make up the model MAC portfolio we have already looked at these in the separate chapters on each. There is, however, one other factor that we need to consider in the interests of making our simulations as realistic as possible.

PARAMETERS OF THE MODEL

The period we must consider is more or less chosen for us since meaningful hedge fund performance data is only available from 1994 onwards. However, while we will be running our first analysis based on 1994 vintage year numbers, this would assume that our model investor already had at this time a mature programme in respect of both private equity and property (since in practice each of these would take some years to implement). Given that the Yale Model began some 10 years before this, I do not think this assumption would be invalid; after all, we are looking to compare the performance of a Yale-like portfolio with a traditional (i.e. non-Yale) one. Also, there were plenty of people around in both the USA and the UK (including myself) who were advocating that institutional investors should be giving meaning-ful capital allocations to asset classes such as private equity well before 1994.

However, I am aware that such an approach might be criticised despite the facts of the case, and so as an alternative we will assume that private equity and property investment programmes had already begun, but were not yet fully mature and that, say, another five years was required to put the remainder of each allocation to work. Let us further assume that in the meantime the cash awaiting investment would be held in the NASDAQ and FTSE 100 indices respectively.

However, let us first run a straight comparison between a Yale and non-Yale portfolio from 1994. We will assume that the non-Yale port-folio was the typical 1994 UK public pension plan portfolio, which was about 16% bonds, 5% in property and the rest split 60/40 between domestic and foreign equities. The foreign equities were in turn split roughly 20/40/40 between the USA, Europe and Asia/Japan and we will use the S&P 100, the DAX and the Nikkei indices respectively to sim-ulate these. The total of bonds rose steadily throughout the period to a high of about 21%, but we will ignore this in the interests of trying to be as generous to the portfolio as possible (it would in any event prob-ably have little impact since we are using compound returns and the combination of time and extra amount involved are small).

Relative Performance

You will see from Figure 12.4 that by taking the 1994 vintage year return for each asset class in question and compounding them forward,

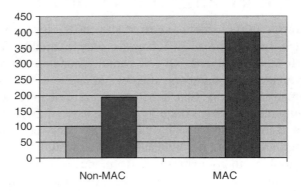

Figure 12.4   MAC versus non-MAC UK portfolio from 1994

the difference in the results of the two portfolios is little short of staggering. The MAC portfolio has produced over twice the value of the traditional, non-MAC portfolio, which is, alas, entirely representative of the actual UK pension fund portfolio during the period in question. This is a very important (though somewhat sensitive) point, since the average UK pension plan is said currently to be about 50% in deficit. In other words, had UK pension plans been using MAC investing throughout the 1990s, the current UK pension funding deficit would never have come into existence and all British occupational plans would be substantially fully funded.

This in turn has very significant implications for our consideration of investment strategy generally, since the bulk of final salary schemes have been closed and many employees now face the prospect of living out their retirement years in very straightened circumstances – very different to what they were promised when they joined their employer's pension plan. Great efforts have been made to portray this as an Act of God, some sort of Tsunami which has swept away pension funds despite their best efforts to preserve value for their members. The reality, as we have just seen, is very different. This was actually a man-made disaster, not an Act of God (a Bhopal rather than a Tsunami, if you will) and we should make sure that the blame is placed where it rightfully belongs. The present crisis has been brought about by fundamentally and tragically mistaken asset allocation, nothing more and nothing less. Had proper planning and implementation of investment strategy been carried out then the crisis would simply not have arisen.

As for the argument that it could not have been wrong because everyone else was doing the same thing at the same time, I think this has already been exploded by Swensen when he says:

> Many investors simply allocate among the asset classes popular at the time in proportions similar to those of other investors, creating uncontroversial portfolios that may or may not address institutional needs. By relying on the decisions of others to drive portfolio choices, investors fail to consider the function of particular asset classes in a portfolio designed to meet specific goals.[3]

But let me add two other cogent points here, both of which will, I hope, be obvious. Firstly, it is simply not true that everyone was doing the same thing at the same time. People such as Yale were already operating a fully diversified portfolio model by the mid-1980s, and the

---

[3] *Pioneering Portfolio Management*, see reference in Chapter 2.

example was there for anyone who cared to look. Secondly, if you carry the argument to its *reductio ad absurdam*, then it becomes 'I should never do anything that all my peers are not also doing, because that way I can never be proved wrong'. Well, I have news for those who may believe this. It is just plain silly to have over two-thirds of your assets in one asset class. It always was silly, and it always will be silly. No amount of posturing or theorising can change this.

But *retournons à nos moutons*. If we look more closely at our MAC portfolio we see that by far the biggest contributor has been private equity, creating nearly half the total value. Let me reiterate, by the way, that I am using the global capital weighted average figures here, not the upper quartile. It can, however, be argued that this way of evaluating private equity returns is not fully realistic, and I will return to this point later.

Property and hedge funds, under-represented or even ignored completely by the traditional portfolio, have also performed very well. The worst performer in the MAC portfolio (and thus also the biggest cause of the difference between the two portfolios) has been UK equities, which falls to less than 10% of portfolio value by the end of the period, having started out at 18.4%.

The real killer point is that the IRR of the MAC portfolio over the period has been very nearly 15%, compared to just 6.78% from the non-MAC portfolio. If you ever wanted evidence of the need for investors to think in terms of compound returns over a long period, then look no further. The traditional investor, doubtless obsessed with annual returns and the need to fit any possible asset class into the traditional risk model, will have produced a money multiple of 1.9× over the period, while the MAC counterpart, thinking in terms of compound returns over the whole period, has delivered 4×. The traditional investor has probably just about matched the escalator factor and perhaps contributed some marginal amount of return on top. The MAC investor has made a very significant contribution indeed to future funding requirements.

At the risk of becoming a crashing bore on the subject, I come back once again to the idea of a train journey. All I care about is whether my train arrives on time at the end of the journey. I should be much more swayed in my choice of train by one that exhibits consistent ability to perform the journey on time than by one that may, from time to time, exhibit a startling top speed. If the available evidence clearly suggests – as it does in the case of many so-called 'alternative' assets – that they have a greater likelihood of delivering an investor's desired rate of return over a long period of time than do traditionally mainstream ones, then why are they still being thought of as 'alternative' rather than forming the core of an investor's portfolio?

In the world of investment performance, compound returns are king. What is important is not so much that you invest in a particular asset class but that you stay in it over time, reinvesting where necessary in order to allow the return to compound upon itself year after year. All that should be necessary is to separate off those cash inflows that you need to top up your three-year liquidity reserve, and then use the remainder to rebalance your asset classes as far as may be possible within the parameters of reasonable cashflow expectations. The liquidity structure of the overall portfolio should mean that you never need be a forced seller of any asset class, and thus never need to sell into a falling market. This again works in favour of compounding, since the powerful arithmetic of this means that losses can be quite easily made good, provided the investor has the courage and singleness of purpose to continue investing, including rebalancing any underperforming asset to keep it as near parity as possible.

As I pointed out earlier, the only possible theoretical objection to such an approach is the assumption that our model investor's private equity and property programmes are already fully funded. Although this presumably would actually have been the case with the Yale Endowment by 1994, let us now make allowances for a slower (or later) adoption of the relevant asset classes and assume that they were only, say, 40% funded by 1994 with the remainder of the money going into the portfolio over the next five years (Figure 12.5).

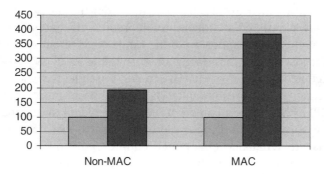

Figure 12.5 Non-MAC versus MAC with delayed option of private equity and property

Before performing the analysis that lies behind Figure 12.5, I was expecting the delayed adoption of private equity and property to make quite a significant difference to the overall performance of the MAC portfolio and it therefore came as a very pleasant surprise to be proved wrong. The money multiple declines from about 4× to about 3.9×, while the IRR is about 14.5% compared to about 14.9%. In this particular case this is due partly to UK property vintage year returns having remained very robust throughout, and private equity returns having held up well until 1999. Whatever the case, it does prove beyond per-adventure that even if UK investors had started on the process as late as about 1990 (in order to have 40% at work by 1994) their returns would have been barely impacted at all.

WHAT ABOUT REBALANCING?

The traditionalists still have another arrow in their quiver, however. It is clearly unrealistic to suggest that any investor would allow any one or more asset class to become a disproportionate share of the portfolio just because of outperformance. In our example, private equity, if left to its own devices, could become anything up to 48% of total portfolio value, which is clearly undesirable, although it must be remembered that putting nearly 50% into just one asset class (domestic equities) is exactly what many investors have actually done in real life. However, I think I can safely assume that, having read nearly to the end of the book, you will readily accept that any such approach is illogical and fraught with all the dangers of lack of diversification.

So far, so good. However, let us also recognise that rebalancing in a situation like this is not nearly as easy at it might at first seem. As we will see below when discussing how to model private equity returns, the cashflows involved are inherently unpredictable, and since we need to have roughly equal exposure to the funds of different vintage years, we cannot just stop committing money to the asset class. On the contrary, accepted wisdom is that wherever possible we should try to commit exactly the same amount every year. Furthermore, this process will usually have to be planned at least three years in advance, since that is the normal fundraising cycle of the typical private equity fund. If we wish to rebalance our quoted equities position, then a simple phone call can achieve this; but other asset classes may be much more complex and require a more flexible approach.

What might this flexible approach be? Well, we have already seen that our percentage target investment in an asset class such as private equity will always be very different from the amount that we intend to commit to it. Indeed, at the very beginning of such a programme the latter could be 10 times the amount of the former, or even more. We also know that even our percentage of total portfolio value represented by capital invested in private equity will fluctuate, and that both the timing and numerical significance of such fluctuation will be uncertain (uncertain because the timing and amount of the underlying cashflows are uncertain). We have already noted in an earlier chapter the problems that even such a sophisticated investor as Yale has experienced in this regard.

A venture fund, in particular, might suddenly make a distribution that represents the sale proceeds of a company sold for, perhaps, a hundred times its cost, and perhaps amounting to two or three times the total committed capital of the fund as a whole. Indeed, it is not unknown for a mature programme to return in cash, in the space of a single year, the total value of the capital actually invested in the programme at the beginning of the year.

Imagine the effect for allocation purposes of having to move that sort of amount out of an asset class and into cash (or, more likely, quoted equities as the most convenient short-term home for it) in the space of a single year. I think you will also see that this would make a mockery of any decision we might have made the previous year to cut back our pace of commitment to private equity funds; we might have made that decision in good faith on the basis of having, say, 25% of value in private equity, only for this sort of 'double whammy' to slash that figure to maybe 15% or less.

So we need to be able to allow our amount actually invested in private equity as a percentage of total portfolio value to move within a fairly broad range. We also need to be able to disregard this so far as possible (although we obviously cannot do so completely) when mapping out our commitment policy for the next three years. I would suggest that it makes sense to try to keep the former as far as possible within a range of 15% to 25%, adjusting our commitment amounts only when either end of this range is threatened.

So, let us look at what would happen to our model MAC portfolio if we were periodically to rebalance it by removing money from private equity and any other outperforming asset classes and redistributing it

Table 12.1 Comparing the performance of the traditional portfolio to a 'rebalancing' MAC portfolio

	Money multiple	IRR
'Traditional' portfolio	1.93×	6.78%
'Rebalancing' portfolio	2.77×	10.96%

to underperforming asset classes. Remember that we have chosen asset classes with as low correlation to each other as possible, which is why it is logical for us to pursue this approach. Hopefully we will be moving the proceeds of some good years in one asset class into another in time for its own period of good years.

Let us look again at the model portfolio set out in Figure 12.3 and see what would have happened in practice if we had rebalanced every time the value of our private equity programme had got to 25% of the total. We will compare this with the performance of the same 'traditional' portfolio that we have used so far.

You will see from Table 12.1 that even using these parameters there is a very significant difference between the performance of the two portfolios. The MAC 'rebalancing' portfolio has generated a money multiple of about 2.8× and an IRR of about 11%. The traditional portfolio has generated about 1.9× and less than 7% respectively. Again, I have bent over backwards to be as conservative in my treatment of the MAC portfolio as possible. I have assumed, for example, that one could actually have seen into the future and reduced private equity commitments in time to avoid a serious allocation issue, whereas in reality it would not have been possible simply to slam on the brakes. Similarly, I have rebalanced religiously at the 25% level, whereas in reality one might have had to live with anything up to 35% (or perhaps even more for very brief periods) as a result of extra value being generated by private equity outperformance. Thus in practice this portfolio would almost certainly still have produced a money multiple of well over 3× and an IRR that might have been roughly double that of the traditional portfolio.

In practice, I think one could in fact live with temporary values in excess of 25%, particularly in the case of private equity, since logically sooner or later the excess will be distributed as cash, in which case it can be fed straight into other asset classes, thus giving a double whammy reduction effect. We should also bear in mind that such fluctuations can occur without any action on our part whatever. For example, if venture firms decide to reduce their fund sizes (as many did between 2001 and 2003), this will arbitrarily reduce the amount that an investor has committed to the asset class. Another factor to consider would be a fall in quoted market values, which could have the effect arbitrarily of increasing the value of other asset classes as a percentage of total portfolio value without the investor actually having altered the targets or commitment pattern in any way.

ARE PRIVATE EQUITY RETURNS MODELLED REALISTICALLY?

This may seem a strange question to pose since in the second example above I have specifically allowed for the continuing investment of an incomplete private equity programme over the following five years. This is fine, but it could be argued that even this does not go far enough towards simulating the way in which private equity investment actually happens in practice.

Let me make one thing quite clear before we start this discussion. The way in which private equity investment and divestment happens is so complex and unpredictable that any attempt to model it must accept certain compromises or trade-offs. I am happy to make the attempt but please bear in mind that if someone is blindly prejudiced against the asset class then it will always be possible to find some way of playing devil's advocate, no matter how sincere the attempt may have been. There are also those in any profession who revel in being negative, since they mistake cynicism for intelligence. It is not impressive to find 20 reasons why something cannot be done. It *is* impressive to find one way in which something can be done, particularly if it might be the only way. In my experience, the 'cynics' are seldom prepared to take responsibility for their actions and decisions (which is why they prefer to find reasons for doing nothing) while the 'doers' are quite the reverse. Bear in mind, too, that in this case much criticism is borne of lack of understanding of the asset class – it will be these same people, for example, who argue against the use of upper quartile performance figures. Well, I have deliberately not used them in this exercise, so at least that is one argument they cannot suggest!

Why is it complex and unpredictable, and how does this make performance modelling so difficult? Private equity differs from all the other asset classes we have been considering in that it is a pure cashflow business. You do not make profits by buying and selling assets (although this is done at an underlying level) nor by receiving dividend yields (yes, these are cashflows, but they are generally fairly predictable as to amount and to timing). Money goes out in the form of drawdowns to limited partnerships, and comes back by way of distributions from these same limited partnerships. Since the timing of these cashflows is uncertain, the levels of cash within the programme at any one time will be unpredictable. (Without wishing to confuse things further, one also needs to distinguish between (1) invested cash, (2) committed but uninvested cash and (3) free cash.) Since any private equity programme is designed to be self-financing, this means that it is also impossible, strictly speaking, to say how much money can be committed in any particular vintage year. It is for these reasons that annual returns are irrelevant to private equity. The only way in which a return can be measured is by looking at the compound return (IRR) represented by the relevant cashflows over time.

I say 'strictly speaking' because, as you might expect, experienced practitioners evolve rules of thumb over time to cope with these uncertainties as best they can and, in particular, to be able to impose a fairly rigid framework of commitments on top of them. The situation will vary slightly according to the precise mix being adopted at any one time between venture, buy-outs, and secondaries, but a rough rule of thumb is to multiply the amount of your allocation by about 1.6× and then commit this steadily over an eight-year period. Experience strongly suggests that by the end of this period the programme will not only be fully self-funding, but should also be throwing off large amounts of surplus cash. Hence my comments earlier in the book about the essential differences between a fully mature private equity programme and a non-mature one, and also about the impossibility of holding the amount of the allocation steady; as the amount of surplus cash grows this will have to be accommodated, at least in part, by making larger and larger fund commitments in future. Sadly, none of this is well understood outside the asset class.

The nature of the cashflows to which I refer above poses two specific problems for any attempt to model private equity returns. Firstly, we are assuming that all the capital invested in private equity at the beginning of our period will grow by the vintage year return of the year in question. In practice this is not the case, since much of that money will have been committed to funds of previous vintage years and the vintage year return measures only the return of those funds actually formed in that particular year. The second conceptual problem is that not all the capital committed to a fund will remain within it for the full amount of the period in question. Indeed, most of it will be distributed before the end and committed to and invested in other funds in turn, and so on ad infinitum. Happily I think we can safely ignore this second point since the figures show the returns of the actual cashflows of the funds formed in a particular year (i.e. both inflows and outflows and when these actually occur) so that provided we can match our ongoing pattern of commitment against each relevant vintage year, we should still arrive at a valid result.

The first objection is obviously a stronger one, but falls into the area of uncertainty bordering on impossibility to which I referred earlier. Unless one knew the precise commitment pattern of a particular investor it would be impossible to know how much money had been committed in each vintage year, particularly since, in the case of a mature programme, that amount would almost certainly have been increasing from year to year. At the end of the day all we can do is make assumptions. However, one thing is clear; the critics cannot have it both ways. If we are assuming a mature private equity programme then we may have to go back to the vintage year returns of some years earlier, but it will not be necessary to run the same process many years in advance, since the programme must be assumed to be more or less fully committed. On the other hand, if a programme is not fully mature then we must go forward a number of years (as we have in our second example) but do not have to go back very far. I hope it will be understood from a reading of the earlier chapter on private equity that the disproportionate effect of the J-curve on the 'non-mature' programme will make this a very unfair comparison, but so be it.

Let us model two different private equity portfolios. The first will have been fully mature by 1994, and we will assume it to have been committed across the eight vintage years 1987 to 1994. The second will not have been fully mature in 1994, and so committed across vintage years 1990 to 1997. Finally, let us see what would have happened to a private equity programme that actually commenced in 1994, and so committed across vintage years 1994 to 2001. I hope it will be obvious in the light of what we know about the J-curve that we should expect this latter exercise to be particularly unrealistic in terms of an expectation of likely final value. In each case we will assume that the money committed in each vintage year represents an annuity and is compounded for the relevant number of years to the end of the period.

There is unfortunately yet another problem in respect of older vintage years. By 1994 the 1987 vintage year funds would have only a small part of their investment and divestment circle left, and so it is simply unrealistic to think of the capital committed in 1987 continuing to compound merrily all the way to the end of 2004 although, strictly speaking, the present value of all the relevant cashflows is exactly what the vintage year return claims to measure (I did say this was difficult!). I will therefore make an assumption that each vintage year comes to the end of its useful life after 12 years, and that the relevant cash is reinvested in the vintage year that occurs 12 years later. Yes, this too is misleading since in practice the cash would have been committed continually over the ensuing period, but it is an assumption that will understate rather than overstate returns and I am frankly nervous about the possibility of calculating returns which, though correct, are so high that the non-believers may even be driven to doubt the veracity of the benchmark itself. I recognise that this method is open to all sorts of objections, but even the objectors must accept that the inherent artificiality is likely to lead to very conservative results. For example, I am assuming only that the original capital amount is recommitted, not the amount of cash actually generated (which is dramatically higher).

I am also aware that it may be artificial to assume that all the money committed to a particular fund should be counted from the beginning of the life of the fund, since in reality it will get drawn down over its life. But remember that the vintage year return is the compound return of all the cashflows that the fund comprises over its entire lifetime, and that once a private equity programme becomes fully mature then the full amount of at least the original allocation should by now be fully invested. To attempt to track the individual cashflows of an individual investor is fine if you are that individual investor and have all the data to hand, but it would surely be an impossible task for our present purposes. I am also assuming that inflows to the investor occur only at the end of the fund's life, or at the end of our analysis period. The overall effect of all this may be to slightly overstate money multiples, but equally it should understate compound returns. I acknowledge that this is not a perfect outcome, but this is a book about investment strategy, not private equity, and I fear we may already have given a disproportionate amount of attention to this issue.

The results of the analysis are set out in Figures 12.6 and 12.7.

You will see that the three portfolios generate potential money multiples of 6×, 7.5× and 4× and IRRs of 24%, 23% and 15% respectively.

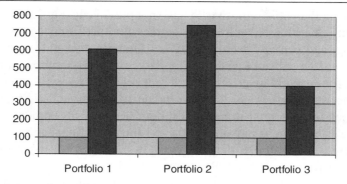

Figure 12.6   Different private equity scenarios

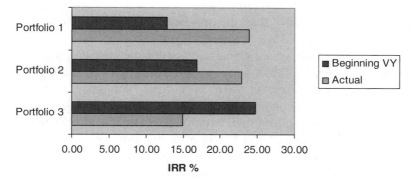

Figure 12.7   IRRs of different private equity scenarios

I am aware that these figures may seem high to those who are not accustomed to private equity returns, but let me draw your attention to two facts. Firstly, we know from the Yale annual report that their 10-year compound return from private equity to the same date was 35%, and I once worked for a firm that enjoyed an even higher return. Secondly, the same firm managed a well-known private equity fund of funds that had a money multiple of about 10×. These sorts of figures can thus be proved to be achievable in the real world.

CONCLUSIONS

We are drawing to the end of the chapter and, indeed, the book and I hope these illustrations of possible portfolio performance have been useful in putting some flesh on the bones of the theory we have been examining thus far. To those who have not previously considered MAC investing as a strategic option, the degree of outperformance may seem startling, and perhaps even incredible – literally, too good to be true. However, I have been asked over the last few years to prepare presentations for different investment conferences using various assumptions, and one incontrovertible common thread has emerged. MAC investment has the potential dramatically both to boost investment returns and lower risk when compared to the existing, traditional approach. We have seen, for example, that any pension fund that had been using a MAC portfolio model by 1994 (or even moving towards it) might have doubled its final value. Given the extraordinary lengths to which some investors are prepared to go (portable alpha schemes, for example) for just the possibility of an extra 1% of performance, it does seem extraordinary that a low-risk diversified approach which has the potential to deliver very much more than this has been in some cases completely ignored.

The German philosopher Hegel saw knowledge as emerging from a process of thesis, antithesis and resultant synthesis. The problem with investment theory in recent years is that the 'antithesis' part of the process has never happened. Everyone has been content simply to accept what they have been told, with the result that theory has not only stood still, but petrified, and has become the equivalent of religious dogma. Early thinkers who dared to suggest that the earth travelled around the sun were persecuted and ridiculed for their beliefs. Yet because they had the courage to stand up and be counted, the sum total of human knowledge advanced and the heresies of yesterday became the orthodoxy of today.

Many writers on psychology have described how, when one is faced with a 'reality as it is' compared to a 'reality as we would like it to be', the natural human reaction is to impose a filter on our view of reality to bring it into line with our beliefs, since it is easier to do this than to admit that we are mistaken. Gradually as the gap between the two becomes wider, our reactions will increasingly be seen as irrational, delusional and perhaps bordering on fantasy. At some point the difference between the two will reach the stage that no rational person could seek to cling to her belief any longer, and she will be forced to change her belief system to match perceived reality. Sadly in a very small number of cases this does not happen, and mental illness can be the result.

I would suggest that portfolio theory, particularly insofar as it deals with the question of financial risk, has reached a point where the disparity between the theoretical and the practical has become too wide a gulf to bridge. This is extremely harmful, as it has led to perfectly valid investment approaches being rejected as they cannot be justified by traditional beliefs (the 'it may work in practice, but will it work in theory?' school of behaviour). We are now ready for the next big leap forward in thinking. We can no longer pretend that the old theories will help us in the new world in which we find ourselves. We need to jettison the artificially theoretical in favour of a logical, commonsense approach based on the real concerns of real investors, and MAC investing points the way ahead.

The way will not be easy, since there are many who have a vested interest in propping up the existing system, and they will spare no effort in attempting to belittle and discredit an alternative approach. Yet we can draw comfort from three things. Firstly, our approach, unlike the existing system, does not rely on the comforting world of artificial assumptions but on common sense and logic. Secondly, David Swensen and the Yale Model have proved beyond any possible dispute that such an approach can be brilliantly successful in practice. Finally, the potential prize is immense.

By implementing MAC investing among our pension funds we can give today's working population their best possible chance of enjoying the comfortable retirement they deserve, and were promised when they first joined their occupational pension scheme. At the same time, we can ease the burden on the sponsoring employers, enabling them to devote their money to the purposes for which it was originally intended rather than being thrown with increasing desperation into an ever-shrinking pensions pot. This is surely an objective worth fighting for, and worth enduring a few brickbats for.

So let us go out into the marketplace and start telling people that the earth really does go round the sun. You never know – we might find a few people who will actually believe us.

Appendix 1
Tables of Performance Figures

Table A1.1 Annual returns (%) of possible MAC portfolio components

	1984	1985	1986	1987	1988	1989	1990	1991	1992	1993	1994
S&P 100	4.51	27.87	15.20	7.20	14.58	28.25	-2.59	27.11	5.21	10.54	2.61
FTSE 100		19.23	23.00	6.60	9.70	39.34	-6.05	21.16	18.41	23.62	-6.09
NASDAQ	0.00	31.58	7.38	-5.16	15.11	19.42	-17.80	56.68	15.53	14.77	-3.22
HF composite											-4.36
HF market neutral											-2
UQ PE			13.90	11.22	9.96	13.80	10.71	19.02	16.83	27.63	25.13
CWA PE			15.00	-25.26	13.58	30.45	2.04	10.83	3.97	18.11	16.29
UK property	8.69	8.19	11.00	24.92	28.35	14.92	-7.63	-2.38	-0.88	19.34	11.60

	1995	1996	1997	1998	1999	2000	2001	2002	2003	2004
S&P 100	38.97	24.66	29.23	32.49	32.31	-12.32	-13.49	-21.91	25.59	6.32
FTSE 100	24.22	15.54	27.85	16.91	19.84	-8.02	-13.58	-20.93	16.83	10.69
NASDAQ	39.89	22.72	21.61	39.68	85.54	-39.30	-21.05	-31.54	50.04	8.59
HF composite	21.69	22.22	25.94	-0.36	23.43	4.85	4.42	3.04	15.44	9.64
HF market neutral	11.04	16.6	14.83	13.31	15.33	14.99	9.31	7.42	7.07	6.48
UQ PE	44.25	49.32	39.07	31.07	83.88	40.62	2.17	-0.62	14.26	23.22
CWA PE	24.65	35.29	34.32	8.72	53.58	14.78	-6.76	-11.89	8.06	17.60
UK property	3.86	9.89	16.17	11.48	14.05	10.24	6.79	9.47	10.62	17.68

Source: UK property figures reproduced by kind permission of IPD; private equity figures reproduced by kind permission of Thomson Financial; hedge fund figures reproduced by kind permission of CSFB/Tremont; all quoted equity figures are in the public domain.

Table A1.2 Vintage year returns (%) of possible MAC portfolio components

	1984	1985	1986	1987	1988	1989	1990	1991	1992	1993	1994
S&P 100	12.15	12.55	11.80	11.61	11.88	11.71	10.69	11.70	10.60	11.06	11.10
FTSE 100		10.83	10.40	9.74	9.93	9.94	8.22	9.32	8.46	7.66	6.32
NASDAQ	10.91	11.49	10.52	10.70	11.71	11.50	10.99	13.40	10.61	10.21	9.81
HF composite											10.98
HF market neutral											10.27
UQ PE	11.85	15.28	12.51	16.74	16.59	19.13	19.58	21.54	24.64	28.06	26.98
CWA PE	13.59	18.96	11.61	12.79	11.54	16.11	16.80	14.28	23.31	22.57	24.74
UK property	10.47	10.56	10.69	10.67	9.88	8.82	8.43	9.68	10.66	11.68	11.01

	1995	1996	1997	1998	1999	2000	2001	2002	2003	2004
S&P 100	11.99	9.34	7.56	4.78	0.76	-4.58	-2.55	1.40	15.55	6.32
FTSE 100	7.65	5.95	4.81	1.87	-0.44	-4.06	-3.04	0.75	13.72	10.69
NASDAQ	11.20	8.40	6.74	4.77	-0.14	-11.77	-3.13	3.71	27.64	8.59
HF composite	12.64	11.68	10.43	8.38	9.90	7.38	8.03	9.26	12.50	9.64
HF market neutral	11.58	11.64	11.03	10.50	10.04	10.70	7.56	6.99	6.77	6.48
UQ PE	31.90	35.05	18.78	10.44	2.90	1.04	8.07	3.34	7.79	-12.43
CWA PE	25.11	17.88	12.22	6.36	-1.86	-0.93	1.65	-0.75	10.38	-25.48
UK property	10.95	11.77	12.01	11.43	11.42	10.90	11.07	12.53	14.09	17.68

Source: UK property figures reproduced by kind permission of IPD; private equity figures reproduced by kind permission of Thomson Financial; hedge fund figures reproduced by kind permission of CSFB/Tremont; all quoted equity figures are in the public domain.

Table A1.3 Correlation of the total return of MAC model asset classes

	S&P 100	FTSE 100	NASDAQ	DAX	HF composite	HF market neutral	CWA PE	UK property
S&P 100		86%	88%	76%	65%	37%	62%	8%
FTSE 100	86%		71%	87%	74%	44%	58%	15%
NASDAQ	88%	71%		70%	60%	28%	59%	1%
DAX	76%	87%	70%		71%	44%	71%	40%
HF composite	65%	74%	60%	71%		60%	72%	11%
HF market neutral	37%	44%	28%	44%	60%		47%	1%
CWA PE	62%	58%	59%	71%	72%	47%		7%
UK property	8%	15%	1%	40%	11%	1%	7%	

NB: In the case of quoted equities, this shows the correlation of the total returns of any year, NOT the correlation of the movement of the different indices.

Table A1.4   Return risk of potential model MAC portfolio components at rates of target return

	8%	9%	10%	11%	12%
S&P 100	38%	46%	56%	64%	72%
FTSE 100	55%	66%	75%	83%	89%
NASDAQ	45%	52%	58%	65%	70%
HF composite	8%	21%	42%	66%	84%
CW PE	7%	9%	13%	17%	22%
UK property	1%	7%	27%	59%	86%

NB: The above figures are calculated using time-weighted vintage year returns and show the percentage probability that the return over time will NOT at least equal the target rate of return.

Table A1.5   Correlation of major quoted indices

	S&P 100	FTSE 100	NASDAQ	Nikkei	DAX
S&P 100		97%	97%	−46%	97%
FTSE 100	97%		94%	−39%	98%
NASDAQ	97%	94%		−38%	94%
Nikkei	−46%	−39%	−38%		−48%
DAX	97%	98%	94%	−48%	

NB: This shows the correlation of the movement of the different indices, NOT the correlation of the total returns of any year.

Appendix 2

Investment Strategy for DC Schemes and Mature Pension Plans

One of the many reasons why I was reluctant to engage in discussion on this subject within the confines of this book was that it is a much wider subject than is commonly realised. It is human nature that we all see our world from an egocentric point of view. I use this word not in its pejorative everyday sense but in its proper psychological sense of meaning viewing the world with ourselves at its centre; after all, that is the basis for all our everyday perceptions. The early reviewers of the manuscript of this book were all from the UK, and their everyday experience involved working for and with UK pension schemes.

In the period before publication of this book most UK employers closed their final salary scheme to new members, and reports were starting to circulate that some employers were looking to go further and close their final salary scheme altogether. Rentokil were the first to announce that they were actually doing so. The question of the change from a DB to a DC scheme therefore dominated discussion in the UK. What was frequently lost in the 'noise' of this debate was that the question of the logicality and morality in closing a final salary scheme was totally separate from the question of how a DC scheme should seek to set its own investment strategy, and that the first question was largely UK-centric, while the second was universal (DC schemes have been an important part of the pension landscape in other countries for many years).

For those who may have studied philosophy, there is also a further distinction to draw in that the second issue is largely one of logic while the former also strays heavily into the field of ethics. I do not feel it appropriate, therefore, to discuss the first reason at all in any detail, since there is no place in a book on investment strategy to discuss the ethics or morality of people's actions. I would simply say that, in my view, the moral imperative (i.e. to provide the members with a comfortable retirement) remains the same whatever the legal nature of the scheme's obligations may be and, therefore, I see little reason in switching from DB status, particularly since many sponsors seem to regard their 'obligations' as little more than voluntary guidelines in any case.[1] Further, the switch to DC status produces a substantial extra cost, namely the profit made by the annuity provider, and that cost comes straight out of the members' retirement pot.

However, as I have said elsewhere in the book, I do not see sponsoring employers as rapacious robber barons intent on stealing bread out of the mouths of impoverished peasants. Rather, I see them as commercial or public bodies whose main concern is not the provision of pension benefits but the effective pursuit of their business interests, or their public responsibilities. Sadly, reality has intervened and turned the established state of things upside down; various large multinationals, such as General Motors and British Airways, could now be described as 'a company attached to a pension fund' rather than vice versa.

The real tragedy of the present retirement funding crisis is that it has thrown into sharp relief government policy in many parts of the world (most notably the UK) of encouraging or even forcing the same people to take both sets of decisions when it is no longer possible for them so to do (if indeed it ever was) except in grave conflict of interest. Pension trustees and sponsors alike deserve our sympathy for the impossible situation in which they have been placed by public policy. That does not mean that one is not allowed to be critical of decisions they have taken, but it does mean that such criticism is intended to be objective (i.e. based on analysis of the facts), academic and non-specific.

Ethics is in any event a complex area. It is entirely possible that even Plato would have been taxed by the present situation; my reading of his work is that human well-being is the yardstick against which ethical judgement should operate and that a laudable human should strive for excellence in whatever he or she does. Yet he was considering the well-being only of a small number of free-born individuals in a society that depended on widespread slavery, and he also mentions the rather Japanese concept that the interests of the individual should be subordinated to the needs of society as a whole. Thus, you could make a

---

[1] It is interesting, though, that the switching process has been allowed to pass virtually unchallenged, particularly by those whom pension plan members have a right to regard as protecting their interests, e.g. politicians and trade unions. In other countries, such as the Netherlands, sponsors are being forced to make large penalty payments into the scheme as the price for switching to DC status.

convincing argument for his coming down on either side of this particular debate.

DC SCHEMES GENERALLY

I can remember being somewhat surprised, when I first started dealing with US pension funds, by the large amount of money they typically administered in DC schemes, since this was very much at variance with my experiences in the UK, where the DB scheme dominated. Of course, at the time (the early 1990s) there seemed a good argument in favour of the UK system. With a DB scheme it was possible for the sponsor to take contribution holidays provided the pension plan's consultant (who usually just happened also to be the pension consultant to the sponsor) could be persuaded to give a 'fully funded' calculation. As pointed out above, to be fair to sponsors this approach was also encouraged by government in the UK (a Conservative government at the time, lest anyone think I am seeking to make a Party Political point as opposed to a simply, political, point), which heavily taxed any surplus of plan assets above 105%. With a DC scheme, where it was the amount of money paid in plus accrued investment performance that counted (and which indeed is the legal entitlement), such an option is not available.

Recent history has thrown a rather different light on this difference of approach, but such a discussion lies beyond the scope of this book. What is more relevant is the other aspect of the US approach which surprised me, and one which I think rests on rather more sandy soil. There appeared to be a marked difference in the investment strategy applied to DC and DB schemes within the ambit of the same sponsoring employer, particularly insofar as it concerned their attitude to so-called alternative assets. It seemed to me then, and it still seems to me now, that this difference of approach is difficult to justify, at least to the extent to which it appears to be applied.

DC Scheme Funding (1)

The Passive Approach

I will be showing below how the Total Funding Model can be applied to a DC scheme, but let us first consider how existing DC schemes typically approach the business of investing. As I said, this is a huge subject in its own right and part of the price that one pays for trying to consider it within a single chapter is that we immediately have to draw another distinction.

In many cases (and particularly in the USA) people will have a DC scheme and a DB scheme at the same time. This may be because they have moved employers and have an accrued pension benefit that has been transferred into a DC scheme, or it may be because they have chosen to contribute to a DC scheme themselves in the nature of making voluntary additional contributions. (In fact the situation is even more complicated than that, as most people will have a 401K, but in the interests of brevity I do not propose even to acknowledge their existence here; I must keep things simple or even one chapter will be insufficient.)

Where one is making contributions to a DC scheme – or holding an accrued DC benefit which must be invested – alongside an existing DB scheme, there is a valid argument that this is in the nature of financial markets disaster insurance; that is, in effect a reserve parachute and that the scheme manager's main obligation is to preserve the scheme's integrity, even to the extent of missing out on superior performance. I do not say that this argument is correct, or even that it is possible to say whether it is correct or not, but it is certainly a valid argument. If one adopts such an approach then clearly a bond style of investment approach will be adopted.

Where one is looking to a DC scheme to provide all one's retirement benefits then clearly such an approach cannot be justified on any grounds. The accepted view now becomes that it is the scheme's obligation to invest this money wisely, but still fairly prudently, and that the accumulated value on the date of the individual member's retirement will be whatever it is; it is in the lap of the Gods and largely beyond the scheme's control apart from the overall responsibility to invest it prudently. I will be arguing that there is in fact an alternative to the accepted view, but let us first look at something that could at first blush be seen as yet another alternative, but which I think is simply a particularly scientific and thoughtful application of what I have just described. It does not have a name, as far as I am aware, and I am unsure of what to call it. Perhaps 'the phased approach' will do as well as anything.

The Phased Approach

This is something that I discovered while talking to people in a particular European pension fund, and it struck me immediately as a very interesting policy. I am aware of others who have given some thought to proceeding on these lines, but nobody who has adopted it so wholeheartedly.

It rests on the recognition that, with DC schemes, the pension fund itself has no real relevance. If one analyses what it is, it is really no more than a money box containing lots of individual little personal pension plans. If this is so, runs the argument, then why not treat each individual's contributions differently based on the person's age, and thus on the length of time that may be assumed to elapse before he or she retires?

Thus, you take the contributions and the reinvestable gains of individuals in their twenties and thirties and put them largely into what could be considered long-term investments, such as private equity and property. As they move into their forties these elements decrease, being replaced largely by hedge funds and quoted equities. As they move into their fifties, the mix changes again, with alternatives starting to disappear in favour of bonds. The nearer one gets to retirement, the greater the proportion of bonds becomes, until by the age of about 60 they are probably making up the bulk of the portfolio, with the balance in shares.

If one accepts the passive approach then it strikes me that this is definitely the way to do it. It is intelligent and attractive. It maximises the opportunity for outperformance in the early years when the time value of money can be most effective (i.e. those high returns can be compounded for a long period, even if at lesser rates) and offers security and certainty when they are most needed. If the passive approach is to be adopted then I would enthusiastically endorse this approach.

The crux, though, is that phrase 'if the passive approach is to be adopted'. Admirable though the phased approach may be (and it really is), it has one conceptual flaw. There is still no direct connection between the supply side and the demand side. It could be argued that this is implicit in the nature of a DC scheme – your entitlement is whatever you get – but this seems to me unsatisfactory for two reasons. Firstly, like it or not this is simply not how individuals think; they will have a certain level of expectation and in an ideal world investment strategy will be devoted to satisfying that expectation if at all possible. Secondly, the phased approach is intelligent but not necessarily logical or scientific. Suppose it becomes apparent to the late forties group that the projected value of their benefits is going to be much less than what they require? To take a less likely example, suppose that by their early forties they were dramatically overfunded? Does it really make sense to go on blindly applying asset allocation by way of a preset formula rather than looking to change it to make good the imbalance?

DC Scheme Funding (2)

The Total Funding Approach

A member of a DC scheme will have an expectation of a certain base level of retirement benefits and this is likely to be expressed as a percentage of salary, partly because of the long traditional dominance of DB schemes, and partly because the level of an individual's current income will provide the yardstick for his or her future expectations.

There must be a level of present funding that is likely to end up satisfying a member's reasonable expectations (Total Funding). If it is apparent that the level of present funding is not sufficiently high, then something has to be done about it. Either the member's expectations must be managed downwards (although there must be a certain minimum below which it is unreasonable to expect these to fall), the level of contributions must be increased, or the investment return must be managed upwards. In reality, of course, a combination of all three is likely to be indicated, and the contentious issue of delaying the retirement age could also be considered.

Yet until the level of Total Funding is known, this exercise, and the form it needs to take, cannot properly be considered. Thus the need and the ability to calculate the target return using a version of the Total Funding Model is just as important in the case of a money purchase (DC) scheme as it is for a final salary scheme.

How Does the Total Funding DC Model Work?

We know, or can assume, the amount of money a member will expect to receive by way of an annuity by compounding that person's current salary by the expected rate of inflation for the period between now and his or her retirement and then taking the appropriate percentage of that.

Thus if a member is expecting 50% of final salary we can use the basic compounding formula:

$$\mathrm{PMT} = 50\% \left[c \left(\frac{1+r}{1} \right)^{n} \right]$$

where r is the expected rate of inflation, c is the current salary, and n is the number of years.

So we can calculate the periodic amount required (PMT). We now need to decide upon an appropriate annuity rate to apply. Current annuity rates can be found in most newspapers, but we have to consider whether today's annuity rates are still likely to be appropriate in, say, 20 years' time.

The main determinants of annuity rates are (1) discount rates, and (2) life expectancy. The higher the discount rate, the more an annuity provider can afford to pay. The longer the life expectancy, the less he can afford annually (since he will have to pay the annuity for longer).

As we have already seen, longevity is a crucial factor in just about every aspect of pension scheme planning and analysis. It is also the one factor that could change quite dramatically over the next 30 years or so; exactly the period over which pension funds need to be modelling. In other words, it is the one thing that could make a mockery of even the most careful and considered planning. Clearly we need to take this into account in some way. Let us see what happens if we try to model this.

At the time of writing (late 2005) men and women aged 65 in the UK can expect to live to 81 and 84 respectively. Each of these figures is expected to increase by three years over the course of the next 16 (having increased by about four years over the last 20). Thus, if a man retires at 65 and buys an annuity, the provider of that annuity would expect on average to pay it for 16 years. However, if life expectancy was to increase more dramatically than forecast (perhaps as a result of breakthroughs in medical science) to, say, 95 for men and 100 for women then the annuity would have to be paid not for 16 years but for 30. This would have a very significant effect on the present value of the annuity; it would be much higher. In other words, to fund the same payment for a longer period requires a larger pot of pension money.

Annuity providers seem currently to be using a discount rate of about 2% (you can calculate this by trial and error in order to arrive at the advertised rate), so the present value of a £10 000 annuity over a 16-year period would be:

$$PV = £10\,000 \left[\frac{1 - (1.02)^{-16}}{0.02} \right]$$
$$= £135\,777$$

For a 30-year period it would be:

$$PV = £10\,000\left[\frac{1-(1.02)^{-30}}{0.02}\right]$$

$$= £223\,964$$

Thus, in the case of the 16-year annuity, the annuity quoted would be something less (since the annuity provider is in business and aiming to make a profit on the deal) than £7365 for a £100 000 pot of pension money, but after extending the likely payment period to 30 years your £100 000 would bring you only £4465 a year.

Remember too that these calculations take no account of index linking for inflation, or of including your spouse for a 'joint life' quote, both of which would of course decrease the annuity rate that a provider was able to offer.

So how should we model the effect of this? Well, once we know roughly what discount rate the annuity providers are using, we calculate exactly what difference an increase of any given number of years would make to the annuity rate offered. I would suggest that we adopt broadly the UK Government Actuaries assumptions, and add three years to life expectancy if we are modelling a 20-year period, and five years if we are modelling a 30-year period (and adjust this pro rata for other periods).

THE COMPLETE DC MODEL

Now we are in a position to assemble the whole model. Let us assume an average member of the scheme, although we could perform this calculation for any individual member based on his or her particular circumstances.

We know how old our member is, and thus the number of years to retirement. We can model the current salary increasing by the anticipated rate of inflation to give us a final salary figure at that date. Let us assume that our member is 45 years old and that the scheme's retirement age is 65. If his present salary is £30 000 and we expect inflation to run at 3%, then by the time he is 65 we assume it to be:

$$£30\,000\left(\frac{1.03}{1}\right)^{20} = £54\,183$$

Let us assume that the member's expectation is for an index-linked, joint life annuity of 50% final salary, say £27 000 a year.

We know that the current annuity rate advertised for this sort of situation is just over 3% (i.e. £3000 of annuity for each £100 000 of pension pot). Adding on another three years of life expectancy brings it down to just under 3%, but let us assume an annuity rate of 3% for the sake of simplicity.

By my calculations, the required pension pot in 20 years' time will be £903 056.

We know the contributions that are due to be made during this period. Let us say they are 12% of salary and, like the salary itself, they will of course increase by the anticipated rate of inflation each year. Now all we need to know is the current value of the member's pension pot and we can calculate the IRR required to meet the target amount. For a current pot of £45 000 in the present example, the target rate of return is 13%.

What Does This Mean for Asset Allocation?

Now that we know the target rate of return for the period between now and the individual member's scheduled retirement date, we can select the mix of assets most likely to satisfy the target rate of return. The MAC investing model will serve as a useful template although, unlike the case of a DB model, we will be looking to vary this to stay on track with our target rate of return. It is rather like the pilot of a plane using the throttle rather than the joystick to control the rate of descent of a plane, thus keeping it on its approach path. With a DC scheme we have truly arrived at the situation where asset allocation is a knob on the control panel that can be used to control (or at least with reference to) a dial on the dashboard.

This may seem an awful lot of trouble to go to, but in fact it is relatively simple. If necessary, members' profiles can be categorised into one of four or five classifications of required allocation profile and then all the members of each category can then be treated as one single group.

It may seem that, at the end of the day, there is little practical difference between what I am suggesting and the phased approach. It is true that it is likely to work in much the same way in practice, at least in a steady-state environment. The essential difference is that with Total Funding we have restored the connection between the supply side and the demand side. We are now using asset allocation in an attempt to match actual investment performance with target investment performance, rather than doing so in an arbitrary (though intelligent) manner.

MATURE PENSION PLANS

A great deal is talked about the nature of mature pension schemes, much of it unfortunately misconceived. In particular there is a common misconception that the mere fact of a pension plan being mature makes it somehow inherently unsuitable for it to be investing in so-called alternative asset classes.

We started this appendix by talking about two branches of philosophy: ethics and logic. Let us end it by considering another: linguistics, which, like logic, has its origins in the classical Greek study of rhetoric.[2] Some philosophers have suggested that most philosophical problems boil down to problems with the meaning of words. I do not go so far, but in this case the reference is probably apt. For example, just as the basic concept of 'liquidity', which we considered earlier, is understood, the host of implied associations that always accompany the word are also fundamentally mistaken.

I have had various pension insiders tell me that their scheme is 'mature', and on further enquiry I found out that what they meant was that the last payment out is likely to occur within the next 30 years. I hope it will be obvious from what we have considered in the book as a whole that a period of 20 years or so is ample for the implementation of a MAC investing model. Of course, if such a scheme can be conclusively shown to be fully funded, even allowing for the escalator factor, that is a different matter, but what pension plan can honestly say that today?

I would therefore state as a principle that alternative assets have a part to play in the asset mix of any pension plan unless it is almost certain to pay out all its assets within the next 10 years and/or it is fully funded even after making full allowance for the escalator factor.

Remember too, that the MAC investing model automatically compensates for the growing maturity of a scheme (this is what I refer to in various places as changing liability profiles). The next three years'

---

[2] For the interested, the exchanges between Alice and Humpty Dumpty in *Through the Looking Glass* by Lewis Carroll are intended as rather warped and humorous examples of linguistics.

net outflows are always held in bonds by way of a liquidity reserve, so, to take an extreme example, it is quite possible that towards the end of a scheme's life this reserve could rise to as much as 30% or so of the total. Similarly, each of the five asset classes is adjustable on a sliding scale of between about 15% and 25%, and one would obviously weight the portfolio more and more in favour of quoted equities the more mature the scheme became. Thus, to continue the example, one could easily reach a situation where up to about 65% of the portfolio was in assets that would satisfy even the most hardened liquidity fetishist.

Private equity is the asset that most often comes in for this sort of attack and sadly such criticism displays not only a lack of understanding of the full implications of maturity, but also a less than full understanding of how private equity can operate as an asset class. I have referred in the chapter on private equity, for example, to the practice of tuning a programme with secondary investments, and these could quite easily be a large part, or even all, of a private equity programme that had to cater for a short timescale.

SUMMARY

- The switching by sponsors from a DB to a DC scheme has many ethical implications which render it unsuitable for full discussion in a book of this nature.
- However, it does not seem to confer any significant financial benefit. On the contrary, it imposes a significant extra cost in the form of the annuity provider's profit.
- Where an individual is running a DC scheme alongside a DB scheme, it is a valid argument (though not necessarily correct) that the contributions to the DC scheme should constitute a 'reserve parachute' and be largely restricted to bonds.
- Where an individual is wholly dependent on a DC scheme for his or her retirement benefits, however, such a position is clearly untenable.
- Existing practice is to invest a DC scheme passively, and best practice in this regard is undoubtedly the phased approach, which allocates contributions and reinvested gains purely on the basis of the age of the participant.

- Even the phased approach is not ideal, however, as it makes no connection between the supply side and the demand side of the situation. Use of the Total Funding Model restores this connection.
- For a DC scheme, the target investment return is calculated by reference to the amount of money that will be needed at retirement to provide an annuity which is in line with the member's reasonable expectations, calculated as a percentage of final salary.
- Just as with liquidity, the implications of maturity are often widely misunderstood. In fact, the MAC investing model is appropriate for any pension fund unless it is genuinely fully funded, even allowing for the escalator factor and/or has less than 10 years to run.

Index

Index compiled by Terry Halliday